Macroeconomic Theory and the Eurozone Crisis

The financial crisis of 2007 required the economics discipline to thoroughly re-evaluate its prevailing theories about economic cycles and economic growth. With a focus on Europe, this volume identifies the latest strands of research on business cycles, monetary theory, the evolution of social policies and public spending, and the institutional context of the European Union. It also considers whether these new ideas could have helped us avoid the crisis, and how they might reshape the current economic paradigm.

This book will be of interest to advanced students and researchers in European economics, macroeconomics and economic history.

Alain Alcouffe is Professor Emeritus at Toulouse University, France. He has published many articles and book chapters on industrial and regional economics, economics of knowledge, economics of education, and the history of economic thought. He has served as head of Toulouse University Network (2001–2005) and president of the International Walras Association (2013–2015).

Maurice Baslé is Emeritus Professor at the University of Rennes 1, France, and an active researcher at the CNRS. He has published two textbooks and numerous articles on the history of economic thought and holds a Jean Monnet ad personam chair in European integration. He continuously searches for improvements in Public Policy Evaluation Methods and Public Finance. He promotes the digital revolution in public service.

Monika Poettinger teaches economic history and history of economic thought at Bocconi University, Milan, Italy. She has published many articles and book chapters on the industrialization process in Italy, merchant networks and German entrepreneurial migrations. Her research interests include economic and cultural history, particularly in the eighteenth and nineteenth centuries.

Routledge Studies in the History of Economics

Aristotle's Critique of Political Economy
With a Contemporary Application
Robert L. Gallagher

Otto Neurath and the History of Economics
Michael Turk

A Brief Prehistory of the Theory of the Firm
Paul Walker

Unproductive Labour in Political Economy
The History of an Idea
Cosimo Perrotta

The History of Money and Monetary Arrangements
Insights from the Baltic and North Seas Region
Thomas Marmefelt

Business Cycles and Economic Crises
A Bibliometric and Economic History
Niels Geiger and Vadim Kufenko

A Contemporary Historiography of Economics
Edited by Till Düppe and Roy E. Weintraub

Money, Finance and Crises in Economic History
The Long-Term Impact of Economic Ideas
Edited by Annalisa Rosselli, Eleonora Sanfilippo and Nerio Naldi

Macroeconomic Theory and the Eurozone Crisis
Edited by Alain Alcouffe, Maurice Baslé and Monika Poettinger

For more information about this series, please visit: www.routledge.com/series/SE0341

Macroeconomic Theory and the Eurozone Crisis

Edited by Alain Alcouffe, Maurice Baslé and Monika Poettinger

Routledge
Taylor & Francis Group
LONDON AND NEW YORK

First published 2019
by Routledge
2 Park Square, Milton Park, Abingdon, Oxon OX14 4RN

and by Routledge
52 Vanderbilt Avenue, New York, NY 10017, USA

First issued in paperback 2020

Routledge is an imprint of the Taylor & Francis Group, an informa business

British Library Cataloguing-in-Publication Data
A catalogue record for this book is available from the British Library

Library of Congress Cataloging-in-Publication Data
A catalog record for this book has been requested

ISBN 13: 978-0-367-66519-7 (pbk)
ISBN 13: 978-0-8153-6404-7 (hbk)

Typeset in Bembo
by Apex CoVantage, LLC

Contents

Figures

Tables

Contributors

Nicolas Barbaroux is Associate Professor in Economics at the University of St Etienne, France. His research interests are mostly oriented around monetary policymaking and the monetary history of economic thought.

Fanny Coulomb is Senior Lecturer in Economics at the University of Grenoble, France. Her fields of study are international political economy, defense economics, the arms industry and the history of economic thought on war and peace.

Arnaud Diemer is Associate Professor at Clermont Auvergne University, France. He manages an observatory of sustainable development (OR2d) and is Vice-President of CIFEODD (Network of sustainable development from AUF). His research is focused on the history of economic thought, diversity of European capitalism and sustainable development.

Antonio Forte is Economist at Centro Europa Ricerche, Rome, Italy. He obtained his PhD in Economics from University of Bari in 2010. His research interests include Central Banking, euro area banking system and public debt.

Sandrine Michel is Professor in Economics at the University of Montpellier, France. She teaches economic history and macroeconomics. She has published articles and book chapters on the relationship between education and economic growth, drawing on European studies.

Peter Nedergaard is Professor in the Department of Political Science at the University of Copenhagen, Denmark. His key research interests are comparative politics and the political economy of European integration, Nordic cooperation, and international political economy.

Bertram Schefold is Senior Professor at Johann Wolfgang Goethe-University, Frankfurt, Germany. He was Dean at the Faculty of Economics, J.W. Goethe-University from 1981 to 1982. He has published more than 40 books and 250 articles on economic theory, history of economic thought, energy policy and general economic policy.

Preface

The turn of the millennium brought to Europe a calamitous financial and economic crisis. The economic downturn spread the awareness of an increasing inequality (Van Treeck, Sturn 2012), fuelling social unrest and the rise of populist and nationalist political movements. Capitalism was perceived, not for the first time, as lying in its deathbed or in need of deep changes (Jacobs, Mazzucato 2016; Kocka, Van der Linden 2016). Economics reacted to the crisis with a profound rethinking of the current paradigm and a revival of innovative researches (Sepp, Frear 2011; Blanchard, Romer, Spence, Stiglitz 2012; Brancaccio, Fontana 2013; Bordo et al. 2016). This volume addresses the challenge posed by the crisis by analysing recent changes in macroeconomic theorizing in Europe. The European Union, with its supra-national economic institutions and regulatory framework, coped with the economic crisis in ways that stimulated peculiar debates among economists (Arestis, Sawyer 2012a; Farkas 2016). Especially controversial were questions related to the international management of the financial sector and of central banking prerogatives, development policies and trade imbalances (Fiorentini, Montani 2012).

The recent economic crisis, though, didn't just influence economic research and theorizing, but also the reception of economic theories in common thinking and their further transformation in policy recommendations and institutions. Looking at the European Union is relevant also in this case (Farkas 2016). The variety of national cultures and traditions of economic thought present in the Union reacted to the economic downturn with exceptional violence on newspapers as in academic journals, in parliaments as in specialized think tanks. This volume offers innovative analyses of the interaction between the crisis and economic culture, highlighting how past ideas still influence economic discussion and economic policies, but revealing also how contemporary economists participated to the public debate offering alternative explanatory views and policy recommendations.

A crisis of macroeconomics?

There is no doubt that economic crises, since their first calamitous appearance, accelerated the theoretical debate in economics. Already at the beginning of the 19th century, the possibility of widespread poverty and need while manufactures lied idle stuck a wide wedge of doubt in the belief of universal economic harmonies (Alcouffe, Poettinger, Schefold 2017). The eve of the new millennium and the ensuing grave financial crisis made no exception.

Since the 1980s, the different macroeconomic approaches developed in the decades after World War II had evolved into a modelling practice with converging characteristics (Woodford 2009). To offer realistic projections of short- and long-run responses to economic disturbances, models had to be structural, based on intertemporal general-equilibrium hypotheses and econometrically validated. Models also endogenized expectations, assumed to be rational and accounted for the stickiness of prices, market imperfections and limited information. These dynamic stochastic general equilibrium (DSGE) models were developed and adopted by many central banks, including the European Central Bank (ECB) (Christoffel, Coenen, Warne 2008).

The main result of the testing of such models on data[1] was that aggregate variability followed only marginally, in 10% of the cases, from monetary disturbances while real shocks, as changes in technology, preferences and fiscal policy, were much more frequent and relevant than previously thought (Woodford 2009). Monetary policy, though, was still considered important in stabilising the business cycle, mainly in its structural component, and for inflation targeting.

DSGE modelling and the related economic policies came soon to be known as New Consensus Macroeconomics or New Neoclassical Synthesis (Goodfriend, King 1997; Woodford 2009). The truce among macroeconomists, though, was soon jeopardized by a financial crisis that the entire profession had failed to predict or expect. While voices of dissent had always been present (Mankiw 2006), after the crisis they became a loud chorus (Paul Krugman's London Lectures 2009; Stiglitz 2009; Leijonhufvud 2009; Acemoglu 2009). Even the then president of the ECB, Jean-Claude Trichet, underlined that:

> The key lesson I would draw from our experience is the danger of relying on a single tool, methodology or paradigm. Policy-makers need to have input from various theoretical perspectives and from a range of empirical approaches. Open debate and a diversity of views must be cultivated – admittedly not always an easy task in an institution such as a central bank. We do not need to throw out our DSGE and asset-pricing models: rather we need to develop complementary tools to improve the robustness of our overall framework.
>
> (Trichet 2010)

Critics concentrated on how DSGE models represented the financial sector, hypothesizing away its potential fragility, and on how they relied on homogeneous rational expectations (Timbeau 2012; Wieland 2012, 41). Solutions to these problems were offered both inside the framework of DSGE models and outside of it (Ragot 2012). In the case of financial intermediation and risks modelling, several economists attempted to extend the standard DSGE framework in order to better represent the relation between financial risk and business cycles and to evaluate the effectiveness of monetary policy in crises such as the one experienced in 2008 (Wieland 2012, 42). Jean-Claude Trichet went even further in his requirements:

> [W]e need to better integrate the crucial role played by the financial system into our macroeconomic models. One approach appends a financial sector to the existing framework, but more far-reaching amendments may be required. In particular, dealing with the non-linear behaviour of the financial system will be important, so as to account for the pro-cyclical build-up of leverage and vulnerabilities.
>
> (Trichet 2010)

Another perceived weakness of pre-crisis DSGE models was the assumption that households and firms shared homogeneous expectations about future events and that these expectations were rational. "Rational expectations theory – affirmed Jen-Claude Trichet – has brought macroeconomic analysis a long way over the past four decades. But there is a clear need to re-examine this assumption" (Trichet 2010). Trichet himself hinted at the most promising lines of research: adaptive learning and rational inattention. While some economists have begun to incorporate in their DSGE models forms of adaptive learning, the general framework remains that of homogeneous expectations (Wieland 2012, 43). Heterogeneity of expectations and diversity of beliefs, though, might be a key to better explain business cycles and phenomena of high volatility, modelling, for example, variances in the degree of optimism and pessimism of households and firms. Attempts in this direction have been done only by some New-Keynesian models (Wieland 2012, 44).

A more radical attempt at abandoning rational expectations would require alternative explanations to human behaviour as offered by behavioural economics (Akerlof, Shiller 2010; De Grauwe 2012) or a completely different methodology of research as that of agent-based modelling. Both these strands of research, though, have yet to be translated in structural macroeconomic models that could be used by institutional actors to evaluate the impact of different policies and forecast business cycles.

The first section of this volume is dedicated to the aforementioned literature and research. Bertram Schefold analyses the macroeconomic debate on business cycles from the new neoclassical synthesis to the resurgence of new Keynesian views. He underlines how the main difference between these opposite positions consists in the influence that crises might have on the long-term trend of an economy: a mere disturbance in one case, a lasting impact – by the name of hysteresis – in the other. In consequence of a crisis, the trend could even experience a permanent slow-down and so necessitate structural reforms to improve again, while mere Keynesian demand management would be ineffective. Interestingly, Schefold, by applying this framework of analysis to the recent Euro-zone crisis, convincingly explains both the failure of standard anti-cyclical Keynesian policies and the divergence in labor unit costs among European countries since the year 2000 (Schefold 2014).

In the second chapter of the volume, Arnaud Diemer goes even further by trying to update economists' methods and tools by using system dynamics. In believing that system dynamics can bring a new perspective on business cycle and crisis' analysis, Diemer follows the advice of Jean-Claude Trichet.

> Scientists – affirmed Trichet – have developed sophisticated tools for analysing complex dynamic systems in a rigorous way. These models have proved helpful in understanding many important but complex phenomena: epidemics, weather patterns, crowd psychology, magnetic fields. Such tools have been applied by market practitioners to portfolio management decisions, on occasion with some success. I am hopeful that central banks can also benefit from these insights in developing tools to analyse financial markets and monetary policy transmission.
>
> (Trichet 2010)

Diemer delineates the main analytical tools of system dynamics and applies them to the Euro-zone crisis.

Economic policies after the crisis

Theoretical debates were only a small part of the academic and public discussion following the most recent economic crisis. Much effort and research was spent in discussing the most appropriate policies to restore the stability of the financial sector and sustain the level of production and employment. The crumbling of New Consensus Macroeconomics led to a revision of the policy practices that had characterized the action of institutions in the decades before. The International Monetary Fund (Blanchard, Romer, Spence, Stiglitz 2012) as the European Central Bank (Trichet 2010) called for a reassessment of economic policy indications. As Olivier Blanchard put it: "There are many targets and many instruments. How the instruments are mapped onto the targets and how these instruments are best used are complicated problems, but we need to solve them" (Blanchard 2012, 7).

The European Union was a major theatre of discussion due to the presence of multiple institutional actors with different attributions regarding economic policies. Moreover, national traditions of economic thought still coexist among member states (Brunnermeier, Landau, James 2016), justifying the insistence on different sets of policies to foster growth and counter the business cycle. The crisis, calling for timely and incisive policy answers, revealed the fragility and inadequacy of European institutions while national political actors attempted to impose their view on other member states or on supra-national institutions like the ECB. The second section of this volume deals with the theoretical and political debate inside the European Union on major policy issues, from monetary policy to fiscal stimuli and social spending.

Inflation targeting, as 'the' monetary policy, had been a major part of the pre-crisis consensus. Otmar Issing, though, justly remembers how the theoretical and normative content of that policy became blurred and questionable over time: "the concept turned out to become more and more complicated. It soon was called inflation targeting with judgment and later flexible inflation targeting" (Issing 2012, 26). The crisis complicated the picture by calling central banks to expand the scope of their policy actions.[2] Questions that had long been excluded from the reach of central banks, as asset-price developments, the zero lower bound on nominal interest rate and the unemployment rate, resurfaced as potential targets (Blanchard 2012). All the while theory lagged behind the exigencies of policy action.

> Despite a widespread recognition of the importance of introducing channels for money and credit into structural models, – affirmed the ECB in 2010 – their formalisation is still at an early stage. Admittedly, over the last years, there has been extraordinary research activity, partly done at, and largely encouraged by, central banks themselves. The absence of a role for money and credit has been perceived by central banks as a major limitation in the ability of available structural models to inform policy decisions. While substantial progress has been achieved, the modelling of money and credit is still highly stylised. However, some important implications for the conduct of monetary policy can already be drawn.
>
> (European Central Bank 2010, 50)

Relying more on empirical investigations than theoretical foundations,[3] central banks devised innovative measures, other than the policy-rate rule, to aim at the new targets of monetary policy. Instruments ranged from increased supervision and regulation of financial actors to quantitative easing, from enhanced monetary analysis to unconventional measures (Gabor 2014).

Antonio Forte depicts in detail this evolution of the monetary policy in the euro area. Forte describes the transformation of the traditional tools of the ECB in order to sustain the banking system and to avoid liquidity risk and the implementation of unconventional measures to reactivate the monetary policy transmission mechanism, to avoid the risks of a prolonged period of deflation. Empirical research, examined by Forte, sustains the view that all these measures have prevented the worst scenario, that is the end of the Eurozone (Arestis, Sawyer 2012b), but their effectiveness has not been as expected. Problems remain: the multiplying of targets and policy instruments can damage the perceived independence of a central bank, given that some measures favour precise economic and/or social groupings – inside the EU, even precise nations – over others, and could also have perverse cumulative effects (Blanchard 2012, 11). Economic theory will have to catch up with the widespread consensus over the new monetary policies practiced after the crisis by central banks.

More theoretical research should also be dedicated to new types of money that are spreading internationally and lie outside the control of central banks. Cryptocurrencies have not only entered the imaginary of people as highly speculative objects, but during the recent economic crisis have also been used by popular and nationalist movements inside the euro area as a symbol of regained independence from the ECB and international financial institutions. Left to such a political discourse, cryptocurrencies have been the object of value judgements with no theoretical content. Nicolas Barbaroux dedicates a chapter of this volume to the theoretical debate over the new decentralized currencies, starting with the position expressed in 1976 by Frederich von Hayek. Hayek saw 'Denationalized money' in the light of an enhanced competition among currencies – a view already championed by Francesco Ferrara in the middle of the 19th century (Ferrara 2013). Barbaroux also evaluates if and how Hayek's monetary theory can still be a useful framework to understand the functioning of latest private currencies based on encryption.

Another main field of dispute in the academic and in the political arena after the onset of the crisis of 2008 has been fiscal policy. While the former macroeconomic consensus left little space for fiscal policy measures in stabilizing the cycle or fuelling economic growth, in the wake of the crisis most countries applied some kind of discretionary fiscal plan to alleviate the worst effects of the economic contraction (Blanchard, Romer, Spence, Stiglitz 2012, 45–47). In the words of Robert Solow:

> The general belief then was that monetary policy was an adequate tool for taking care of minor blips. During long and deep recessions, however, it has become evident that monetary policy may reach its limits without being able to generate enough aggregate demand to close the excess supply gap. So governments have turned more or less instinctively to discretionary fiscal policy, even if the latest refined theory cannot approve.
>
> (Solow 2012, 73)

While theory, again, lost pace, the political cycle heavily influenced economic policies and was influenced by them (Shome 2012, 49).

The fight over fiscal policy measures and the weight of the political cycle were particularly harsh among European Union members (Arestis, Sawyer 2012a). Given the loss of control over monetary policy, national governments fought bitterly over budgetary constraints, easily blaming the Union for being incapable to effectively relieve populations from the consequences of the crisis. The lack of agreement on a common economic policy theory (Hein, Truger, Van Treeck 2012) and the absence of a crucial institution as a European treasury gave rise to a colourful array of anti-cyclical actions without any coordination that worsened the cycle instead of reducing it (Semieniuk, Van Treeck, Truger 2011). Maurice Baslé dedicates a chapter of this volume to a careful analysis of the institutional construction and regulation of the euro area and its flaws. Among them, he identifies the unrealism and ineffectiveness of the European

Commission's supervision of national budgets at least since 1999. The present combination of procedures – budgetary supervision, macro-economic imbalances procedure and coordination of economic policies – is still not an optimal one. The only viable alternative, in Baslé's view, would be to introduce one or more actors, such as a European monetary fund or a European treasury or a stabilization mechanism in the European budget, which would assume the crucial function of overall macroeconomic stabilization.

Also, regarding social protection and anti-cyclical safety nets (Ferreiro, Serrano 2011), there still isn't a general agreement in favour of a common European social policy nor a large consensus that such policy could be a positive and very useful guardrail, particularly in times of crisis. Sandrine Michel examines the issue in the last chapter of the second section of the volume. Results are mixed. Trends in the rise of social expenditures remain sensitive to business cycle variations, and countercyclicality is still their main characteristic. Social expenditures thus play an important role in income stabilization through public transfer policies. Education and healthcare expenditures, though, emerge form Michel's analysis as insensitive to the fluctuations of business cycles. In the European countries, in spite of considerable national differences, these expenditures have assumed an increasing role in economic growth, independent from the cycle, through the qualitative development of the labour force and better living standards.

Economic thought, politics and culture

There are many explanations for resistance to innovations in the post-crisis period, both in theoretical reasoning and policy implementation. The lack of understanding of the dynamics of crises is not the only cause. Political ideas and economic cultures are the basis for the creation of new economic institutions and are used by different interest groups to 'dress', 'design' and prioritize economic policies (Palley 2012). Advances in scientific research are useful to foster change, but these advances should not hide the preconceptions, implicit modelling or proto-analytic narratives that always serve as the basis for interested economic policy recommendations. Economic ideas, good or bad, to paraphrase Keynes, have political power.

The third section of this volume focuses on the confrontation between the political and cultural representations of neoliberalism, ordoliberalism and Keynesian ideas during and after the crisis. In the Eurozone, this means tackling with the growing political influence of Germany, spreading its own economic ideas (Brunnermeier, Landau, James 2016, 27–32). The first chapter in this section, by Peter Nedergaard, explores the linkages between ordoliberalism and how the Eurozone perceived the crisis and reacted to it. Nedergaard observes that even if ordoliberalism was the ideational philosophy in the backdrop of the construction of the Economic and Monetary Union (EMU), in some critical moments of the existence of EMU ordoliberal recommendations were not followed by the member states, even by Germany. Nonetheless, when in 2011 Germany became de facto hegemonic in the European Union, it began to shape the EMU's constitution according to ordoliberal principles, causing extreme reactions on part of other member states and even the rise of populist and nationalist movements (Hein, Truger 2013).

In the following chapter, Alain Alcouffe and Fanny Coulomb investigate the influence of French economists on the construction and strategic management of international economic institutions from the World Trade Organization to the EMU and the International Monetary Fund since the end of World War II. Paradoxically, French views – for a long time in the minority – seem to have been vindicated by the recent economic crisis.[4] Many of the policy indications championed by the likes of Jacques Delors, Henri Chavranski and Pascal Lamy have re-entered academic discussion in consequence of the failing of New Consensus Macroeconomics (Arestis, Sawyer 2013).

The last chapter of the volume, by Monika Poettinger, analyses the debate over economic theory and economic policies that took place on main newspapers in France, Germany and Italy during the crisis years. The research confirms the relevance of economists long dead and of the historical past in the structuring of present categories of thought and symbolic imagining. It also shows how economic theories were used in relation to the political cycle and to ignite nationalistic sentiments. Lastly, it testifies how economists interacted with media and politics, as a critical voice against a judgmental evaluation of theories or as part of the political decision process, even participating in governments.

In sum, this volume presents the ten years period following the 2008 crisis as pivotal for both the modelling and the characterization of the last economic, theoretical and, ultimately, political cycle in Europe. The volume relates the increasing dissatisfaction with the belief that the economic cycle had been vanquished by the adoption of reckless and widespread neo-liberalist policies, underlining the current debate in economics and the enlargement of the policy choices available at state and inter-state levels to avoid future breakdowns and foster economic growth. Choices must be made – many at an international level – on financial markets regulation, regulations for a banking sector responsive to risk and granting responsibility, monetary regulation and coordination in a growing competitive environment among major international currencies and potentially between such currencies and new private forms of money, and the institutionalization of the macroeconomic stabilization function at interstate level in the euro area. All of this implies, obviously, a better knowledge of economic theories and better economic theories, particularly on business cycles (Coyle 2012). In this regard, this volume aims to favour a more widespread understanding of different European traditions of thought, not exclusively at scholarly level, fostering a more conscious scrutiny of economic policy indications and a clear understanding of the choices available.

Notes

1 An accurate listing of these models for the US and the euro area can be found in Wieland (2012, 39–40).

2 According to the ECB:

> The financial crisis has proven to be a powerful reminder that policy-makers need to be attentive to the build-up of imbalances in the nominal sphere of the economy. Monetary analysis endows the ECB's monetary policy strategy with a framework to always be attentive to the build-up of financial imbalances, which ultimately bear risks to price stability. Finally, the monetary analysis in the context of the two-pillar strategy ensures that no perspective and no information set is overlooked in the decision-making process. This notion of cross-checking has many dimensions, including the consideration of the long-term perspective in addition to the shorter-term one and the assessment of financial as well as real developments.
>
> (European Central Bank 2010, 109)

3 According to the ECB:

> In conclusion, the changing patterns of influence with which money acts upon the economy and price formation – at times more directly through expansions or contractions in purchasing power, at other times in a more roundabout fashion, through asset prices, liquidity constraints and the pricing of risk – remain largely unexplained.
>
> (European Central Bank 2010, 55)

4 On the different traditions of economic thought in Germany and France and the respective policy indications, see: Brunnermeier, Landau, James (2016, 40–83).

References

Acemoglu, D. (2009). "The Crisis of 2008: Structural Lessons for and from Economics", *CEPR Policy Insight*, 28.

Akerlof, G., Shiller, R. J. (eds.) (2010). *Animal Spirits: How Human Psychology Drives the Economy, and Why It Matters for Global Capitalism*, Princeton, NJ: Princeton University Press.

Alcouffe, A., Poettinger, M., Schefold, B. (eds.) (2017). *Business Cycles in Economic Thought: A History*, London: Routledge.

Arestis, P., Sawyer, M. (eds.) (2012a). *The Euro Crisis*, New York: Palgrave Macmillan.

Arestis, P., Sawyer, M. (eds.) (2012b). "Can the Euro Survive after the European Crisis?", in Id., *The Euro Crisis*, New York: Palgrave Macmillan, pp. 1–34.

Arestis, P., Sawyer, M. (eds.) (2013). *Economic Policies, Governance and the New Economics*, New York: Palgrave Macmillan.

Blanchard, O. (2012). "Monetary Policy in the Wake of the Crisis", in: Blanchard, O., Romer, D., Spence, M., Stiglitz, J. E. (eds.) *In the Wake of the Crisis: Leading Economists Reassess Economic Policy*, Cambridge, MA: MIT Press, pp. 7–14.

Blanchard, O., Romer, D., Spence, M., Stiglitz, J. E. (eds.) (2012). *In the Wake of the Crisis: Leading Economists Reassess Economic Policy*, Cambridge, MA: MIT Press.

Bordo, M. et al. (eds.) (2016). *Central Banks at a Crossroads: What Can We Learn from History?*, Cambridge: Cambridge University Press.

Brancaccio, E., Fontana, G. (eds.) (2013). *The Global Economic Crisis: New Perspectives on the Critique of Economic Theory and Policy*, London: Routledge.

Brunnermeier, M. K., Landau, J., James, H. (2016). *The Euro and the Battle of Economic Ideas*, Princeton, NJ: Princeton University Press.

Christoffel, K., Coenen, G., Warne, A. (2008). "The New Area-Wide Model of the Euro Area a Micro-Founded Open-Economy Model for Forecasting and Policy Analysis", *ECB Working Paper Series*, 944.

Coyle, D. (ed.) (2012). *What's the Use of Economics: Teaching the Dismal Science after the Crisis*, London: London Publishing Partnership.

De Grauwe, P. (2012). "Booms and Busts: New Keynesian and Behavioural Explanations", in Solow, R. M., Touffut, J.-P. (eds.) *What's Right with Macroeconomics?*, Cheltenham: Edward Elgar Publishing, pp. 149–180.

European Central Bank (2010). *Enhancing Monetary Analysis*, Frankfurt: European Central Bank.

Farkas, B. (2016). *Models of Capitalism in the European Union: Post-Crisis Perspectives*, New York: Palgrave Macmillan.

Ferrara, F. (2013). *Moneta e credito*, Carnago: Libreria San Giorgio.

Ferreiro, J., Serrano, F. (2011). "Long-Term Uncertainty and Social Security Systems", in Arestis, P., Sawyer, M. (eds.) *New Economics as Mainstream Economics*, New York: Palgrave Macmillan, pp. 154–189.

Fiorentini, R., Montani, G. (2012). *The New Global Political Economy: From Crisis to Supranational Integration*, Northampton: Edward Elgar Publishing.

Gabor, D. (2014). "The ECB and the Political Economy of Collateral", in Goodhart, C., Gabor, D., Vestegaard, J., Ertürk, I. (eds.) *Central Banking at a Crossroads: Europe and Beyond*, London: Anthem Press, pp. 157–176.

Goodfriend, M., King, R. G. (1997). "The New Neoclassical Synthesis and the Role of Monetary Policy", in B. S. Bernanke and J. J. Rotemberg (eds.), NBER Macroeconomics Annual, Cambridge, MA: MIT Press.

Hein, E., Truger, A. (2013). "Future Fiscal and Debt Policies: Germany in the Context of the European Monetary Union", *Working Paper Institute for International Political Economy Berlin*, 24.

Hein, E., Truger, A., Van Treeck, T. (2012). "The European Financial and Economic Crisis: Alternative Solutions from a (Post-)Keynesian Perspective", in Arestis, P., Sawyer, M. (eds.) *The Euro Crisis*, New York: Palgrave Macmillan, pp. 35–78.

Issing, O. (2012). "Lessons for Monetary Policy", in Blanchard, O., Romer, D., Spence, M., Stiglitz, J. E. (eds.) *In the Wake of the Crisis: Leading Economists Reassess Economic Policy*, Cambridge, MA: MIT Press, pp. 25–30.

Jacobs, M., Mazzucato, M. (eds.) (2016). *Rethinking Capitalism: Economics and Policy for Sustainable and Inclusive Growth*, Chichester: John Wiley & Sons.

Kocka, J., Van der Linden, M. (eds.) (2016). *Capitalism: The Reemergence of a Historical Concept*, London: Bloomsbury.

Leijonhufvud, A. (2009). "Macroeconomics and the Crisis: A Personal Appraisal", *CEPR Policy Insight*, 41.

Mankiw, N. G. (2006). "The Macroeconomist as Scientist and Engineer", *Journal of Economic Perspectives*, Fall, 29–46.

Palley, T. I. (2012). *From Financial Crisis to Stagnation: The Destruction of Shared Prosperity and the Role of Economics*, Cambridge: Cambridge University Press.

Paul Krugman's London Lectures (2009). "The Nobel Laureate Speaks on the Crisis in the Economy and in Economics", *The Economist*, 11 June.

Ragot, X. (2012). "The Economics of the Laboratory Mouse: Where Do We Go from Here?", in Solow, R. M., Touffut, J.-P. (eds.) *What's Right with Macroeconomics?*, Cheltenham: Edward Elgar Publishing, pp. 181–194.

Schefold, B. (2014). "The Economic Crisis and the Euro: Theoretical and Political Reactions to a Singular Historical Experiment", in Varsori, A., Poettinger, M. (eds.) *Economic Crisis and New Nationalisms: German Political Economy as Perceived by European Partners*, Bern: Peter Lang, pp. 67–98.

Semieniuk, G., Van Treeck, T., Truger, A. (2011). "Nothing Learned from the Crisis? Some Remarks on the Stability Programmes 2011–2014 of the Euro Area Governments", *IMK Working Paper*, 11.

Sepp, J., Frear, D. (eds.) (2011). *The Economy and Economics after Crisis*, Berlin: BWV Verlag.

Shome, P. (2012). "Fiscal Stimuli and Consolidation", in Blanchard, O., Romer, D., Spence, M., Stiglitz, J. E. (eds.) *In the Wake of the Crisis: Leading Economists Reassess Economic Policy*, Cambridge, MA: MIT Press, pp. 49–56.

Solow, R. (2012). "Fiscal Policy", in Blanchard, O., Romer, D., Spence, M., Stiglitz, J. E. (eds.) *In the Wake of the Crisis: Leading Economists Reassess Economic Policy*, Cambridge, MA: MIT Press, pp. 73–78.

Stiglitz, J. E. (2009). "The Current Economic Crisis and Lessons for Economic Theory", *Eastern Economic Journal*, 35(3), pp. 281–296.

Timbeau, X. (2012). "The Fireman and the Architect", in Solow, R. M., Touffut, J.-P. (eds.) *What's Right with Macroeconomics?*, Cheltenham: Edward Elgar Publishing, pp. 8–32.

Trichet, J.-C. (2010). *Reflections on the Nature of Monetary Policy Non-Standard Measures and Finance Theory*, Opening Address at the ECB Central Banking Conference, Frankfurt, 18 November.

Van Treeck, T., Sturn, S. (2012). "Income Inequality as a Cause of the Great Recession? A Survey of Current Debates", *Conditions of Work and Employment Series*, 39.

Wieland, V. (2012). "Model Comparison and Robustness: A Proposal for Policy after the Financial Crisis", in Solow, R. M., Touffut, J.-P. (eds.) *What's Right with Macroeconomics?*, Cheltenham: Edward Elgar Publishing, pp. 33–67.

Woodford, M. (2009). "Convergence in Macroeconomics: Elements of the New Synthesis", *American Economic Journal: Macroeconomics*, 1(1), pp. 267–279.

Acknowledgements

The original idea of the volume stemmed from a trilateral Villa Vigoni Colloquium, held in 2016. Given the multidisciplinary character of the conference's theme, participants included economists, historians of economic thought and economic historians from France, Germany and Italy. We wish to thank the Secretary General Prof. Dr. Immacolata Amodeo and all the staff of Villa Vigoni for precious support and the encouragement to pursue our researches. We further thank Routledge for publishing the resulting studies with its renowned professionality. Thanks also to all anonymous reviewers, to translators and editors who helped to make out of scattered essays a well-structured volume.

Part I

Developments in business cycle theory

1 Business cycles without periodicity?

Bertram Schefold

Introduction

This book is concerned with economic and theoretical cycles during the "long" 21st century which – the authors agree – starts with the downfall of the Soviet Empire and ends with the present. This means a time for most of the contributors that they have lived through. For myself, the "long" 21st century began in the middle of my academic career. Personal experience makes it tempting to recount history in subjective terms. Since the number of economists has grown considerably and communication among them has intensified in the same period, choices have to be made anyway: a book would not suffice if all important approaches were to be mentioned. At the time when this essay was planned, one felt overwhelmed by the impact of the last crisis. At the time of publication, one still strives to understand it better in order to overcome it definitely. For all these reasons, the authors were in danger of being historically and geographically parochial, but recent researches have made us aware of what one can discover only with some effort: that many crises of very different characteristics took place in all parts of the world during this quarter of a century. They include the crises in East Asia of the emerging markets, crises resulting from speculative activities in domestic or international markets and crises connected with the new markets based on information technologies, but also crises of the countries in transformation in Eastern Europe and crises associated with dramatic forms of inequality in developing countries, in particular in Africa. Reinhart and Rogoff (2011) have taken such a broader view, but we are concerned with the contrasts and the continuities between the revival of the theory of business cycles during the period under consideration and the older traditions of business cycle theory, which had been discussed in two previous meetings at Villa Vigoni.

Even with this traditional European (and American) focus, business cycles theory has become more diffuse. The idea of a regular cycle of given length (like the ten-year cycle of the 19th century) has disappeared almost completely, and the trigger of the cycle can apparently turn out to be quite different. One need not look to exotic places to see it. Relatively small events such as the housing bubble in the United States in the present case or stock market crashes in the 1980s can lead to worldwide disruptions. But it is a question whether the economies are always so vulnerable. Is there a fundamental weakness in the growth process, which is the real cause of the depth of the present crisis? Why can an event such as an overproduction of houses in the United States, which would hardly have been noticed during the years of strong growth in the immediate post-war era, now lead to stagnation and recession? What are the channels of propagation? And finally, what are the costs of these crises? It is an outcome of the historical investigations (Reinhart and Rogoff 2011) that crises associated with a major disruption of the financial markets are costlier and take longer before a full recovery sets in. The broad result is that the origins of crises can be quite heterogeneous, but there are characteristic patterns of how they develop. It seems impossible to predict the outbreak and very difficult to predict the time it takes for recovery, but fundamental connections can be described and identified. In the beginning of the period under consideration, there was a strong opposition between Keynesian and neoclassical approaches. The latter had begun to incorporate the theory of rational expectations. Today we find that compromises between those approaches have been struck which almost form a continuum.

Selective, as we have been and must be, we shall start with some broad ideas of the rational expectations revolution. We shall confront this with the radical Minskyian position and with the compromise struck by the French disequilibrium school (Malinvaud), thus going back to the 1970s and 1980s. It can incidentally be shown that a simple variant of that theory can be used to compare and confront a Keynesian and a neoclassical interpretation of the present European crisis, as it affects the North and South unequally. We then recount a simple model of real business cycles and indicate where new Keynesian elements may come in. We conclude with a novel model by Blanchard and others explaining "reverse causality" as an expression of how weak growth processes may render the economy more vulnerable and lead to cyclical behaviour.

Rational expectations

It is impossible to deny the importance of the rational expectations revolution, for which Lucas (1988) was largely responsible. (He also was one of the progenitors of the endogenous theory of growth by introducing human capital to explain total factor productivity in the neoclassical growth model.) He opposed the Keynesian assumption that agents have given static expectations so that policymakers can rely on them, anticipating given reactions in order to influence the course of events by introducing discretionary measures. According to the theory of rational expectations, agents use all information at their disposal; they therefore adapt their expectations according to the policies pursued by the authorities. Agents anticipate, for instance, the consequences of a rising quantity of money, which follows from central bank policies. If the policy is known, they expect prices to rise, and activity and employment stay constant. This meant that the well-known Phillips curve was modified. It had consisted in a negative correlation between inflation and unemployment, based on historical observations. But if the consequence of the rise of the money supply is anticipated, prices rise at once and the Phillips curve becomes inelastic. Friedman (Phelps 1967) had predicted a similar final outcome on the basis of adaptive preferences. Rational preferences meant that this outcome was realised immediately.

It took some time before it was discovered that a similar idea had already been used by the mediaeval bishop and scholar Oresmius, who said that the depreciation of a currency by means of debasement could lead to a gain of the prince, who ordered the debasement, only if the merchants were surprised by this move and did not know about the debasement, for otherwise they would raise prices at once, so that the debased coins had only as much purchasing power as corresponded to their reduced content of precious metals (Schefold 1995). Our present experience (up to January 2018) contradicts the scenario envisaged by Lucas completely: the European Central Bank dramatically augments credit and the money supply by buying securities, and yet the markets do not react with notable increases of either inflation or output. We shall return to this point in a new Keynesian context in the next section. Here it may suffice to say that it can, in the face of a monetary expansion, also be rational not to raise prices under the pressure of competition, in particular from foreign countries, if many prices are set by organs of the state, the state being slow to react, and if trade unions are weak. And it is rational not to increase output if one foresees that other agents do not raise demand. Lucas himself admits in his book of 1987 (Lucas 1988, p. 13) that "rationality" can be defined precisely only in the context of a given model. He even says in an associated footnote that the definition of "rational" as a "use of all information" is "vacuous" and that the identification of "rational" with the hypothesis that people "know the true structure of the world they live in" is "silly" (Lucas 1988, p. 13).

Lucas argues, in essence, that the process of accumulation should be seen as a dynamic game, in which the actors take into account the actions of all others, including the policymaker. He introduces a "useful" economic model where states of the economy s_t at time t are transformed into future states by a function F:

$$s_{t+1} = F(s_t, e_t) \tag{1}$$

Here e_t are exogenous shocks from some fixed distribution. Both s_t and e_t are vectors. A policy change means the transition from one F to another F'. This is described as a policy action $z_t = z_t(s_t)$. The agents i also act according to s_t: $a_{it} = a_i(s_t)$. Hence:

$$s_{t+1} = F(s_t, e_t) = H(z(s_t), a(s_t), s_t, e_t) \tag{2}$$

The agents choose their actions from a set of possibilities, they evaluate the result of the actions taken in each period and a representative agent eventually maximises the return generated over an infinite horizon, according to his expectations and discounting the future.

There is no room here to reproduce the result of the intertemporal maximisation. The main point Lucas wanted to make can be stated without going into the details and without adding the specifications needed to render the calculation feasible (for instance, introducing the Phillips curve).

Keynesian policy is identified by Lucas with the discretionary fixing of certain numbers, like the magnitude of a budged deficit, in order to influence specific situations, each of which is historically unique. The theory of rational expectations, by contrast, is concerned with deriving policies that lead to repetitive patterns of reactions. The result of the intertemporal maximisation can, on the one hand, be used to estimate the growth process with the characteristic deviations from the trend that results from the shocks. The triumph of the rational expectations revolution was in part due to the fact that real business cycle models (RBC) were or seemed quite successful in reproducing the curious mixture of regularity and irregularity in the deviations from the trend. On the other hand, Lucas affirmed in his book that these deviations were small and should not be a major concern for the economist, for to make them still smaller by discretionary means – as opposed to policy rules – would only detract from the major structural problems. He noted that unemployment in the United States was of the order of magnitude of seven per cent at the peak of the cycle. These seven per cent were the problem, he thought, not the one or two per cent added during a recession. Consumption smoothing was inefficient, as Kydland and Prescott had shown (Lucas 1988, p. 106). The book ends with the assertion that macroeconomics was going to be dissolved into microeconomics: "The term 'macroeconomic' will simply disappear from use and the modifier 'micro' will become superfluous." In the end, the economists did not go quite as far.[1]

Keynesian approaches and rationing

I here want to discuss Minsky and Malinvaud. They were active essentially prior to 1990, but their work was an important influence on economic thought around 1990 and may be discussed here. It was very important at least for my perception of macroeconomics in those days.

A theory of rational expectations in the sense of Lucas is not possible if uncertainty is such that rational expectations cannot be formulated and economic action must be based on other assumptions. Hyman Minsky described the situation as follows:

> Keynes wrote that in dealing with uncertainty, "in practice we have tacitly agreed, as a rule to fall back on what is, in truth, a *convention*" (Keynes 1936, p. 152, emphasis in the original). But in a capitalist economy the aspect which is least bound by technology or by fundamental psychological properties, which is most clearly a convention or even fashion,

> subject to moods of optimism and pessimism and responsive to the visions of soothsayers, is the liability structure of both operating and financial organisations.
>
> (Minsky 1976 [1975], p. 128)

Minsky continues saying that ingenuity is used to develop and introduce financial innovations just as it is used in production. In each state of the economy, one acts as if it were to continue indefinitely. Credit is easily granted in the boom, but in the depression, people have experienced the dangers of being in debt and are afraid of incurring new debts. However, neither boom nor recession last indefinitely. "Each state nurtures forces that lead to its own destruction" (Minsky 1976 [1975], p. 128).

Uncertainty means that the action of the agents cannot be based on the anticipation of the action of others over a long period of time. Since the future is unknown, only the short run behaviour of others can be guessed; hence, one is trapped in states of optimism during the boom and of pessimism during the recession. As recent experience shows, even prolonged efforts of a central bank to change the state of mind of the public can be in vain. Minsky then was led to consider a consequence, which had also been observed by others such as Clower (1965) and Garegnani (1964): the decisions on consumption and investment are constrained by the budget available to households and entrepreneurs. Both could spend more than is available from their current income, using own wealth or credit, and both can – and mostly do – to some extent spend less and save. However, according to the neoclassical equilibrium conception, households spend exactly as much as corresponds to their equilibrium income at full employment, saving being taken into account by means of an intertemporal allocation over a given time horizon, and the actions of firms adapt to the demand for goods and the supply of factors of households over time. It can be shown that a general equilibrium exists in the form of prices for goods and factors such that full employment obtains, the corresponding income can be spent and leads to production such that the expenditure buys the commodities produced, and the incomes so generated are equal to the full employment income.

Unemployment is the main manifestation of the fact that the market clearing which we observe in reality (not always, but on average and as a tendency, market clearing for goods may be granted) does not correspond to the full employment equilibrium predicted by the neoclassicals. As for labour, there are effective budget constraints. If we neglect saving and credit taking by households, they can spend wages only, if they get them; that is, if they are employed. The unemployed have no access to credit and can only spend what they get by some form of social security or private charity. The budget constraint is vey flexible for firms.

Minsky was most successful in his description of the boom phase, during which an ever-more-daring liability structure is being built up, using financial innovations. The real growth is constrained by technical possibilities and by the rise of real wages. The debt base by contrast may grow and accelerate, being constrained only by mutual trust, and the growth of the financial system overtakes that of the real economy. Hence, financial crises become possible when this liability structure is fragile; they can, but need not, be triggered by overinvestment in the sense of real capital growing faster than demand for it. As I argued in Schefold (2017), the economists of the 19th century, even Marx, doubted the possibility of a crisis triggered merely by financial factors. Why should trust suddenly wane? Why should a loss of trust affect many, if it affects a few? Earlier economists sought the explanations in factors exogenous to the financial system such as bad news (a war, a natural calamity) or, as a recurrent possibility, overinvestment in the "real" economy. Keynes's explanation was ambiguous. He wrote that, "when disillusion falls upon an overoptimistic and overbought market, it should fall with sudden and even catastrophic force" (Keynes 1936, p. 316). Why is the market "overoptimistic and overbought"? This could be interpreted as the traditional – and, I repeat, even Marxian – overinvestment theory (Spiethoff 1925).[2] But Minsky thought that Keynes meant an overexpansion of the financial system which could, in principle, take place even during a phase of reasonably steady growth of the real economy.

More or less contemporaneously with Minsky and post-Keynesian research, there arose a school of neoclassical economics that took up the question of the effective budget constraints in order to modify general equilibrium so as to take Keynesian states of unemployment into account as states of disequilibrium due to quite different causes than the financial system, namely due to price and wage rigidities. Malinvaud wrote an influential synthesis of this approach. It was criticised by Cambridge economists, and I myself got involved in the debate at one point (Malinvaud 1977; Kahn 1977; Schefold 1983). I here want to summarise an aspect of the discussion which may help to shed light on a current debate.

The model is as follows: there is a production function to produce output Y by means of labour, capital being constant in the short run so that we may write $Y = F(L)$. The value of output is distributed as wages and profits. Kahn introduced the post-Keynesian theory of distribution, i.e. the idea to have profits determined by the expenditure on investment and by the government, so that we may write:

$$pF(L) = wL + P = wL + G \tag{3}$$

with p price level, w wage rate, L labour employed, P profits and G exogenous expenditure (government and investment). The equality, causally interpreted, means that exogenous expenditure determines profits and employment, since all profits are saved and all wages spent on consumption. The equality holds as an equilibrium condition and defines a curve in the space of prices and employment, with the wage rate regarded as given:

$$p = wL / F(L) + G / F(L) \tag{4}$$

Assuming diminishing returns, this curve is *U*-shaped; it divides the plane into two areas; below the curve where prices are low, there is excess demand at given prices, and above, demand is deficient.

On the other hand, the real wage p/w is equal to the marginal product $F'(L)$ in competitive conditions. One can introduce an element of imperfect competition by assuming a mark-up. In the simpler case, if there is no mark-up, $p = w/F'(L)$. This marginal cost curve rises and cuts the *U*-shaped equilibrium curve in the minimum of the latter, as can easily be shown. The point of intersection of the two curves may be called the point of effective demand *PED*; here the *two* conditions formulated by Keynes in the *General Theory* in the Chapter III on effective demand are simultaneously fulfilled. The Keynesian underemployment equilibrium has employment corresponding to effective demand, which depends on the level of exogenous expenditure and the level of expenditure out of wages. Keynes assumed that the Marshallian condition of price equalling marginal cost was also fulfilled. In the present construction, this condition corresponds to his supply curve. There was unemployment, if the labour supply $\bar{L}$ which we here assume to be inelastically given, is to right of the point of effective demand. This is drawn in Figure 1.1.

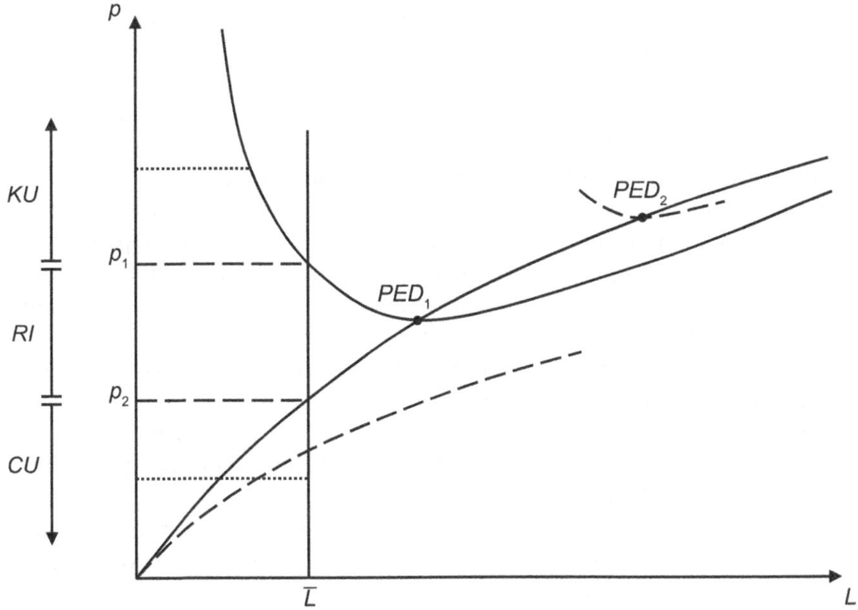

Figure 1.1 Different kinds of equilibria according to Schefold (1983), based on Malinvaud (1977) and Kahn (1977). *KU* domain of prices leading to Keynesian unemployment, *RI* domain of prices leading to repressed inflation, *CU* domain of prices leading to classical unemployment. PED_1 point of effective demand initially. PED_2 point of effective demand resulting if autonomous expenditure *G* is increased. This reduces Keynesian unemployment resulting at price p_1. The price level is lower at p_2, where classical unemployment results. This is lowered if the marginal cost curve moves to the right, drawn as dotted curve.

Different kinds of disequilibria result, given exogenous expenditure, depending on the level of prices. At an intermediate level of prices, the point of effective demand is, with the labour supply assumed here, to the right of full employment. At these prices, there is repressed inflation: excessive demand leads to full employment at prices which are above marginal cost. Since we considered the wage rate as given, this situation can be stable only to the extent that it is possible to control prices. If prices are still higher, there is Keynesian unemployment in that an equality of demand and supply of goods obtains at these prices, but they are above costs. Effective demand in real terms is, at this level of prices, too low to employ the entire labour supply. At low prices, such as at p_2, effective demand is high in real terms but, given increasing marginal cost, the level of employment is limited by the condition that the real wage equals the marginal product or that prices equal marginal cost.

This latter constellation was introduced by Malinvaud as "classical unemployment." He claimed to have had an important idea in that he thought to have shown in a unified framework how unemployment could result not only from deficient demand, but also from excessive cost, and he suggested that, in a more general model, there might be deficient demands in some sectors (meaning an equilibrium of demand and supply of the corresponding goods such that labour was not fully employed as here at prices p_2) and classical unemployment in other sectors, due to excessive costs, as here at prices p_2 . His intended model was much more complicated than the present simplification, in that it was fully disaggregated. A generation of especially French economists struggled with the task of representing the various disequilibria properly with their interconnections. By contrast, Kahn took the main step to simplify the model, but it was not fully transparent, because he reckoned in wage units. He criticised Malinvaud for a variety of shortcomings. He criticised the lack of a representation of expectations, of a proper investment function and of an explicit dynamics. Malinvaud would answer to these criticisms with new ideas which we cannot discuss here (Malinvaud 1980). But the main point made by Kahn was that classical unemployment could not exist, because, he thought, prices could not be kept constant. In our diagram we are, at p_1, far in the region of excessive demand. So it seemed natural to assume that prices would rise, and a process of inflation might eventually lead into a situation of Keynesian unemployment, if not to repressed inflation.

I found Kahn's argument entirely convincing, although a similar argument could be advanced against repressed inflation: what assumption would suffice to demonstrate that prices could be controlled and actually would stay constant? In the happiest days of Postkeynesianism, we were content to believe that the essential outcome was Keynesian unemployment. Of course, the arguments were all based on real balance effects and given monetary investment. These assumptions could be and were doubted, and the doubts gave rise to further discussions.

Is there anything to be learned from these controversies, which few young economists know today? Going through the old papers, I was struck by the observation that there was something, after all, in Malinvaud's ideas, if we reconsider them in the light of recent experiences, especially in Japan and Southern Europe. For we find that prices *can*, after all, be kept constant in the face of excessive effective demand. Governments run deficits, especially in Japan, but also in Europe, where governments repeatedly overstep the constraints by the Maastricht Rules. This is counteracted to some extent by private saving to pay for old debts. Would it help to stimulate demand even more, in line with the attempts of central banks to ease credits?

The price level is fairly constant,[3] in part because of falling oil prices and in part because many prices are administered by the state, but I think primarily because of worldwide competition. Whoever wants to sell cars on the world market can do so, provided they are sufficiently cheap and of adequate quality. And so countries are in many sectors in a situation resembling that of p_2. In order to sell more, productivity would have to increase, and/or the wage rate would have to fall. This is indicated in the diagram by a shift of the marginal cost curve to the right. If productivity could be raised sufficiently, which would be better than lowering real wages, full employment would be reached.

But politicians and many economists argue that government expenditure should be raised instead, so as to fight unemployment in the Keynesian manner. This will not help in a situation such as the one drawn in this diagram. If autonomous expenditure G is raised or if other countries increase imports (in the actual situation: if Germany invests more, which would be good for the infrastructure of that country), the point of effective demand for Italy moves up and to the right. That will help to reduce Keynesian unemployment, if one is in a situation such as at p_1. But if one is in a situation such as at p_2, the situation will not be affected at all: the marginal cost curve will not move, if productivity does not improve, and the price level cannot be raised because of global competition.

So this diagram seems to provide an rationalisation of the debate which has been going on since about 2010, when it was discovered that unit costs had developed in very unequal ways in different European countries since 2000, as shown in Figure 1.2 (see Schefold 2014).

I do not claim that this simple model provides a solution to the debate, but it does provide an instrument for diagnosis, which may help to clarify what different authors mean. It is true that classical unemployment vanishes, if there are constant or increasing returns (this was a point made by Schefold 1983, pp. 241–244), and one may object to the use of a production function. But, as stated, the core of the argument remains valid, if mark-ups are introduced instead of the neoclassical marginal cost condition and if firms are in each sector ordered in the short run according to productivity so that a rising cost curve can be drawn for the corresponding market as a whole. What, if not costs and quality, prevents Japan or Italy from returning to the export-led booms of 40 or 60 years ago?

From the new Keynesian model to reverse causality

We return to the mainstream in the history of macroeconomics and business cycles. The real business cycle models have been supplemented by introducing

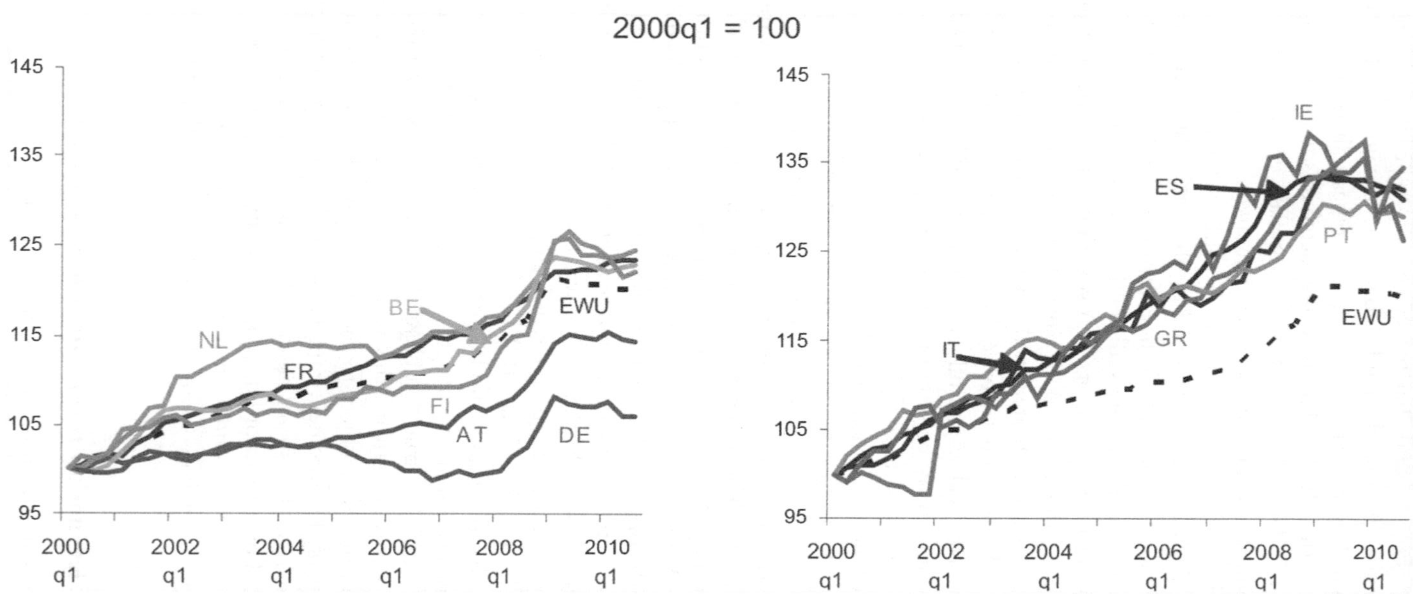

Figure 1.2 Development of unit costs in different European countries between 2000 and 2010, relative to national productivity

Source: Niechoj, Stein, Stephan and Zwiener (2011, p. 13)

market failures, in particular sticky wages and prices, which in turn were explained in different ways by menu costs, imperfect competition, coordination failures, search and matching theory, bounded rationality, efficiency wages, and others. In order to illustrate this intellectual development, it is useful to start from a representative model of real business cycles and to introduce complications successively. The point of departure is a neoclassical growth model with stochastic technical progress. The difference to the Solow model consists in the introduction of a stochastic component for total factor productivity and a labour supply which is responsive to the changes of the wage rate relative to the trend. Such a model has been presented by Robert King and Sergio Rebelo in the paper "Resuscitating real business cycles" (King and Rebelo 1999). The model can be made to fit real data for output rather well (Figure 1.3). It is, unsurprisingly for Keynesians, not equally successful, as far as labour is concerned. A detailed discussion of the paper must be omitted for reasons of space.

We want to conclude with a recent publication which links business cycle analysis and the trend of growth. The deep impact of the recent crisis has here displaced the idea that the business cycle consists of relatively minor fluctuations which, as in Lucas, are thought not to be worthwhile to control. Blanchard, Cerutti and Summers (2015) start from the admission that the great financial crisis entailed a fall of output such that the leading economies have remained far below the prerecession trend. This is not surprising, if one believes that each crisis is a different animal and that growth consists of upswings of different character and duration. But neoclassical theory predicts a trend with small fluctuations. Here, the fluctuation, if it can be interpreted as such, is large. How to explain its lasting consequence? Is it hysteresis? Is "hysteresis" an explanation, or is it just a name for the phenomenon? At any rate, the cost of the output shortfall seems to be much higher than typically assumed. The authors now demonstrate that the same may be said of many recessions. They present a survey of about 23 developed countries over 50 years and find that in two-thirds

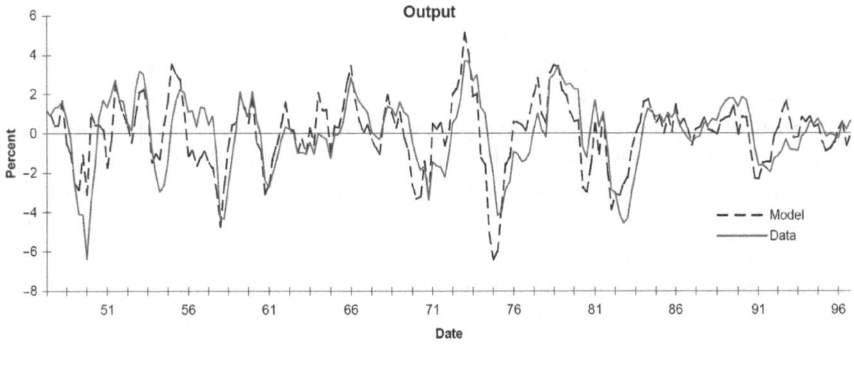

Figure 1.3 Simulation of the model and real output in the King/Rebelo model

Source: King and Rebelo (1999), figure 7, p. 959

of the recessions, output is lower than according to the prerecession trend even after the economy has recovered, and in half the cases output growth follows a lower trend than prior to the recession. Hysteresis is one explanatory hypothesis, if it is taken to mean a reduction of the propensity to invest due to the experience of the crisis or a similar later modification of initial conditions. Another is reverse causality, according to which it is the perspective of a long-term trend of output to fall which causes the recession in the first place.

The set-up expresses a belief in a certain permanence of fundamental data, especially of preferences and the trend of productivity, which are only shattered by shocks, but not changed permanently. Recessions are associated with different shocks. Changes of oil prices and financial crises as triggers are examples. A specific focus is on demand shocks:

> even in the case of recessions associated with intentional disinflations, which probably represent the purest case of demand shocks. We find that still nearly two thirds are associated with lower output later and that a significant fraction of those are associated with lower output growth.
>
> (Blanchard, Cerutti and Summers 2015, p. 4)

Hysteresis had been discussed by Blanchard and Summers earlier (1986). It may be due to institutional changes resulting from the crisis, such as tougher capital requirements or unemployed workers becoming unemployable. The analysis of the empirical basis, not to be described in detail here, is based on the following schematic idea: the sequence of data for actual output is confronted with a trend extrapolated from output during the four years preceding the recession. This is corrected on the one hand for unusual stimulating factors such as unusual growth of credit, and on the other hand a correction takes place to represent a declining trend of growth. This adjusted trend is then compared with actual growth during the four years following the recession so as to discover output gaps relative to this adjusted trend. A variety of tests show that the output gap can be observed across countries and phases of post-war growth, confirming the hypothesis of hysteresis.

Or are initial supply shocks the causes of slower growth, inducing, for instance, long-run changes in the behaviours of banks, more risk aversion and less efficient intermediation? Then, reverse causality is regarded as a possible explanation. It presupposes an exogenous decline of the growth potential that is anticipated by households and firms, and this leads to the recession, which thus initiates the phase of slower growth. "Firms appear to over-accumulate capital during periods of expansion. . . . [This is] what one would expect if firms and households took some time to realise that productivity growth had actually slowed down" (Blanchard, Cerutti and Summers 2015, p. 13). We here find a similarity with the old overinvestment theory (Spiethoff 1925).

The paper contains an extensive attempt to control for these rival hypotheses per type of recession. Among the results, the most important seems to be that lower output relative to the prerecession trend is found in two thirds of the

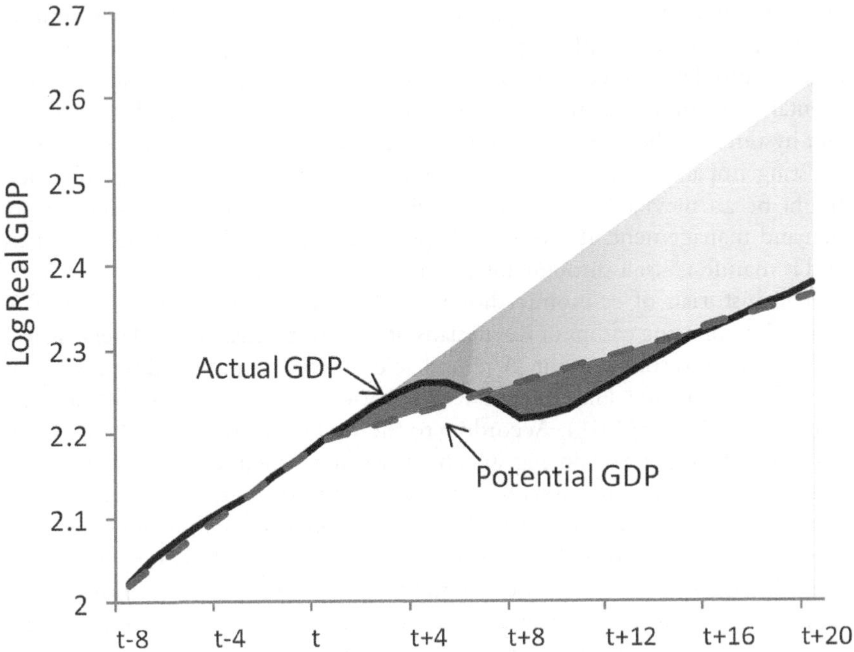

Figure 1.4 Decreases in growth, recessions and output gaps, according to Blanchard, Cerutti and Summers (2015). Agents anticipate the decline in the growth trend ("potential growth"); this causes the recession. But if the authorities calculate the output gap without having noticed the change of the trend, they will overstate it.

Source: Blanchard, Cerutti and Summers (2015, p. 26)

recessions. The phenomenon shows even in the case of deliberate disinflations (recessions caused by a financial policy oriented towards a reduction of inflation). The conclusion is that deviations from the adjusted trend are more dangerous than is usually thought in the case of hysteresis; hence, monetary policy should become more active to avoid lasting increases in unemployment, but a theory of an optimal monetary policy in the case of hysteresis does not seem to exist. If there is reverse causality, there is the danger, according to the authors, that potential output loss is overstated and that the action of the authorities is excessive, for it is their basic belief that the fundamentals of long-term growth cannot be influenced. The case of an overstatement is illustrated in Figure 1.4.

Conclusion

The paper by Blanchard, Cerutti and Summers (2015) can be seen as the expression of a new neoclassical synthesis. Contrary to the view taken by Lucas,

Keynesians do not rule out the possibility that the experience of a crisis has an irreversible effect on the dynamics of investment; crises then determine a trend which is visible only ex post. Here, growth is still represented as a moving equilibrium determined by resources, techniques and preferences; these fundamentals determine a trend, which is only disturbed, not altered by recessions. But hysteresis is the expression of the recognition that accidental crises can have a lasting impact, after all. Reverse causality, by contrast, recognises that there might be an inevitable slowdown of the trend. It is not to be influenced by demand management. It is only perhaps to be improved by structural reforms, and it manifests itself through anticipation in recessions.

The historian of economic thought will note that, over the course of 30 years, the opposing camps of Keynesians of various persuasions and neoclassicals have merged to some extent. A remarkable example is provided by the recent paper "Reconciling Hayek's and Keynes' Views of Recessions" by Beaudry, Galizia and Portier (2018). According to their interpretation, Hayek saw recessions mainly as periods during which an overinvestment of the past had to be liquidated; government intervention could not mitigate this necessary process without causing new distortions. The paper models such a process of liquidation but shows that some Keynesian policies can nevertheless be beneficial.

In this changed environment, "method" seems to have become more important than "ideology." The papers have in common that they do not expound an abstract theory, but formulate models that are in most cases immediately put to empirical tests using historical data. It is these methods with their associated standards of performance that seem to define modern mainstream economics. The elder historian of economic thought may regret that standards of theoretical rigour and elegance as well as of sociological interpretation are partially lost in this merger, but has to accept the fact that younger colleagues do not seem to feel that something is missing. Methods also change because of the growth of research institutes. Spiehoff's famous article (Spiethoff 1925) was edited by Edgar Salin 30 years after its first appearance (Spiethoff 1955) with only small amendments but in two volumes, the first containing the text, the second the statistical materials which Spiethoff had collected in a lifetime of study. It shows what an individual could perceive and may be contrasted with the systematic collection and analysis by the research institutes that originated a little later in the 1920s (Kulla 1996). As a result, after almost a century of institutionalised research, our modern perception starts not from single data but from statistical constructs of increasing sophistication which cannot easily be verified or challenged by a particular observer.

As far as the theory of business cycles is concerned, the diagnosis is clear: the triggers of business cycles can be many and diverse, and so are the propagation mechanisms. The length of the cycle is indeterminate, but they recur, and to speak of boom and recession is still a matter of course despite the absence of regularity in the form of the cycle. It remains to be seen which theory will be adequate as the 21st century actually unfolds.

Notes

1 For a comparison between fictional changes in rates of growth and consumption smoothing, see Section III of Lucas (1988).
2 Two quotes from Schumpeter may suffice to highlight Spiethoff's importance. In his *Theory of Economic Development* (English edition), Schumpeter (1961 [1934], pp. 214–216) compared *his* "theory with by far the most thorough effort in the field, that of Spiethoff – little as it is capable of comparison with the latter in thoroughness and perfection." According to the *History of Economic Analysis* (Schumpeter 1971 [1954]), "Spiethoff was the first to recognize explicitly that cycles are not merely a non-essential concomitant of capitalist life" (p. 1127). Only Marx had a similar insight.
3 The present paper was first presented in April 2016, and completed in January 2018.

Bibliography

Beaudry, P., Galizia, D. and Portier, F. (2018): Reconciling Hayek's and Keynes' Views of Recessions. In: *Review of Economic Studies*, 85 (1), pp. 119–156.

Blanchard, O., Cerutti, E. and Summers, L. (2015): Inflation and Activity: Two Explorations and Their Monetary Policy Implications. *IMF Working Paper* WP/15/230.

Blanchard, O. and Summers, L. (1986): Hysteresis and European Unemployment. In: *NBER Macroeconomic Annual 1986*, edited by S. Fischer. Cambridge, MA: MIT Press, pp. 15–77.

Clower, R.W. (1965): The Keynesian Counter-Revolution: A Theoretical Appraisal. In: *The Theory of Interest Rates: Proceedings of a Conference Held by the International Economic Association*, edited by F.H. Hahn and F.P.R. Brechling. London: Macmillan, pp. 103–125.

Eatwell, J. and Milgate, M. (1983): *Keynes's Economics and the Theory of Value and Distribution*. London: Duckworth.

Fischer, S. (ed.) (1986): *NBER Macroeconomic Annual 1986*. Cambridge, MA: MIT Press.

Garegnani, P. (1964): Note su consumi, investimenti e domanda effettiva (parte prima). In: *Economia internazionale*, 17, pp. 591–631.

Hahn, F.H. and Brechling, F.P.R. (eds.) (1965): *The Theory of Interest Rates: Proceedings of a Conference Held by the International Economic Association*. London: Macmillan.

Kahn, R. (1977): Malinvaud on Keynes. Reprint from *Cambridge Journal of Economics*, 1 (4), pp. 375–388. In: *Keynes's Economics and the Theory of Value and Distribution*, edited by J. Eatwell and M. Milgate (1983). London: Duckworth, pp. 214–228.

Keynes, J.M. (1936): *The General Theory*. London: Macmillan.

King, R.G. and Rebelo, S.T. (1999): Resuscitating Real Business Cycles. In: *Handbook of Macroeconomics*, Volume 1B, edited by J.B. Taylor and M. Woodford. Amsterdam: North Holland, pp. 927–1007.

Kulla, B. (1996): *Die Anfänge der empirischen Konjunkturforschung in Deutschland 1925–1933*. Berlin: Duncker & Humblot.

Lucas, R.E. (1988): *Models of Business Cycles*. New York: Blackwell.

Malinvaud, E. (1977): *The Theory of Unemployment Reconsidered*. Oxford: Blackwell.

Malinvaud, E. (1980): *Profitability and Unemployment*. Cambridge: Cambridge University Press.

Minsky, H.P. (1976 [1975]): *John Maynard Keynes*. London: Macmillan.

Niechoj, T., Stein, U., Stephan, S. and Zwiener, R. (2011): Deutsche Arbeitskosten und Lohnstückkosten im europäischen Vergleich – Auswirkungen in der Krise. Auswertung der aktuellen Eurostat-Statistik bis 2010. *IMK Report*, Nr. 60. Düsseldorf: Hans-Böckler-Stiftung/IMK, Institut für Makroökonomie und Konjunkturforschung.

Phelps, E.S. (1967): Phillips Curves, Expectations of Inflation and Optimal Employment over Time. In: *Economica*, 34 (3), pp. 254–281.

Reinhart, C.M. and Rogoff, K.S. (2011): *This Time Is Different: Eight Centuries of Financial Folly*. Princeton, NJ: Princeton University Press.

Schefold, B. (1983): Kahn on Malinvaud. In: *Keynes's Economics and the Theory of Value and Distribution*, edited by J. Eatwell and M. Milgate. London: Duckworth, pp. 229–246.

Schefold, B. (1995): Nicolaus Oresmius: Die Geldlehre des Spätmittelalters/Anmerkungen zum Text. In: *Vademecum zu einem Klassiker der mittelalterlichen Geldlehre. Kommentarband zur Faksimile-Ausgabe der um 1485 entstandenen Handschrift Oresmius, Nicolaus: Tractatus de origine et natura, iure & mutationibus monetarum (BNF, Ms Latin 8733 A)*, edited by B. Schefold. Klassiker der Nationalökonomie. Düsseldorf: Verlag Wirtschaft und Finanzen, pp. 19–72, pp. 184–195.

Schefold, B. (2014): The Economic Crisis and the Euro: Theoretical and Political Reactions to a Singular Historical Experiment. In: *Economic Crisis and New Nationalisms: German Political Economy as Perceived by European Partners*, edited by A. Varsori and M. Poettinger. Bern: Peter Lang, pp. 67–98.

Schefold, B. (2017): The Growth of Capital in Business Cycle Theories of the Nineteenth Century. In: *Business Cycles in Economic Thought*, edited by A. Alcouffe, M. Poettinger and B. Schefold. Routledge Studies in the History of Economics 191. London: Routledge, pp. 28–38.

Schumpeter, J. A. (1961 [1934]): *The Theory of Economic Development:An Inquiry into Profits, Capital, Credit, Interest, and the Business Cycle*. New Brunswick, NJ: Transaction Books.

Schumpeter, J. A. (1971 [1954]): *History of Economic Analysis*. London: Allen & Unwin.

Spiethoff, A. (1925): Krisen. Entry in Handwörterbuch, Volume 6, edited by L. Elster et al. Jena: Fischer, pp. 8–91.

Spiethoff, A. (1955): *Die wirtschaftlichen Wechsellagen. Aufschwung, Krise, Stockung*. Mit einer Einleitung von Edgar Salin. Tübingen: J.C.B. Mohr (Paul Siebeck).

Taylor, J.B. and Woodford, M. (eds.) (1999): *Handbook of Macroeconomics*, Volume 1B. Amsterdam: North Holland.

2 Business cycle to 2008's crisis

How system dynamics can help the economists to understand financial crisis[1]

Arnaud Diemer

A large number of models have been developed by economists to understand economic growth, economic fluctuations, business cycles, long wave, and economic and financial crises. Each model is usually concerned with some part of the economy and makes different assumptions on the processes that influence that part. In 1923, Joseph Kitchin considered that the movements of economic factors (price and volume) were composed of *minor cycles* averaging 3½ years in length, *major cycles* (so-called trade cycles) which are merely aggregates, usually of two, and *fundamental movements* or trends which are largely straight-line movements. In 1935, Kondratieff argued that the dynamics of economic life in the capitalist social order was not of a simple and linear nature, but rather of a complex and cyclical character. He assumed the existence of long waves of an average length of about 50 years in the capitalist economy. In 1937, Kalecki proposed a theory of the business cycle focused on investment processes (closely allied to the Keynesian theory). His analysis was divided in two parts: the determination of short-period equilibrium with a given amount of capital equipment and with a given rate of investment; and the determination of the rate of investment. The answer to the question "what causes the periodical crisis?" seems obvious – investment considered as capitalists' spending is the source of prosperity. But at the same time, investment drives the capitalist economy to crisis. In 1946, Burns and Mitchell presented a detailed, technical analysis of a method for studying the cyclical behavior of 1,277 individual series (covering production, transportation, employment, prices, inventories, sales and monetary circulation) in the United States, Great Britain, Germany and France. They arrived at the definition that a business cycle:

> consists of expansions occurring at about the same time in many economic activities, followed by similarly general recessions, contractions, and revivals which merge into the expansion phase of the next cycle, this sequence of changes is recurrent but not periodic; in duration business cycles vary from more than one year to ten or twelve years; they are not divisible into shorter cycles of similar character with amplitudes approximating their own.
>
> (1946, p. 3)

More recently, Kydland and Prescott (1982) developed a competitive equilibrium model to explain autocovariances of real output and the covariances of cyclical output with other aggregate economic time series for the post-war US economy. Minsky (1986, 1992) introduced the financial instability hypothesis (FIH) as an interpretation of the substance of Keynes's "General Theory" to argue that the capitalist economy was not reliant on exogenous shocks to generate business cycles. The FIH holds that business cycles are compounded out of the internal dynamics of capitalist economies (profit and debts) and the system of interventions and regulations that are designed to keep the economy operating within reasonable bounds.

Beyond the theoretical and empirical aspects, these models are based on a structural and methodological design well known to economists. Most of these models introduce the concept of equilibrium (existence, unicity, stability), a program of optimization and econometrics techniques. Some models are representing a particular phenomenon at a point of time (static model), while some others are comparing different phenomena at different points of time (comparative static model). Some models are analyzing the process of a particular phenomenon (mathematical model that describes the functions of demand and supply), while some others are trying to reflect changes in real or simulated time and are taking into account that model components are constantly evolving (dynamic model). This chapter is intended to update economists' methods and tools by using system dynamics. We believe that system dynamics can bring a new perspective to the analysis of business cycles (even for long waves) and crises. To explore that assumption, we propose to follow the four next steps. First, we introduce system dynamics as a method to revisit economic models (Meadows, 1973; Low, 1976; Sterman, 2000). Second, we present the roots and the characteristics of the subprime crisis. Third, we apply system dynamics to analyze the mechanisms of that financial crisis. System dynamics may help economists to better understand the strengths (and weaknesses) of systems thinking and improve their own knowledge of economic growth. Fourth, we propose to implement system dynamics by using a scenario planning method.

Applying system dynamics to the economic system

System dynamics was developed at MIT during the 1950s by J.J Forrester. His first book *Industrial Dynamics* (1961) contains the seeds of a method that was to prove successful in the 1970s, notably through the *Limits to Growth* (Meadows, Meadows, Randers, 1972).

For Forrester (1961), industrial dynamics was a way of studying the behavior of industrial systems to show how policies, decisions, structure and delays are interrelated to influence growth and stability. To speak of systems "implies a structure of interacting functions. Both the separate functions and the interrelationships as defined by the structure contribute to the system behavior" (Forrester, 1967, p. 1). To describe a system, we have to describe not only the separate functions, but their method of interaction: "As used here, a system means a grouping of parts that operate together for a common purpose"

(Forrester, 1968a, p. 1). So, to identify the structure of a specific system, one should understand the fundamental nature of the structure common to all dynamic systems. In *Industrial Dynamics*, Forrester integrated the separate functional areas of management, marketing, investment, research, personnel, production and accounting (Forrester, 1968b). Each of these functions is reduced to a common basis by recognizing that any economic or corporate activity consists of flows of money, orders, materials, personnel and capital equipment. These five flows have been integrated by an information network. Industrial dynamics "recognizes the critical importance of this information network in giving the system its own dynamic characteristics" (Forrester, 1961, p. vii).

Forrester considered that industrial dynamics became possible as the result of four fields that were relatively new: (1) information feedback control theory, (2) analysis of decision-making processes, (3) experimental approaches to system analysis and (4) digital computers.

(1) An information feedback system exists "whenever the environment leads to a decision that results in action which affects the environment and thereby influences future decisions" (Forrester, 1961, p. 14). The study of feedback systems deals with the way information is used for the purpose of control. It helps to understand how the amount of corrective action and the time delays in interconnected components can lead to unstable fluctuations. For Forrester, information feedback systems have three characteristics: *structure* (which tells us how the parts of the system are related to one another), *delays* (which always exist in the availability of information, in making decisions based on the information and in taking actions on the decisions) and amplification (which manifests when an action is more forceful than might at first seem to be implied by the information inputs to the governing decisions).
(2) Decision-making processes were achieved in the 1950s during the automatization of military tactical operations. For Forrester, fire control prediction decisions during World War II were made automatically by machine. A few years after, these automatic decisions were accepted and put into practice. So, it was necessary to interpret the tactical judgment and experience of military decision-making into formal rules and procedures:

> It has been amply demonstrated that carefully selected formal rules can lead to short term tactical decisions that excel those made by human judgment under the pressure of time, or with men having insufficient experience and practice, or in the rigidity of large organizations.
>
> (Forrester, 1961, p. 17)

(3) Experimental approach reminds us that mathematical analysis is not powerful enough to yield general analytical solutions to situations as complex as are encountered in business. Simulation is often used to conduct experiments on a model (e.g., the design of an air defense system or an engineering process): "Use of simulation methods will not require great mathematical ability. To be sure, details of setting up a model need to be

monitored by experts because there are special skills required and pitfalls to be avoided" (Forrester, 1961, p. 18).

(4) Electronic digital computers became available between 1950 and 1960. Computing machines (with increased memory, speed and capacity) brought the feasibility of dealing with more complex systems.

These four new fields associated with corporate modeling provided the breeding ground for the development of systems dynamics:

> Chance intervened again when I found myself talking to people from General Electric. They were puzzled as to why their household appliance plants sometimes worked three or four shifts and then, a few years later, had to lay off half their staff. . . . After finding out how the corporation made hiring and inventory decisions, I started to do some simulation, using a pencil and a page in a notebook. At the top, I put columns for inventories, employees, and orders. Given these conditions and the policies being pursued, one could predict how many people would be hired the following week. This produced a new set of conditions for inventories, employment, and production. It became clear that here was the potential for an oscillatory or unstable system that was entirely internally determined. Even if incoming orders remained constant, employment instability could still arise as a consequence of common decision-making policies. This first pencil and paper inventory control system was the beginning of system dynamics.
>
> (Forrester, 1989, p. 5)

In *Industrial Dynamics*, system dynamics can be presented as a form of computer simulation modeling which uses the concepts of information feedback and state variables to model social systems and to explore the link between system structure and time-evolutionary behavior (Forrester, 1968a). To model the dynamic behavior of a system, we have to introduce two new publications from Forrester, *Principles of Systems* (1968a) and *Urban Dynamics* (1969). In these books, Forrester proposed a detailed description of the system dynamics approach and recognized four hierarchies of structure (Diemer, Coelho, Morales, 2017): (1) closed boundary around the system, (2) feedback loops as the basic structural elements within the boundary, (3) level (state) variables representing accumulations within the feedback loops and (4) rate (flow) variables representing activity within the feedback loops (see Table 2.1).

Closed system boundary: To develop a complete concept of a system, the boundary must be established within which the system interactions that give the system its characteristic behavior take place. Forrester states that:

> the closed boundary does not mean that the system is unaffected by outside occurrences. But it does say that those outside occurrences can be viewed as random happenings that impinge on the system

Table 2.1 Four steps in the theory of system structure

A Closed boundary		
1 Feedback loops		
	a Levels b Rates	
		(1) Goal (2) Observed condition (3) Discrepancy (4) Desired action

Source: Forrester (1967, p. 2)

> and do not themselves give the system its intrinsic growth and stability characteristics.
>
> (Forrester, 1969, p. 12)

Feedback loop structure: The dynamic behavior of systems is generated within feedback loops (Roberts, 1975). A feedback loop is composed of two kinds of variables, called rate and level variables. A feedback loop is a structure within which a decision point – the rate equation – controls a flow or action stream. The action is integrated to generate a system level of behavior. Information about the level is the basis on which the flow rate is controlled.

Figure 2.1a is the simplest form of feedback system, whereby there may be additional delays and distortions appearing sequentially in the loop. There may be many loops that are interconnected. Figure 2.1b describes the circular cause and effect structure of the feedback loop when a firm orders replacement goods to maintain an inventory.

So, the aim of system dynamics modeling is to explain behavior by providing a causal theory (Lane, Sterman, 2011), and then to use that theory as the basis for designing intervention policies into the system's structure, which then attempts to change the subsequent behavior and improve performance (Lane, 2008). Each system dynamics study starts with a problematic situation and a set of assumptions that is used to describe the problematic situation (Goodman, 1974). These assumptions are held in a mental model of a dynamic system (MMDS). Each causal link in a model has a polarity, the direction of effect that the influencing variable has on the influenced variable. The nature of that influence depends on the type of causal link being considered. In a system dynamics model, the polarity of each feedback loop is a crucial part of understanding the model behavior. The perturbation of a loop may result in the magnification of the original effect; this unstable response is known as a positive feedback loop polarity. Alternatively, a perturbation may be counter-acted,

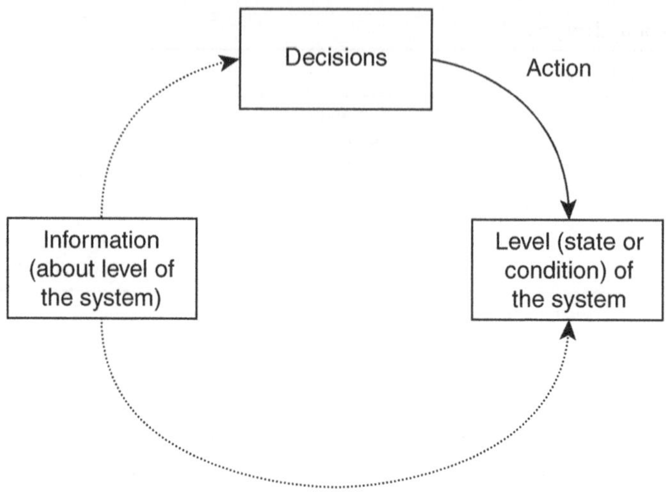

Figure 2.1a Feedback loop

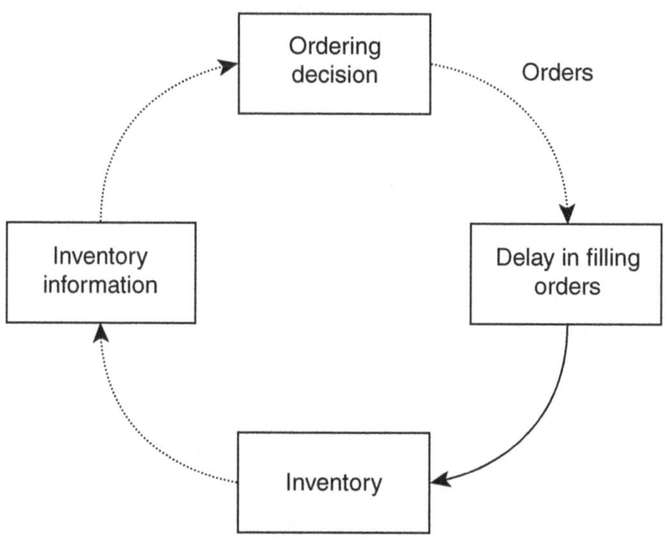

Figure 2.1b Inventory ordering loop
Source: Forrester (1968a, p. 8–9)

or resisted by the operation of the loop. This equilibrating response is known as a negative feedback loop polarity.

Role of simulation: the interaction of these complicated relationships is almost always beyond the capability of the human mind to infer – as mental simulation is deficient. Computer simulation is therefore rigorously needed to deduce the consequences of these relationships and to reveal the counter-intuitive behavior that results from the assumptions in the model.

Diagramming methods: Two diagramming methods are dominant in the system dynamics community (Lane, 2008). Broad representations of the variables and the feedback structure of a model are conveyed using causal loop diagrams (CLD). In contrast, stock/flow diagrams (SFD) are more detailed, discriminating between both state and flow variables.

At this stage of the discussion, it is important to stress two important points relating to the use of system dynamics:

(1) If *Industrial Dynamics* (1961) and *Urban Dynamics* (1969) presented system dynamics as a computer simulation model[2] of how sales or a city grow, stagnate or decay, it's because Forrester's main endeavor was the development of a tool to be used by managers and urban policymakers. But system dynamics is above all a method "of dealing with questions about the dynamic tendencies of complex system, that is, the behavioral patterns they generate over time" (Meadows, 1976, p. 31). System dynamics help us "to learn about dynamic complexity, understand the sources of policy resistance and design more effective policies" (Sterman, 2000, p. 4). As a method embedded in interdisciplinarity, system dynamics gets its roots

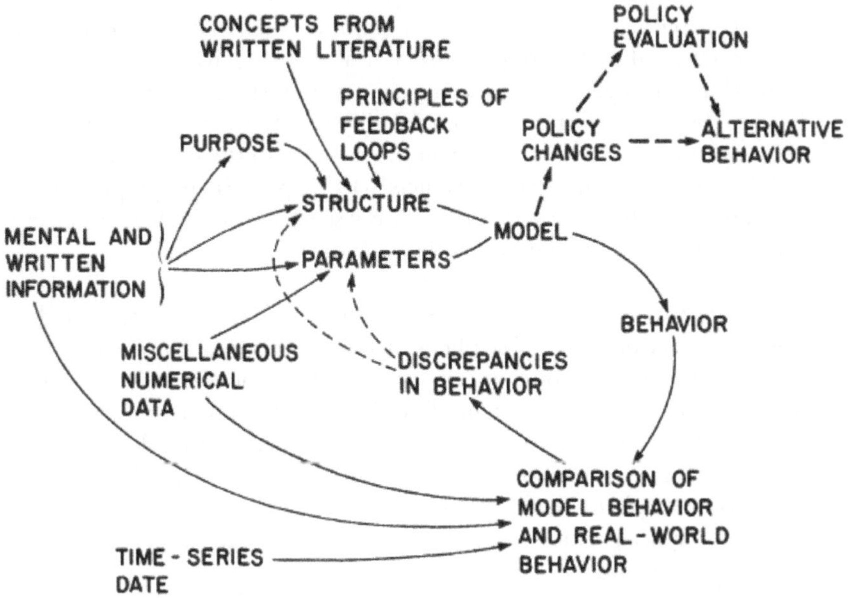

Figure 2.2 Creating a system dynamics model

Source: Forrester (1975b, p. 559)

from the theory of nonlinear dynamics and feedback control developed in mathematics, physics and engineering (Milsum, 1968, Wolstenholme, Coyle, 1983; Wolstenholme, 1985). Because we apply it to understand the behavior of human as well as physical and technical systems, system dynamics has been used in social sciences and economics (Morecroft, 1982, 1985). For the latter, it would seem that the dynamics of systems generated a "paradigm conflict" (Diemer, 2004, 2012), with another method, econometrics (Tinbergen, 1937), developed by economists (Irving Fisher, Ragnar Frisch) in the 1930s. This hostility may be due to the personalities of the methodological founders (whereas J.W. Forrester and Paul Samuelson worked at MIT, no economist from MIT participated in the research project *Limits to Growth*, 1972) and to the natural parochialism of academics (econometrics aims to estimate and test economic models). However, as suggested by Donella Meadows, "a closer examination of the two modeling paradigms reveals a deeper division, one that is not easily bridged" (Meadows, 1976, p. 47). Key words such as predictability vs unpredictability, linearity vs nonlinearity, quantitative vs qualitative, opened structure vs closed structure are symbols of the fierce opposition between the two sides.

(2) System dynamics is focus on general dynamic tendencies, "whether the system as a whole is stable or unstable, oscillating, growing, declining or in equilibrium" (Meadows, 1976, p. 31). So, system dynamics as a method seems a very interesting way to improve theoretical foundations and descriptive analysis of the long waves (and well as the business cycle). This point is developed by Forrester (1977) in his article "Growth Cycles". Considering that most literature of economic cycles falls into two classes, either statistical analysis of past time series or descriptive speculation about how different aspects of the socio-economic system interact to produce cyclical behavior, Forrester argues that "System Dynamics computer simulation models can be used to retain the strength of the descriptive method while overcoming its major weakness" (1977, p. 525) and proposes a new powerful basis for testing theories of how structure and policies interact to produce fluctuations and growth in a socio-economic system.

To explore the dynamic tendencies of systems, it's necessary to include in models concepts from many disciplines or fields of thought – especially those coming from physical and biophysical sciences, social sciences and economics – and to discount theories to the light of our knowledge on system's structure. In *Industrial Dynamics*, J.W Forrester (1961, p. 49) introduced models as "a basis for experimental investigations". Models became largely accepted as means for studying complex phenomena. A classification of models used some key words as abstract – physical, static – dynamic, linear – nonlinear, unstable – stable or steady state – transient.

In the 1970s, Forrester (1975a, 1976, 1977, 1980) discussed growth cycles from the perspective of the national model. This model – supported by MIT

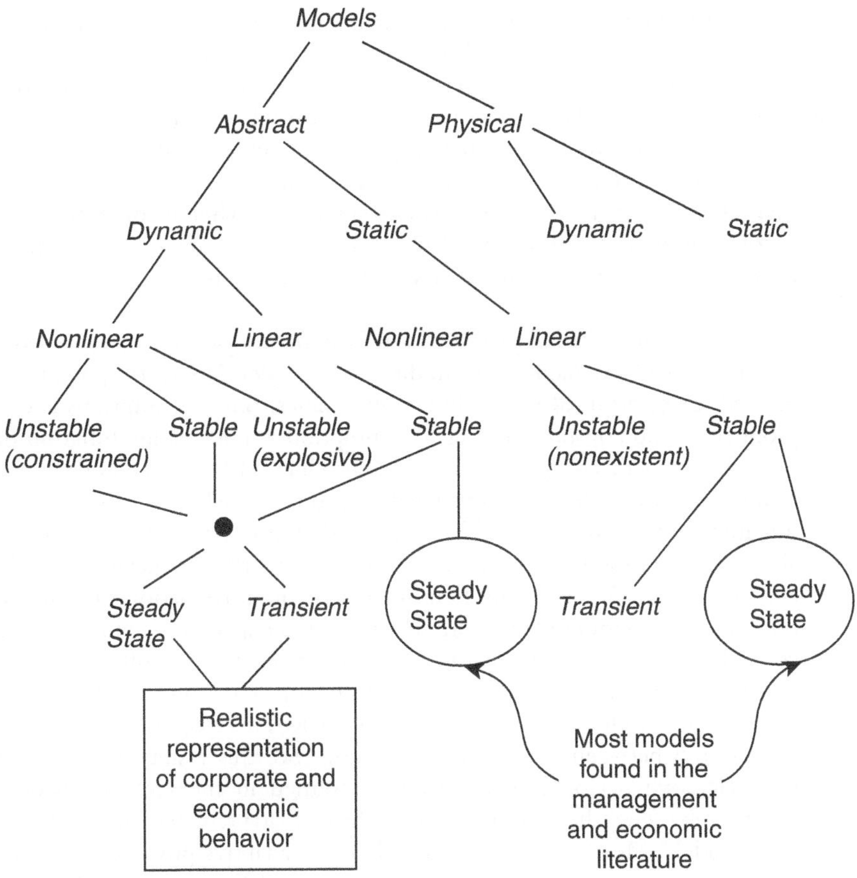

Figure 2.3 Classification of models

Source: Forrester (1961, p. 49)

and the Rockefeller Brothers Fund – was intended to integrate the major sectors of national activity into an explicit dynamic simulation model for investigating how the different parts of the socio-economic system function, how they produce the behavior of the entire system, how alternative policies might yield a more desirable future. The model was composed of six sectors (production, financial, household, demographic, labor, government). These sectors describe the major determinants of production, consumption, investment, employment, prices and government policy, and are interconnected by flows of information, people, money, goods, services and orders. The national model was designed to describe the processes of national social and economic development over approximately a 200-year period, from 1850 to 2050. By comparison with the resulting studies of *Urban Dynamics* (1969), *World Dynamics*

(1971a) and *Limits to Growth* (1972), Forrester, Mass and Ryan (1976, p. 52) considered that the national model was "highly detailed, containing a range of internal structures spanning from short-term inventory management and price setting policies to capital investment policies and long term demographic and environmental forces". The model was able to deal with the long-range issues of economic growth, resources, energy, population and capital investment, as well as with the shorter-term dynamics of the business cycle.

System dynamics as a method, seems very interesting when it comes to revisiting economic models (Meadows, 1973; Low, 1976; Sterman, 2000). Three main cyclical modes of economic behavior are presented here.

(1) Dennis Meadows (1970) proposed a reformulation of the cobweb model and introduced a dynamic commodity cycle model. His starting point is a general formulation of the Cobweb hypotheses, three assumptions about production and consumption: (1) consumption is a decreasing function of the price recognized by consumers, (2) production is an increasing function of the price which was expected by producers when production was initiated, and (3) there is a lag between initiation of production and availability of the resulting commodity. Using the works of Akerman (1957) and Nerlove (1958), Meadows considers that the formulation of adaptive producer expectations plays an important role to explain the stability of the cobweb model. This formulation of expectations is quite different from the investment decision, or the acquisition of production capacity or the maturation (production) of the capacity in its effect upon the dynamic relationship between price and production. So, this result "invalidate(s) the strict one period lagged response assumed in the Cobweb Model and thereby alter the system's stability from that predicted by the Cobweb Model" (Meadows, 1970, p. 17). Because adaptive producer expectations cause important changes in the conclusions about system stability of the cobweb model, Meadows proposes to develop a more realistic model which explicitly represents all the processes relating price, production and consumption: the dynamic commodity cycle model.

The essence of that structure are two coupled negative feedback loops, consumption and production, each acting to adjust inventory coverage to the desired level. When stocks are lower than desired, there are price increases. These increases affect change in both the production and the consumption sectors which act to return inventory to its desired level. The price increases lower per capita consumption of the material. With less consumption drain, inventories will tend to rise. Production relationships act with the same effect. The increase of the current price raises producers' price forecasts and thus the capacity they wish to utilize. After many delays, additions to capacity result in increased production and higher inventory.

So, in the dynamic commodity cycle model, producers may employ any function of current and past prices to form their expectations about future

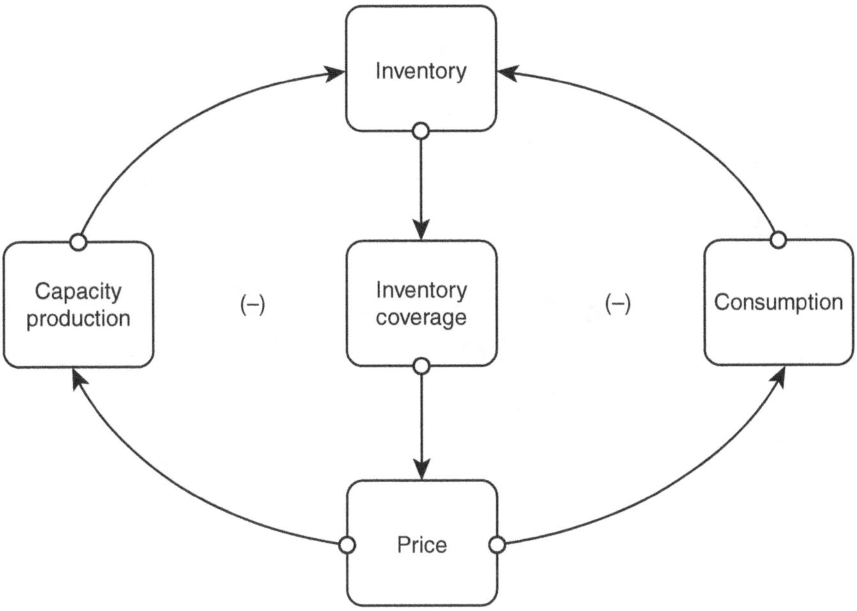

Figure 2.4 Feedback loop structure of production cycles

Source: Meadows (1970, p. 19)

prices. Emphasis is upon actual commodity, capital and information flows. The model includes an inventory of processed commodities, which serves to decouple production and consumption over the short run. Production and consumption are assumed to adjust continuously to price changes, not abruptly from the equilibrium point in one period to that in the next. Price is determined by those who hold inventories through interaction with producers and consumers. As inventories rise above the desired level, those holding stocks will decrease the price to discourage production and raise consumption. When inventories fall below the level desired by those holding them, prices will be increased. Delays that are important in the behavior of real commodity systems are explicitly included in the model: (1) producing commodity, (2) forecasting producers' price, (3) forecasting consumption, (4) recognizing the retail price, (5) responding to price forecasts and (6) transferring productive capacity.

(2) Low ([1976] 1980) proposed to revisit the multiplier – accelerator model to involve information/physical flows and to interpret it in terms of system dynamics.

The smoothed income is an exponentially smoothed value of current income. So, current consumption depends on the weighted income of all past periods

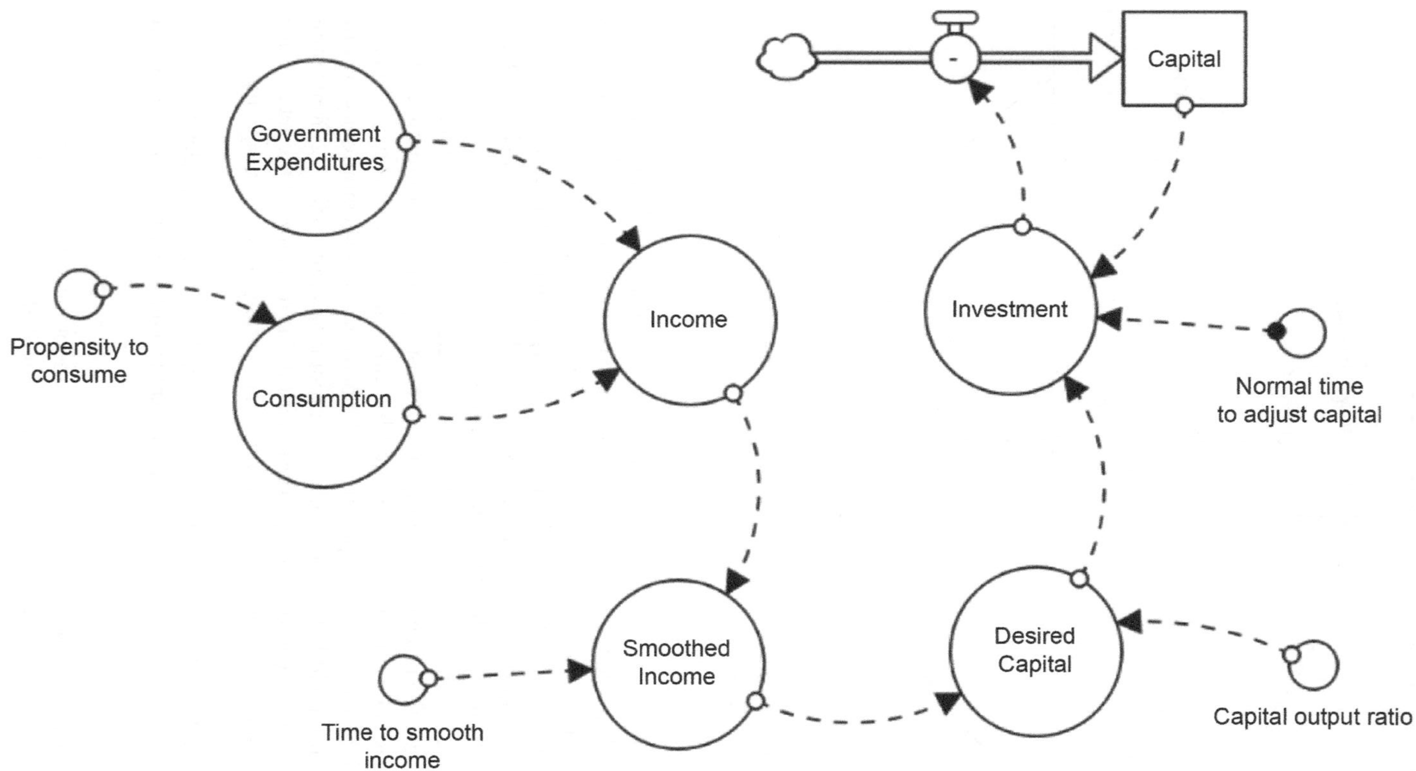

Figure 2.5 The two-level multiplier – accelerator mode revisited

Source: Low ([1976] 1980), p. 83)

rather than on income of one undefined previous period. This formulation "reflects the continuous process by which consumption habits and standards are gradually adapted to the levels dictated by current income and corresponds to the permanent portion of consumption in Friedman (1957) permanent income hypothesis" (Low, op. cit.), p. 83).

Consumption and smoothed income constitute parts of the multiplier loop. This loop is positive, and propensity to consume plays a key role. For the multiplier loops, investment – like consumption – is linked to smoothed income in a positive loop and to capital stock in a negative loop. These two loops together area a two-level system, which can produce oscillatory behavior.

(3) Sterman and Mosekilde (1992) proposed a behavioral model of the long wave. They considered that acquisition of capacity in individual firms involved inherently oscillatory processes. In isolation, these processes are stable, producing damped oscillations when excited by exogenous changes in demand. However, a wide range of self-reinforcing loops exists in the linkages between firms and among production, financial, household and government sectors of the economy, destabilizing the cycle and lengthening its period. These following loops are:

   (1) Demand for capital increases the capacity needs of the capital-producing industries, further boosting orders for capital, so expansion by capital producers raises labor demand and wages, leading to substitution of capital for labor and still greater demand for capital.
   (2) Rising aggregate demand boosts prices, reducing real interest rates and further stimulating investment. Rising output boosts income and aggregate demand, further boosting output. Expansion leads to expectations of future growth, leading to further investment and output growth.
   (3) Rising credit demand in order to finance the boom causes monetary accommodation, additional inflation and still lower real interest rates.

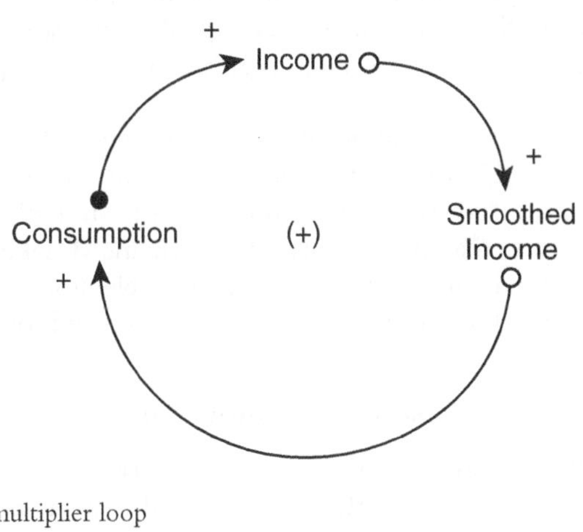

Figure 2.6a The multiplier loop

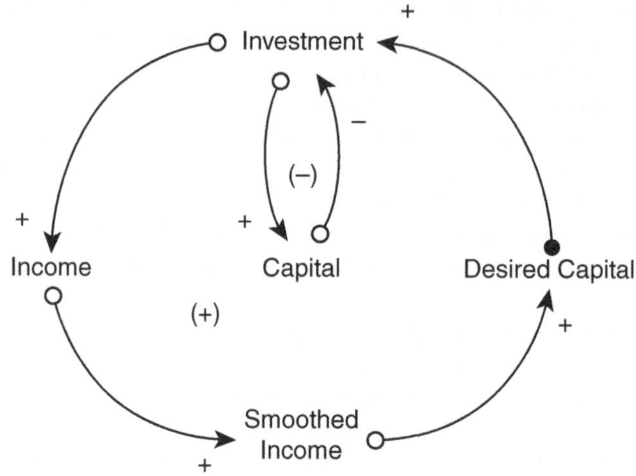

Figure 2.6b The accelerator loops

Source: Low (op. cit.), p. 83)

> Here it can be observed that these positive loops include familiar economic processes from the Keynesian multiplier (1936), the Mundell Effect or the Fisher debt/deflation spiral.

One of the most fundamental self-reinforcing feedbacks is the capital investment multiplier, or capital self-ordering. If the demand for consumer goods and services increases, the consumer goods industry must expand its capacity and so places orders for new factories, machinery, vehicles, etc. To supply the high volume of orders, the capital-producing sector must also expand its capital stock and hence place orders for more buildings, machines, rolling stock, trucks, etc., causing the total demand for capital to rise still further in a self-reinforcing spiral of increasing orders, a greater need for expansion and still more orders.

For Sterman (1985) "in equilibrium, the multiplier effect of capital self-ordering is modest". However, "the long wave is an inherent disequilibrium phenomenon, and during transient adjustments the strength of self-ordering becomes much greater than in equilibrium" (Sterman, Mosekilde, 1992, p. 13). This is partly a consequence of the investment accelerator. A variety of additional positive feedback loops further increase the demand for capital.

The subprime crisis, lessons and comments

In 2007, the US economy entered a mortgage crisis that caused panic and financial turmoil around the world. The financial markets became especially

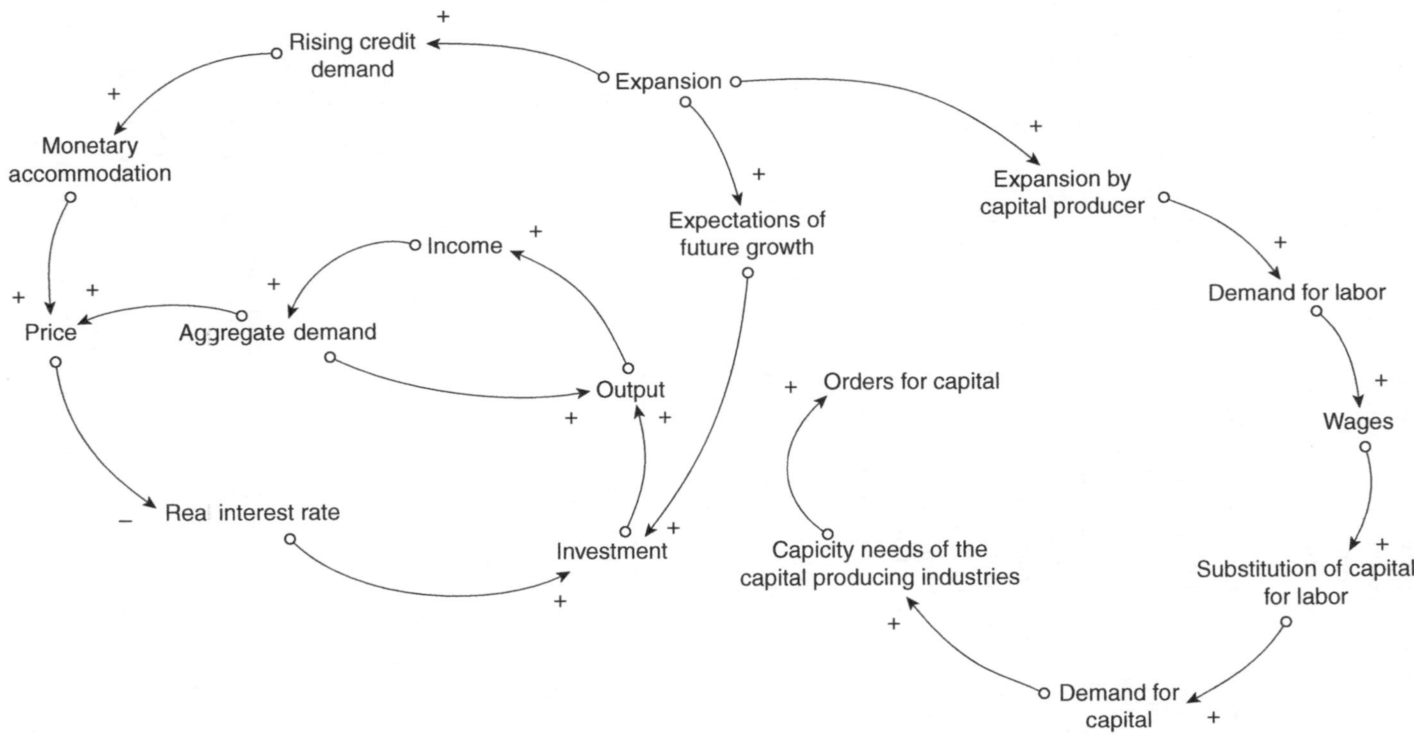

Figure 2.7 Feedback loops and long waves

volatile, and the effects lasted for several years. For many economists, the subprime mortgage crisis was a result of too much borrowing and flawed financial modeling, largely based on the assumption that home prices would only go up. So, what we have come to call the *subprime crisis*, turned the American dream of owning a house into nightmare for millions of Americans.

The subprime crisis, a historical view

This crisis stemmed from loans granted to American households with too little collateral to access normal prime loans. In 2006, this type of credit represented nearly 45% of new mortgage loans. In this system, everyone had something to gain. The least creditworthy households were attracted by a banking policy that allowed them to access home ownership – a policy that was based on low repayments in the first few years, followed by a gradual increase in the debt burden. Financial and real estate advisors earned substantial commissions. Banks took these "bad" loans out of their assets and converted them into securities sold on the financial markets. Investors bought these securities, which offered high returns. However, the machine started to get stuck in the fourth quarter of 2006. As a growing number of households were unable to repay their loans when they reached their maturity dates, default rates on subprime loans increased significantly. As a result, some households were forced to sell their property on the market, which was now in a state of depression. In the first quarter of 2007, the specialized establishments that were too committed to these products also went down. Nearly 20 establishments had to close their doors.

The crisis took on a new dimension in the summer of 2007, when two hedge funds of Bear Stern Investment Bank were unable to meet the withdrawal requests of their depositors and their creditors refused to renew their loans. Although there is no equivalent to the subprime market in Europe, European banks, which had taken many positions in subprime-backed securities, were also affected. Two German banks, IKB and SachsenLB[3], only found their salvation in the credit lines provided by the German public bank, Kreditanstalt für Wiederaufbau, (amounting to almost €9 billion) and a group of regional banks, like Landesbanken (amounting to over €17 billion).

A final step was finally taken in August 2007. The subprime crisis turned into a liquidity crisis (the rate went from 4% to 4.7% overnight). The disappearance of all transactions in certain segments of the US securitization market led to a lack of benchmark prices and virtually total illiquidity of the assets in the funds' portfolios. On 10 August 2007, BNP Paribas, the French banking leader, announced the temporary suspension of the calculation of the net asset value of three funds[4] composed of asset-backed securities (ABS) backed by loan portfolios, in particular mortgage-backed securities – Parvest Dynamics ABS, BNP Paribas ABS Euribor and BNP Paribas ABS Eonia.

In September 2007, it was England's turn to enter the turmoil. Northern Rocks, the UK's fifth-largest mortgage bank (77% of its assets were real estate loans, half of them to individuals), began to face significant difficulties

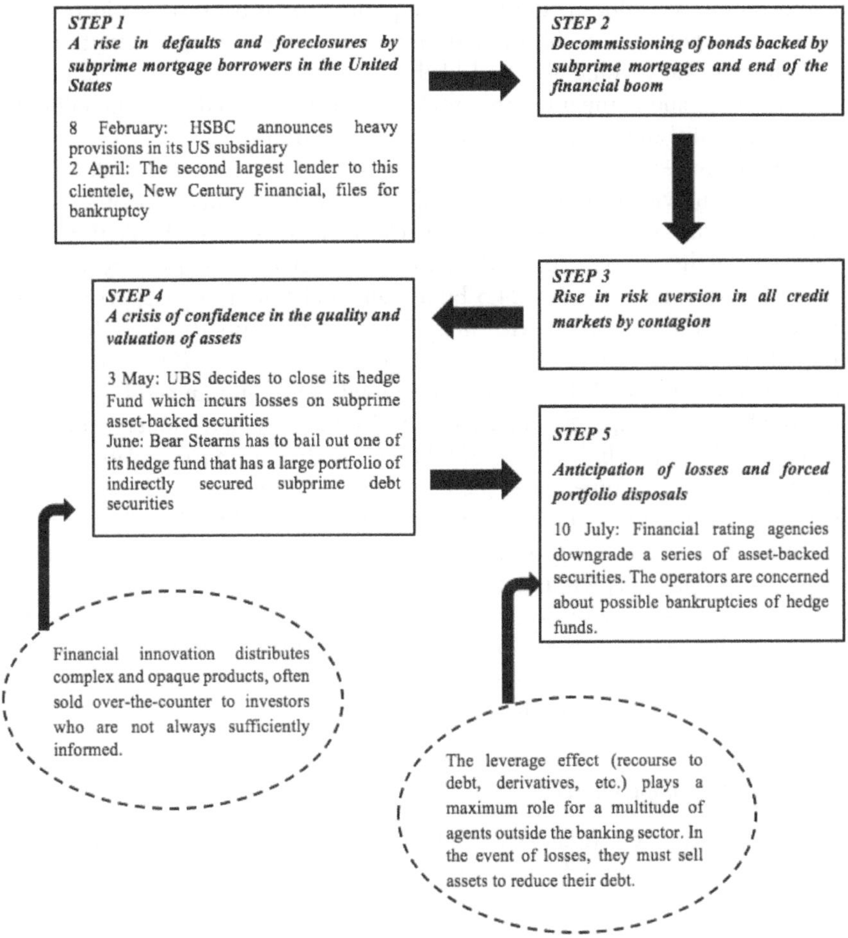

Figure 2.8 Financial crisis, contagion's mechanism

in refinancing itself in the markets. It had no choice but to turn to the Bank of England (BoE) for emergency financing. The American, European and Japanese central banks were thus led to lend widely to commercial banks (US $35 billion, €95 billion and €61 billion, respectively, in the form of a three-day tender; 1,000 billion yen) in order to quickly restore confidence between financial players and safeguard the financing of the economy. While such initiatives are economically justified, their substance is unsatisfactory. On the one hand, central banks, by acting as lenders of last resort, have guaranteed a return to normalcy without resolving the problems. There is a risk of successive financial crises. For some, these "hot spots" would be beneficial. They would make it possible to mitigate the excess credit associated with the various sub-funds of the financial market (real estate assets, financial assets through LBO practices, etc.). It is, however, impossible to forget the irreversible consequences for the banks themselves (due to the lack of liquidity, some banks that did not have unwelcome positions in subprime mortgages, but were dragged into the crisis, and they are now vulnerable and likely to be bought back), households (sale of real estate) and companies (the stock market has suffered from the fall in the shares of banks' and financial institutions' difficulties).

On the other hand, commercial banks consider that any reckless risk-taking will inevitably lead to intervention by central banks. In other words, the European Central Bank (ECB) or the Federal Reserve Bank (FED) will always save them. At a time when many commercial banks were trying to heal their wounds – nearly $24.5 billion and $11 billion in asset write-downs were reported by US banks Merrill Lychn and Citigroup; the Swiss bank UBS recorded a loss of USD $4 billion; the top five UK banks (HSBC, Royal Bank of Scotland, Barclays, RBS, HBOS and Lloyds TSB) announced losses of €6.6 billion; Deutsche Bank recorded a loss of €2 billion; Société Générale in France recorded a loss of €2 billion. It is still difficult to draw up a true balance sheet of the financial crisis (some banks such as Alliance & Leicester or Paragon had to seek costly financing from Credit Suisse or the financial market, issuing highly discounted securities, while others such as Citigroup, UBS or Société Générale had to carry out a capital increase).

There is a good reason to believe that the real losses in the financial system have not all been accounted for or taken out of the accountancy, and that the resurgence in growth over the past two years may well bring out junk bonds or displace problems on other financial innovations.

Causes of the subprime crisis

In its report released in January 2011, the US Commission of Inquiry on the Financial Crisis, chaired by Phil Angelides, stresses the lack of transparency of major financial institutions and the persistence of beliefs:

> Panic fanned by a lack of transparency of the balance sheets of major financial institutions, coupled with a tangle of interconnections among institutions perceived to be "too big to fail", caused the credit markets to seize up. Trading ground to a halt. The stock market plummeted. The economy plunged into a deep recession (United States (2011) p. XVI).

Beyond the numbers (more than 26 million Americans have lost their jobs, cannot find full-time jobs or have given up looking for them; nearly four million families have lost their homes, and 4.5 million have fallen behind in their monthly payments or are being evicted; nearly $11 billion worth of household wealth has evaporated into the air), the report's conclusions are unequivocal:

(1) The financial crisis could have been avoided. The warning signs did exist, and were ignored by Wall Street experts, the Federal Reserve and rating

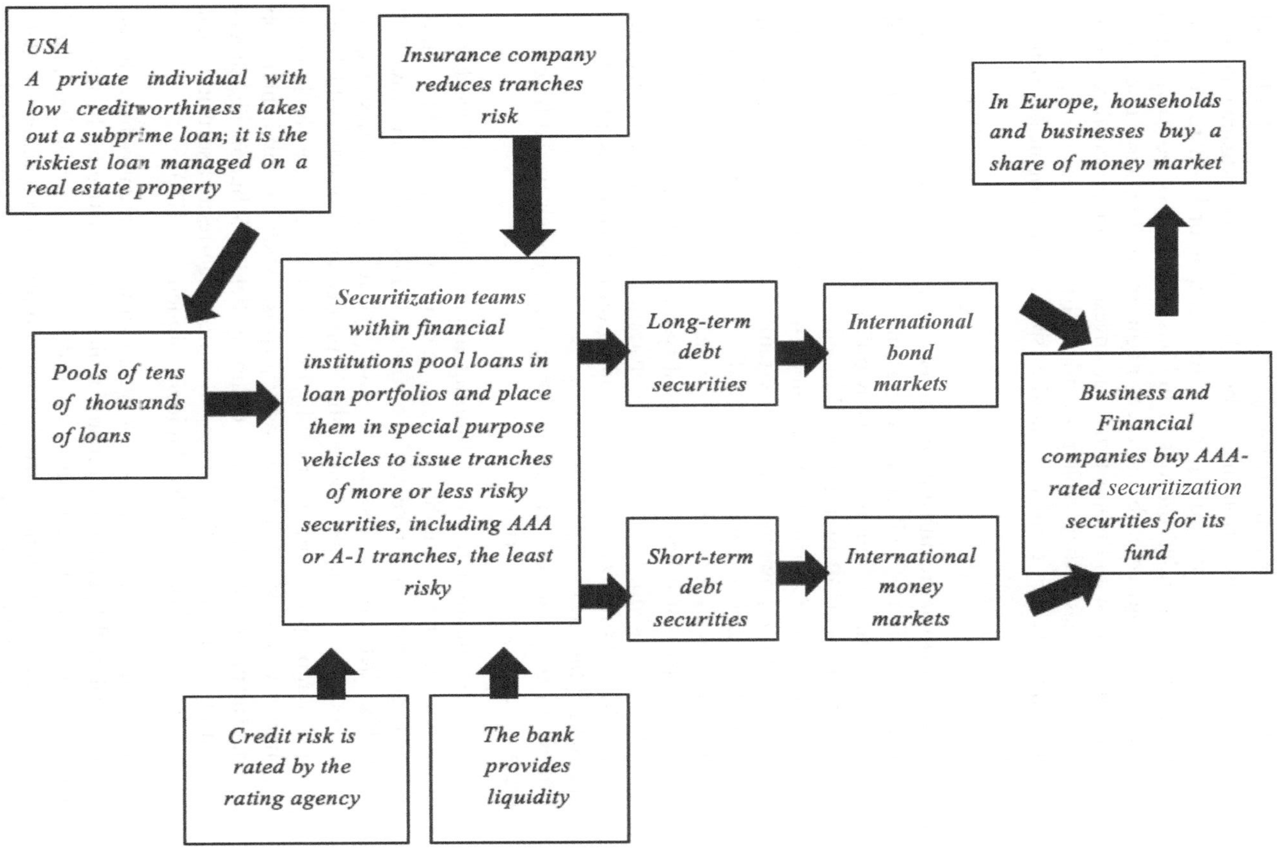

Figure 2.9 How did the subprime crisis get to Europe?

agencies. The generalized failure would thus be based on widespread criminal fraud in which all players in the American financial system would have been immersed:

> The record of our examination is replete with evidence of other failures: financial institutions made, bought, and sold mortgage securities they never examined, did not care to examine, or knew to be defective; firms depended on tens of billions of dollars of borrowing that had to be renewed each and every night, secured by subprime mortgage securities; and major firms and investors blindly relied on credit rating agencies as their arbiters of risk. What else could one expect on a highway where there were neither speed limits nor neatly painted lines?
>
> (ibidem, 2011, p. xvii)

(2) Failures in financial regulation and supervision are the result of a widely accepted belief in the "self-correcting nature of the markets and the ability of financial institutions to effectively police themselves" (2011, p. xviii) and nearly 30 years of uninterrupted deregulation (policy of the former Federal Reserve Chairman Alan Greenspan, various administrations, Congress and the powerful financial system). Laxity on the part of some (the government has allowed financial firms to choose their regulators, resulting in a race for the weakest oversight) is combined with opportunism on the part of others (the financial system has played an important role in the weakening of regulatory constraints on institutions, markets, and products; from 1999 to 2008, spending on lobbying was estimated at nearly $2.7 billion!).

(3) Failures in corporate governance and risk management would be one of the main causes of the crisis:

> Our examination revealed stunning instances of governance breakdowns and irresponsibility . . . among other things, about AIG senior management's ignorance of the terms and risks of the company's $79 billion derivatives exposure to mortgage-related securities; Fannie Mae's quest for bigger market share, profits, and bonuses, which led it to ramp up its exposure to risky loans and securities as the housing market was peaking; and the costly surprise when Merrill Lynch's top management realized that the company held $55 billion in "super-senior" and supposedly "super-safe" mortgage-related securities that resulted in billions of dollars in losses (ibidem, p. XIX)

The five major investment banks – Bear Stearns, Goldman Sachs, Lehman Brothers, Merrill Lynch and Morgan Stanley – were active in the markets with little equity capital and short-term debt. By the end of 2007, Bear Stearns had $11.8 billion in shareholders' equity, $383.6 billion in debt and nearly $70 billion in overnight borrowing. Leverage effects have often been hidden "in derivatives positions, in off-balance-sheet entities, and through 'window dressing' of financial reports available to the investing public" (ibidem, p. xx).

(4) The fact that the government and high financial authorities were very ill-prepared for the crisis added uncertainty and panic to the financial markets (contamination effect). In particular, the report stresses the absence of a comprehensive plan to contain the crisis and a complete understanding of interconnections in financial markets. Although the idea of a financial bubble was regularly raised, senior officials felt that it could not threaten the financial system as a whole. Throughout the summer of 2007, "both Federal Reserve Chairman Ben Bernanke and Treasury Secretary Henry Paulson offered public assurances that the turmoil in the subprime mortgage markets would be contained" (ibidem, p. xxi).

(5) The erosion of accountability and ethical norms has exacerbated the financial crisis. It has created significant financial consequences and eroded investor, business and public confidence in the financial system. Mortgage fraud thus flourished in an environment of lax credit standards and regulation:

> The number of suspicious activity reports-reports of possible financial crimes filed by depository banks and their affiliates-related to mortgage fraud grew 20-fold between 1996 and 2005 and then more than doubled again between 2005 and 2009. One study places the losses resulting from fraud on mortgage loans made between 2005 and 2007 at $112 billion.
>
> (ibidem p. xxii)

As early as September 2004, countrywide authorities recognized that the loans granted could have catastrophic consequences for the US economy. The crisis would thus be the result of human error, errors in judgment and misdeeds.

(6) The collapse of mortgage loan standards combined with their securitization both ignited the flame of contagion and the financial crisis. As soon as house prices fell and borrowers defaulted, Wall Street went into a negative spiral:

> Many mortgage lenders set the bar so low that lenders simply took eager borrowers qualifications on faith, often with a willful disregard for a borrower's ability to pay. Nearly one-quarter of all mortgages made in the first half of 2005 were interest only loans. During the same year, 68% of "option ARM" loans originated by Countrywide and Washington Mutual had low – or no – documentation requirements.
>
> (ibidem, p. 23)

With the blessing of the Federal Reserve and the Thrift Supervision Office, fraudulent practices have become "commonplace" and particularly widespread. Securitization would have only spread fraud throughout America and the world, by increasing the complexity of outstanding products (the so-called CDOs, collateralized debt obligations), increasing their remuneration (profit-seeking) and introducing systemic risk.

(7) Financial innovation, including derivatives in OTC markets, has contributed significantly to the financial crisis. Financial companies, commercial enterprises, farmers, and investors all used derivatives to hedge or speculate on price, interest rate and index fluctuations or even default on potential debts. These uncontrolled products, worth approximately $673 billion, aggravated the situation in three ways. First, some of these products, the CDSs (credit default swaps), were sold to investors who wanted to protect themselves against non-performance or decline in the value of subprime mortgage-backed securities. The companies (in this case, AIG) that offered this protection to investors (nearly $79 billion) generated a powerful stimulus in the financial market and fuelled the bubble. Second, CDSs have been essential to the creation of synthetic collateralized debt obligations (CDOs). These structured finance products are the result of complex arrangements and meet needs such as reduced refinancing costs, the desire to exploit arbitrage opportunities in a portfolio and the desire to get rid of credit risk. CDOs would only bet on the performance of mortgage securities. According to the Commission, they have amplified the losses due to the collapse of the housing's bubble by allowing investors to place multiple bets on the same securities. Thus:

> Goldman Sachs alone packaged and sold $ 73 billion in synthetic CDOs from July 1, 2004, to May 31, 2007. Synthetic CDOs created by Goldman referenced more than 3,400 mortgage securities, and 610 of them were referenced at least twice. This is apart from how many times these securities may have been referenced in synthetic CDOs created by other firms.
>
> (ibidem, p. xxv)

Third, when the housing bubble burst, the financial crisis wiped out everything in its wake. Companies such as AIG have not been able to meet their commitments due to a lack of sufficient capital reserves. The US government had to commit more than $180 billion due to the systemic risks posed by the collapse of AIG (millions of derivative contracts between international financial institutions).

(8) The failures of rating agencies (Fitch Ratings, Moody's, Standard & Poor's) have been the key drivers of financial destruction. Mortgage-related securities could not have been marketed and sold without their approval. It was their upward valuations that exacerbated price volatility and downward revisions that led to the market collapse. In its report, the Commission notes that from 2000 to 2007,

> Moody's rated nearly 45,000 mortgage-related securities as triple-A. This compares with six private-sector companies in the United States

> that carried this coveted rating in early 2010. In 2006, alone, Moody's put its triple-A stamp of approval on 30 mortgage-related securities every working day. The results were disastrous: 83% of the mortgage securities rated triple-A that year ultimately were downgraded.
>
> (ibidem, p. xxv)

The Commission's criticisms are severe here: defective computer models, pressure from the financial companies that paid for the valuations, aggressive policy of winning market share, lack of resources despite record profits, absence of significant public supervision.

In the end, the Commission wished to emphasize three main points:

(1) The first point is the presence of excess liquidity. If all the conditions of the crisis were met (low interest rates, available capital, and investors seeking to invest their money in US real estate), the commission members specify that excess liquidity does not lead to a financial crisis. Thus, it is the inability of players in the financial system to curb mortgage and market excesses that is at stake here.

(2) The second is the role of the para-public organizations (government-sponsored enterprises, or GSEs), Freddie Mac and Fannie Mae. Once again, the verdict is final: these government-sponsored companies have adopted business models similar to those of publicly traded companies when they received subsidies and had a public service mission. Their exposure to real estate credit was significant: nearly $5 trillion. They even used their political power by spending $164 million on lobbying from 1999 to 2007. In the third quarter of 2010, the Treasury Department provided them with $151 billion to put them back on the water. Importantly, the Commission considers that:

> these two entities contribute to the crisis, but were not a primary cause. Importantly, GSE mortgage securities essentially maintained their value throughout the crisis and did not contribute to the significant financial firm losses that were central to the financial crisis. The GSEs participated in the expansion of subprime and other risky mortgages, but they followed rather than led Wall Street and other lenders in the rush for fool's gold. They purchased the highest rated non-GSE mortgage-backed securities and their participation in this market added helium to the housing balloon, but their purchases never represented a majority of the market.
>
> (ibidem, p. xxvi)

Purchases of mortgage-backed securities thus accounted for 10.5% in 2001, rose to 40% in 2004 and fell to 28% in 2008.

(3) The third point addresses the issue of housing targets set by the Department of Housing and Urban Development (HUD) to the GSEs. Too ambitious,

they would have contributed to increasing their investments in subprime mortgages. The housing policy would thus have encouraged home ownership through a combination of incentives and support programs. This policy has been implemented and promoted by several administrations (including those of Bill Clinton and Georges W. Bush). The commission mentions in particular that "As a nation, we set aggressive homeownership goals with the desire to extend credit to families previously denied access to the financial markets" (2011, p. xxvii). In a way, successive governments had failed to ensure that the philosophy of equal opportunities corresponds to a reality on the ground!

While the causes of the financial crisis are both financial and political, the consequences are both economic and social. This raises the question of whether the different models are likely to face such a shock. The financial crisis could both show the limits of the liberal model (in which the shareholder is the king) and lead to a capitalism war.

Holding the subprime crisis to the light of system dynamics

Using system dynamics may be useful to understand the different mechanisms of the crisis, especially the housing bubble (Figure 2.10a). causal loops diagrams (CLD), stock/flow diagrams (SFD) and a presentation of the complex structure of the system give us a new understanding of the facts (Egner, 2009). When the housing supply goes up, the average price of a house tends to go down. When housing prices decrease, more people can afford to buy homes, which increases the demand for housing. But the interest rate also affects the affordability of a house. Thus, if interest rates go up, demand will go down (and vice-versa). In this case, we are tracing increasing demand from lower housing prices. When demand for houses increases, so does the demand for home mortgages. If the demand for mortgages goes up, more mortgages are approved, more houses are sold and the housing supply goes down. This completes the first balancing feedback loop, which we will call B1. We should also consider the relationship between demand and prices. When demand increases, it causes housing prices to increase. When prices go up, both housing demand and mortgage demand go down. This completes a second balancing feedback loop we will call B2. But there is also a link from housing prices to mortgage demand. As prices go up, fewer people qualify for mortgages and demand goes down. If demand for mortgages goes down, fewer homes are sold, causing the housing supply to go up and driving prices back down. This gives us a third balancing feedback loop that we will call B3. There is also a connection from housing prices back to housing supply. When prices are going up, it's more attractive to build and sell homes, causing an increase in supply. When prices are rising, people are also more tempted to sell their existing homes. When houses are in greater supply, the prices tend to go down. This completes a fourth balancing feedback loop we will call B4. A final balancing feedback loop exists between housing price and mortgage demand. We will call it B5.

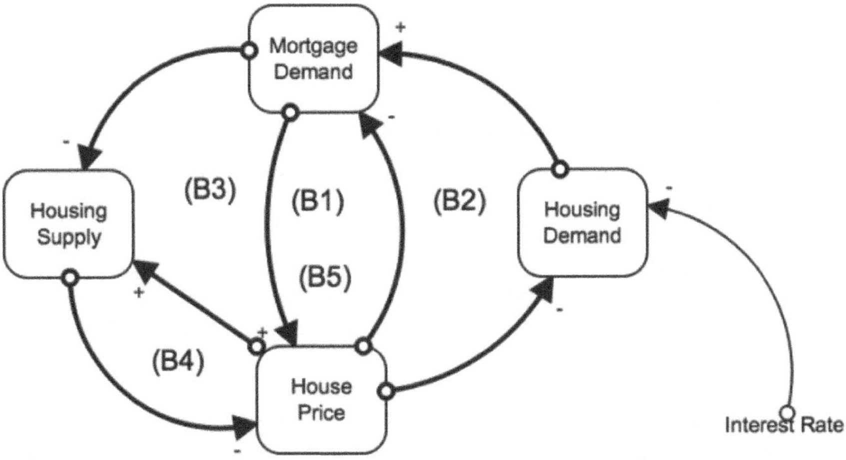

Figure 2.10a Feedback loop structure of the housing bubble

If we explore the model structure, we can identify four modules: (1) housing demand (Figure 2.10b), (2) mortgage demand (Figure 2.10c), (3) housing supply (Figure 2.10d) and (4) house price (Figure 2.10e).

Demand for houses is subject to normal demand (market conditions) and peak demand (subprime demand). For the latter, a low interest rate environment and the prospect of house valuation at a high price condition the dynamics of the market.

By relaxing mortgage requirements, banks allowed a part of the population that could not afford it to become owners. This resulted in increased demand for houses. Demand for houses led to higher prices, which in turn increased defaults (especially when variable rates began to rise).

Rising house prices lead to higher housing starts, and therefore higher house deliveries. Manufacturers need to reduce average delivery times so that homes are available quickly. The demand for new homes interacts with the turnover of existing home sales. Under normal circumstances, new homeowners take possession of their homes, but there is still an unsatisfied demand, which leads to higher house prices. Payment defaults lead to foreclosures and thus to a change of existing homes on the market. The relaxing mortgage requirements lead to unsatisfied demand (which does not necessarily have the wealth to buy a house) for home ownership.

Prices must take into account the time delays between upward and downward trends in the housing market. The supply of houses resulting from new housing starts interacts with the increase in demand for new borrowers' homes (always linked to the relaxing of mortgages requirements). The supply-to-demand ratio increases, which has an effect on prices.

While the signs of the subprime crisis appeared clearly in 2007, an analysis of the US real estate market over a long period of time indicates a turnaround

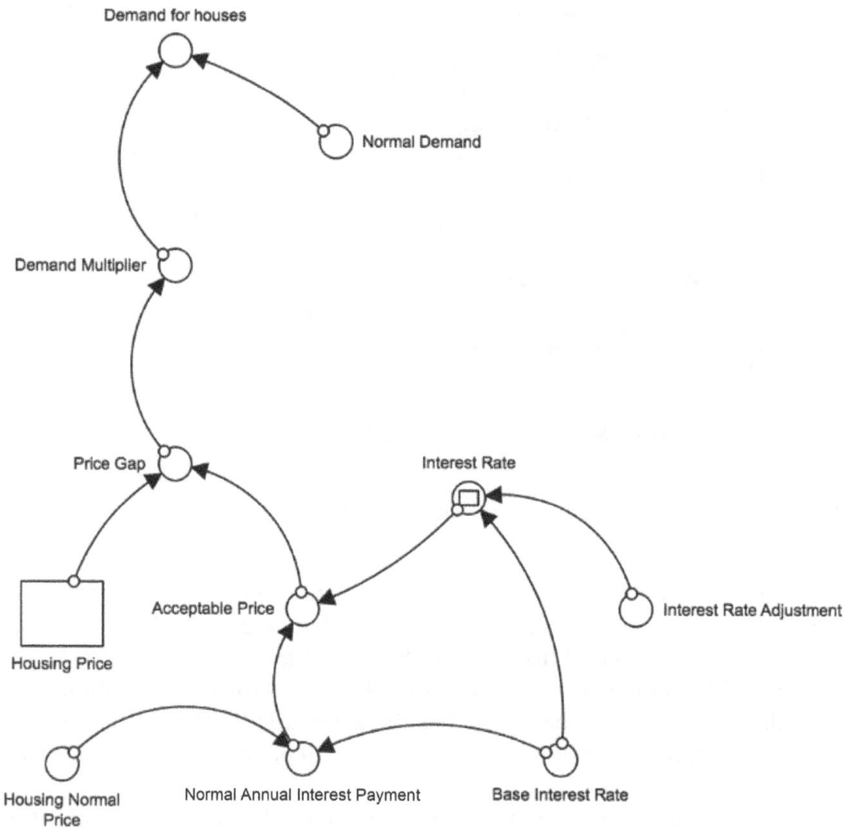

Figure 2.10b Housing demand

in the market from 2005 onwards (Figures 2.11a and 2.11b). Indeed, the existing homes sales followed an upward trend over nearly 23 years, rising from 1.9 million in 1982 to more than 7 million in 2005, despite two slowdowns in 1992 and 2000. The market downturn began in 2006, with a 9% decline, then 30% in 2007 and 40% in 2008. The signs of the housing bubble are even more significant when we are looking at the new home sales. The slowdown began in 2004, after 13 years of euphoria (+ 130%). The market for new homes then fell by nearly 20% in 2006, 40% in 2007 and more than 60% in 2008. If we return to our causal chain introduced in feedback loops (CLD), the tracking of home foreclosures as a result of mortgage default, the slowdown in existing home sales and new homes sales should have been warning signs of the crisis.

System dynamics and scenario planning for 2019

Scenario planning was developed by Pierre Wack in the 1970s for Shell Company just before the big oil crisis of 1973–1974 (Wack, 1985). In his article in

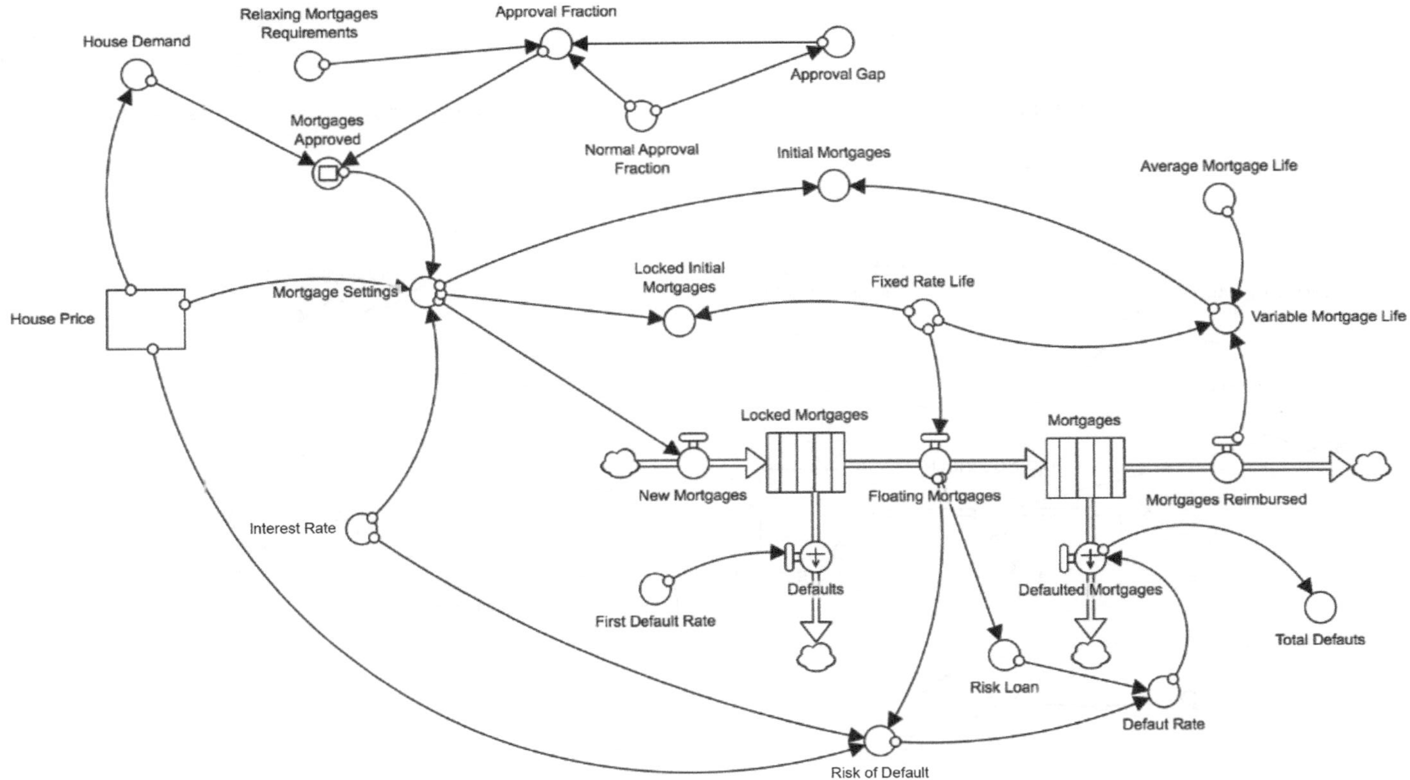

Figure 2.10c Mortgage demand

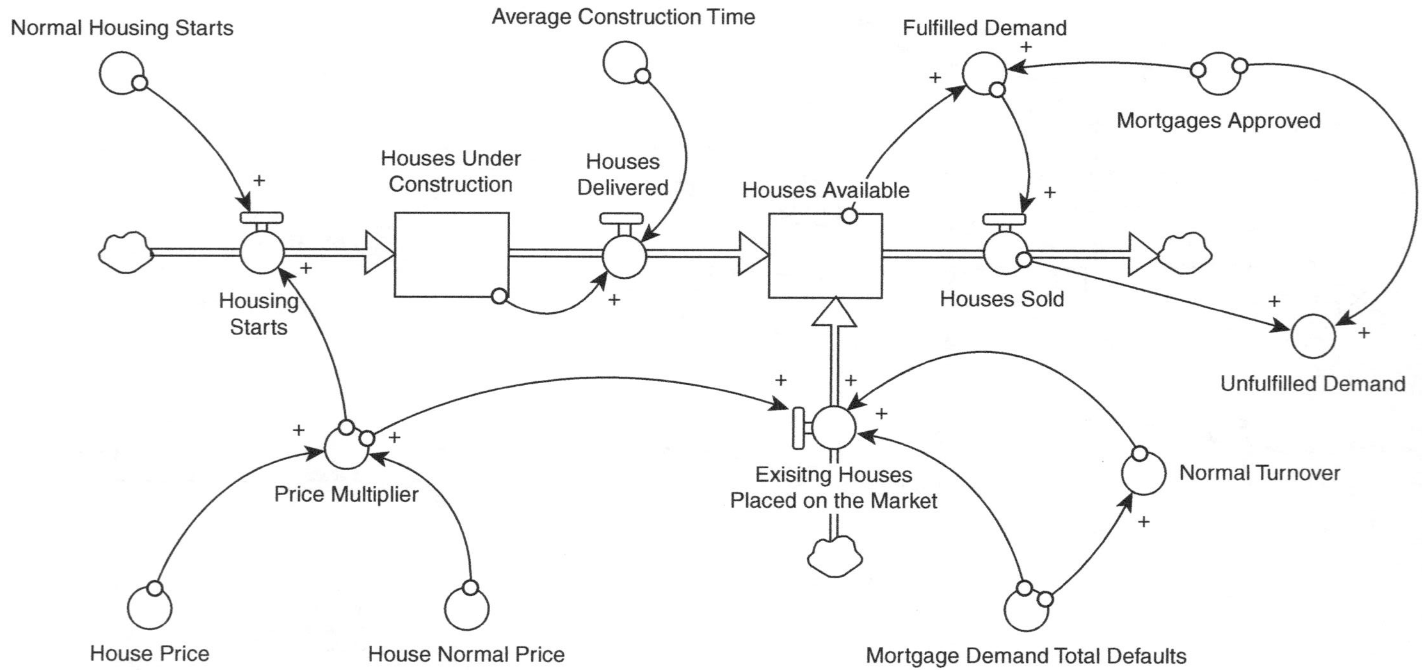

Figure 2.10d Housing supply

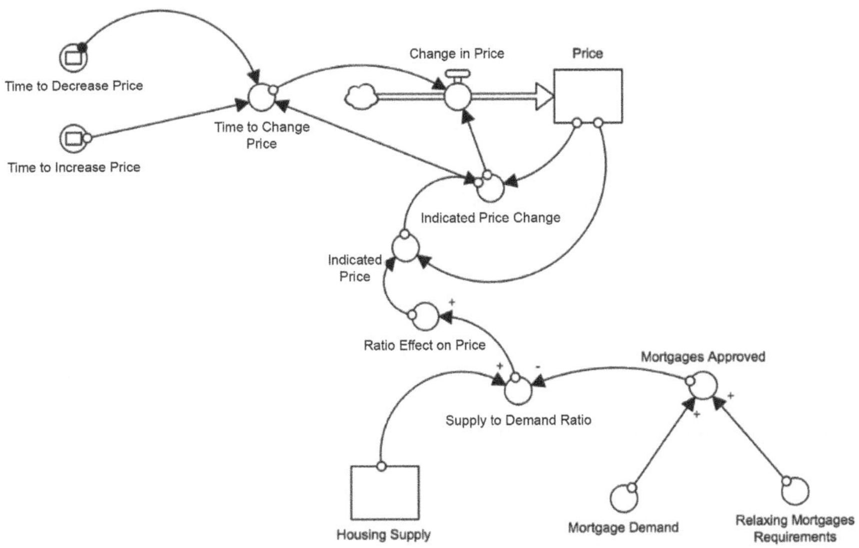

Figure 2.10e Price housing module

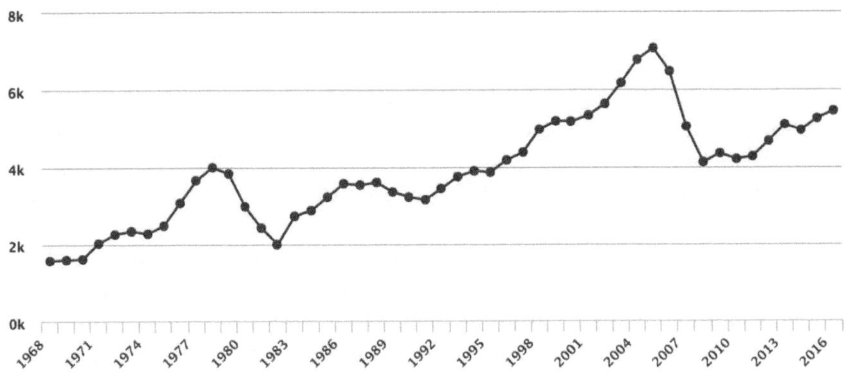

Figure 2.11a Existing homes sold (1,000s), total

Source: US Department of Housing and Urban Development

the *Harvard Business Review*, Wack considered that "scenarios deal with two worlds: the world of facts and the world of perceptions. They explore for facts but they aim at perceptions inside the heads of decision makers" (Wack, 1985, p. 140).

Their purpose is to gather and transform information of strategic significance into fresh perceptions. This transformation process is not trivial – more often than not it does not happen – but when it works, it's a creative experience that leads to strategic insights beyond the mind's previous reach. Scenario

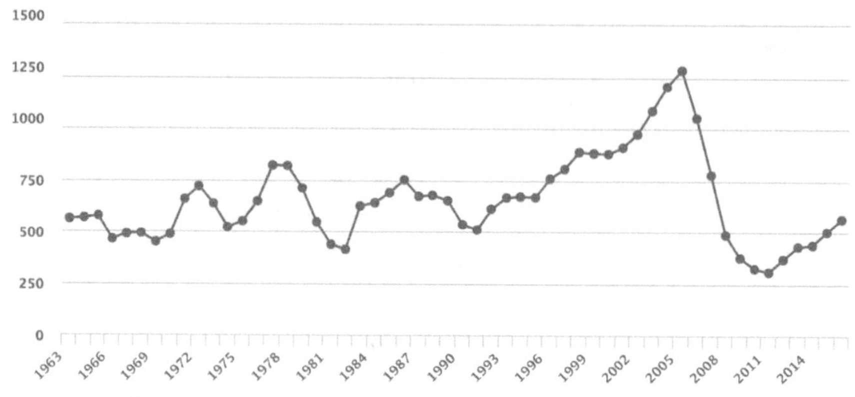

Figure 2.11b New homes sold (1,000s), total

Source: US Department of Housing and Urban Development

planning imagines different possibilities and develops plans to address these possibilities (Diemer, 2004). This approach insists on two points: (1) scenarios describe different worlds, not just different outcomes in the same world, and (2) the purpose is not so much to have one scenario that gets it right as to have a set of scenarios that illuminates the major forces driving the system, their interrelationships and the critical uncertainties.

So, this methodology is used when uncertainty is high, significant change is anticipated, a new long-term initiative has been prepared, cognitive task analysis uncovers a recurring issue with an ongoing process, modeling practices demonstrate an unanticipated outcome or conflicting perspectives yield radically different expectations (Amer, Daim, Jetter, 2013). This method is very interesting for strategic decision-making on social, economic, political, technological and environmental issues (Figure 2.12). Scenario planning will allow a multidisciplinary group to identify the relevant focal questions to be addressed and constructs narratives about the future that will incorporate the broadest imagined spectrum of uncertainties and trends.

Here, we will consider that a scenario for economic growth is defined as: (1) a description of a possible future situation (conceptual future) and (2) including paths of development which may lead to that future situation. We'll describe the development, the dynamics and the moving forces from which a specific conceptual future results. The aim is to generate orientation "regarding future developments through of certain relevant key factors" (Kosow, Gassner, 2008, p. 10). Scenarios have an explorative function (they serve to systematize and deepen the existing understanding of contemporary developments, conditions and influences). The process explores possible future developments with the present as a point of departure. The central question will be: "What if?". But it can also have a normative function, especially when a scenario is able to achieve

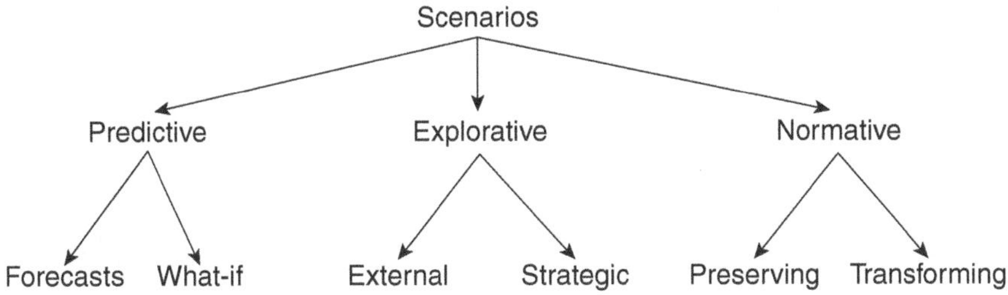

Figure 2.12 Typology of scenarios

Source: Börjeson et al. (2006, p. 726)

a transformation effect (an initially unknown future environment can be transformed into a future environment in which developments are assembled into scenarios). The process identifies desirable futures or investigates how to arrive at future conditions. The central question will be: "How do we get there?"

In today's context, all countries – with few exceptions – are experiencing positive and significant growth rates (Figures 2.13a and 2.13b). The global situation suggests that economic growth is back and many market signals (valuation of financial assets, decline of US foreclosures, low interest rates, etc.) are increasingly reassuring the various governments in their desire to surf on a wave that they do not want to stop. However, it should be remembered that the current situation and the so-called recovery are based on an optimistic but relative analysis of market flows and the failure to take stock trends into account. In other words, financial and economic experts prefer to focus on positive signals on flows' market rather than taking into account negative signals from stock markets.

The return of growth, reflected in profits and the share values of capitalized firms, should not make us forget that global debt stands at nearly 233 trillion dollars, the equivalent of 318 % of world GDP (OECD, 2017). This rise in debt is not felt at the moment because central banks have largely intervened to lower interest rates and keep them at extremely low levels. The European Central Bank is currently in charge of €2 trillion of public debt and plans to continue raising €30 billion each month until September. Thus, the cost of debt service is stable (like Germany and France, for example) or is decreasing in countries with higher debt levels at the beginning of the crisis in 2007–2008 (like Spain and the United Kingdom). Central banks are vigilant in maintaining low interest rates and would intervene if a wind up should occur. The cost of repaying the debts should therefore be controlled until the beginning of 2019, except if the macroeconomic context change. In 2018, financial markets will be focused on inflation (expectations of price rises following the rise in consumption, and increase in the price of oil) and the evolution of exchange rates (in a context of generalized growth, the only way to grow faster than its competitors is to

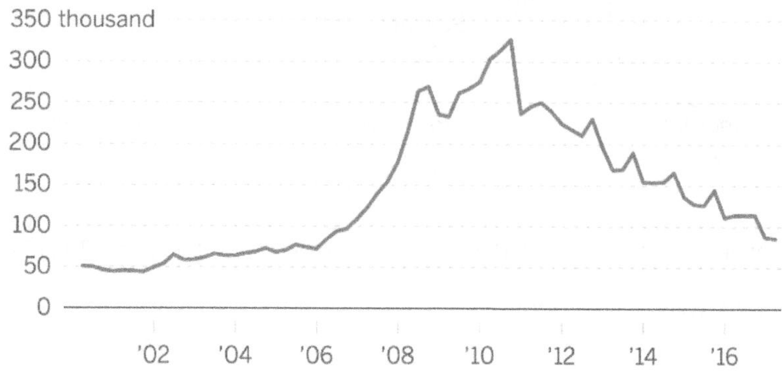

Figure 2.13a Completed US foreclosures[5]

Source: US Department of Housing and Urban Development (2018), Completed US Foreclosures, https://www.hud.gov.

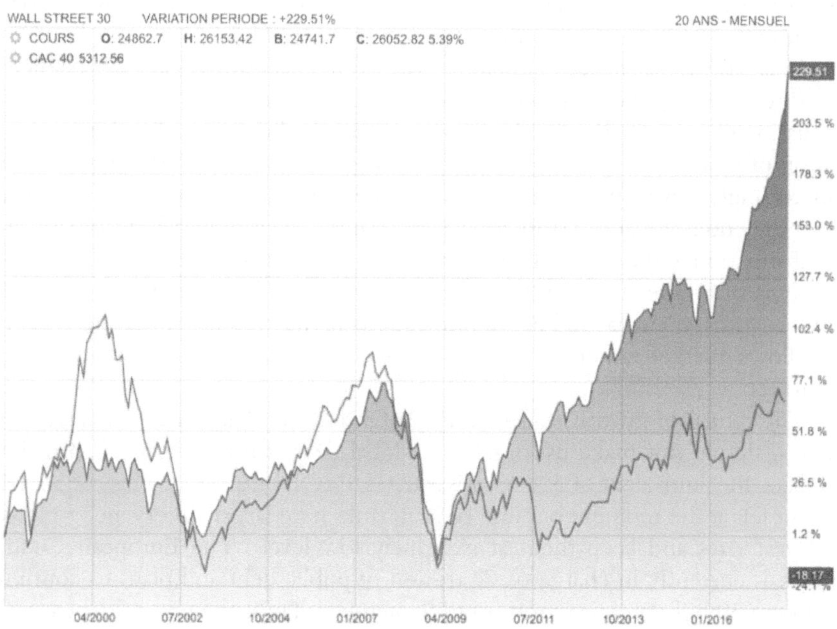

Figure 2.13b Evolution Dow Jones/CAC 40

Source: Boursorama (2018), *Evolution du Dow Jones et du CAC 40*, 19 janvier

generate artificial currency variations; tensions between the euro and the dollar could well engender a currency war and recalibrate the cycle on a shorter monetary cycle) (Figures 2.14a and 2.14b).

For now, the financial cycle seems to be more focused on the government bonds and debts market because it is the market that is most sensitive to interest

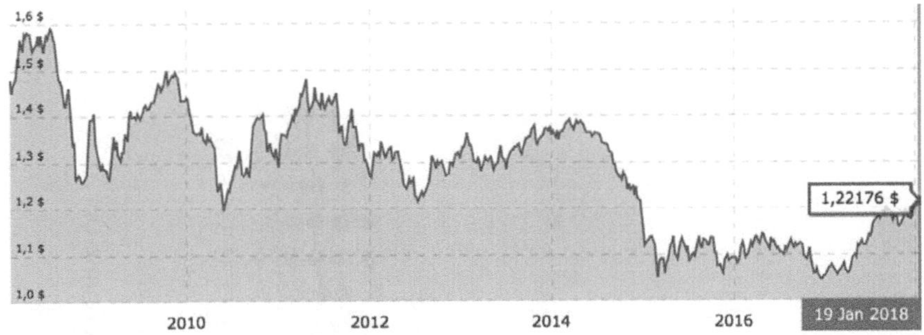

Figure 2.14a Euro/dollar spot

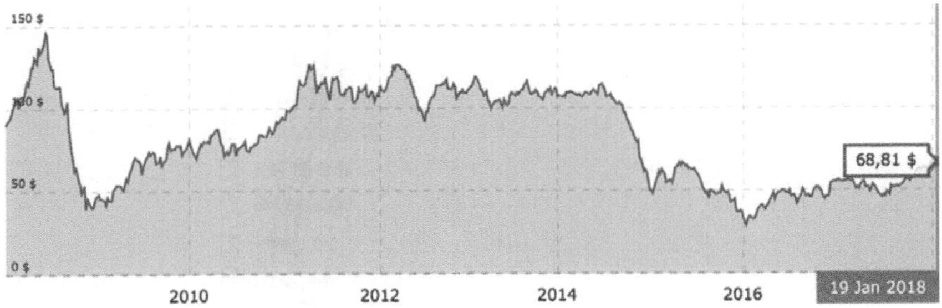

Figure 2.14b Brent crude oil

Source: Boursorama, 19 janvier 2018; see https://www.boursorama.com/bourse/matieres-premieres/cours/8xBRN9F/

rate increases (Figure 2.15). The inverse relationship between the interest rate and the bond price suggests that in a low interest rate environment, any increase in central bank rates (Japan, USA, Europe) will result in a decline in the profitability of these financial products.

This trend is now unavoidable and causes waves of speculation on the bonds market (recent changes in currency parity, including euro/dollar, will also stimulate speculation on monetary markets and changes in values on financial markets, with firms' results being evaluated in euros or dollars).

Once again, system dynamics tools can be useful to understand causal loops and feedback effects of the economic system (Figure 2.16) and to prevent a new crash.

Three loops seem important and create oscillations.

The first one (flows) is linking to inflation. If consumption is high, prices increase (oil price may accentuate the increase of price) and the central bank will increase its discount rate. Short-term liquidity costs will be high and long-term interest rates will grow. Growth could stop, and investment may be reduced.

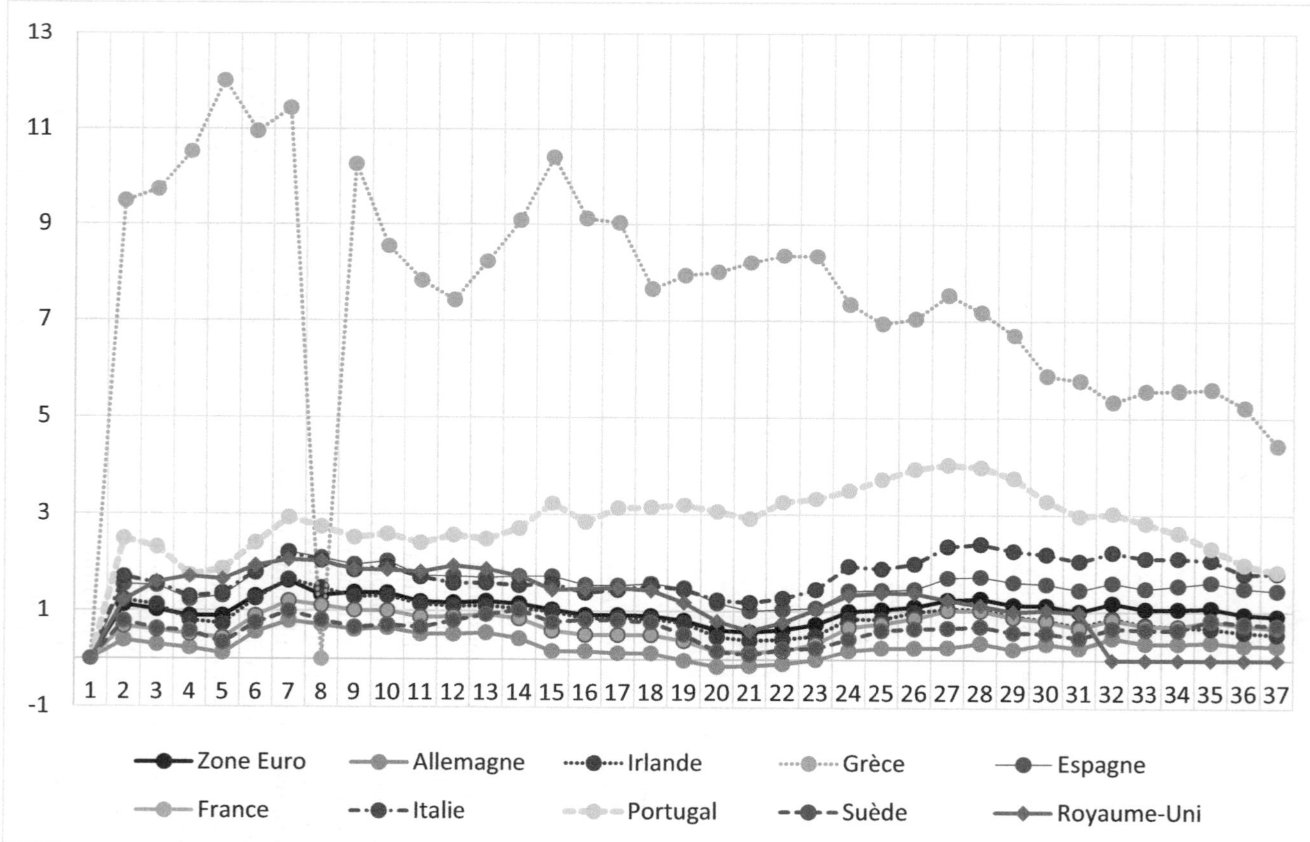

Figure 2.15 Long-term interest rates for government bonds

Source: Eurostat (2018); see http://ec.europa.eu/eurostat/web/products-datasets/-/teimf050

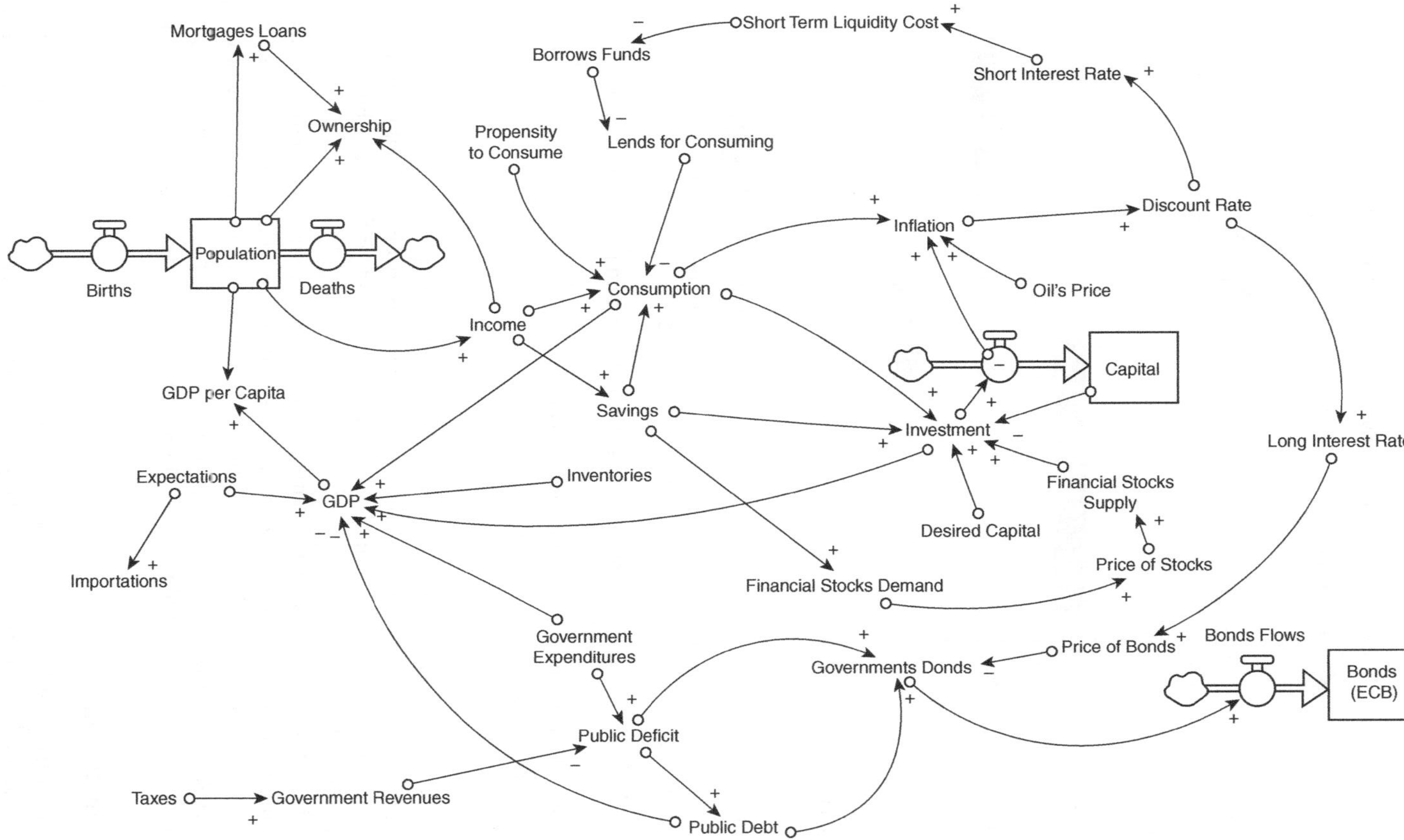

Figure 2.16 Feedback loops of the economic system

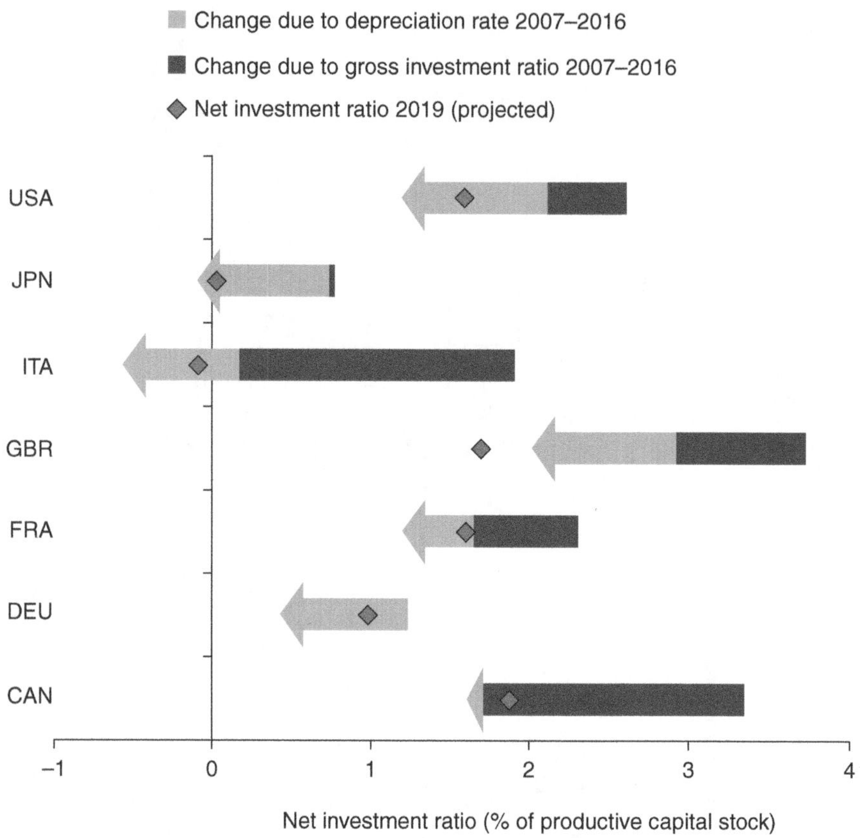

Figure 2.17 Dynamics of the net investment ratio

Source: OECD Economic Outlook database; and OECD calculations, 2017

The second one (stocks) concern bonds. The European Central Bank has a huge stock of bonds, a legacy of the subprime crisis. An increase of interest rate reduces the value of the bonds and increases the cost of financing by government bonds.

The third one is associated with investment and capital. Growth may keep going if investment creates a new stock of capital. Dynamics of the net investment ratio[6] (Figure 2.17) seems to not go to this direction: (1) gross investment rates have declined, (2) faster depreciation has contributed to slow net capital stock growth and (3) the investment recovery projected to 2019 remains partial.

Conclusion

For nearly two centuries, business cycle theories have highlighted the fact that several mechanisms are likely to explain fluctuations and trends. The multiplier-accelerator mechanism, price-quantity dynamics, real cycles linked to productivity shocks or financial cycles based on changes in interest rates are focused on macroeconomic and microeconomic signals. Statistics and econometrics have often been used by economists to highlight long-term cycles and transitions to the different phases (growth, crisis, recession, recovery). In this chapter, we propose to return to some theoretical contributions in the field of cycle theory in order to better understand the causes and facts of the subprime crisis. In order to do this, we have used system dynamics, which – through feedback loops and delays – aims to identify the structure of complex systems. So, mechanisms such as the accelerator-multiplier or price – quantity adjustment can be reinterpreted with that new method. We find this analysis particularly interesting, especially when it comes to identify the mechanisms driving the financial crash or to point to the signs of a future downturn in the cycle.

Notes

1 A first version of that paper was proposed to the "Villa Vigoni Trilateral Conference, Economic and Theoretical Cycles in Europe: The 21st Century" (4–7 April 2016) coordinated by Bertram Schefold, Monika Poettinger and Alain Alcouffe. I thank all the participants of that meeting for proposals and recommendations aimed to improve this paper.

2 According to Radzicki (2008 p. 162):

> System dynamics is a computer simulation modeling technique originally created in 1956 to help corporate managers improve their understanding and control of industrial systems. Over the years, it has been used to address a wide variety of problems in social systems ranging from the transition from fossil fuels to alternative sources of energy in the United States economy, to the growth and decline of cities, to the causes of worker burnout and cost and scheduling overruns in R & D projects, to the diffusion of new medical technologies, to global warming, to the reasons for Hamlet's behavior in the well-known Shakespearean play.

3 SachsenLN was sold to LBBW.

4 Between 27 July and 7 August 2007 (date of suspension of valuation), the three funds saw their total value fall by nearly 23%.

5 US real economy seems to be providing many signals that the purge period has passed. Business Cycles could be useful to understand the macroeconomic context and prevent new crash. Since 2017, completed US foreclosures came back to their 2006's level (75 000).

6 The net investment ratio is defined as the gross investment ratio minus the depreciation rate in percentage of the productive capital stock. It includes business plus government investment.

Bibliography

Akerman, J. (1957), *Structures et cycles économiques*, Paris, Presses universitaires de France.

Amer, M., Daim, T. U., Jetter, A. (2013), A Review of Scenario Planning, *Futures*, February, vol 46, pp. 23–40.

Boot Sweeney, L., Meadows, D.L. (1995), *The System Thinking Playbook*, Chelsea Green.

Börjeson, L., Höjer, M., Dreborg, K.H., Ekvall, T., Finnveden, G. (2006), "Scenario Types and Techniques: Towards a User's Guide", *Futures*, vol 38, pp. 723–739.

Burns, A.F. (1969), *The Business Cycle in a Changing World*, New York, National Bureau of Economic Research.

Burns, A.F., Mitchell, W.C. (1946), *Measuring Business Cycles*, National Bureau of Economic Research, p. 560.

Celasun, O., Milesi-Ferreti, G.M., Obstfeld, M. (2017), *The Year in Review: Global Economy in 5 Charts*, IMF, December 18.

CNUCED (2017), *Rapport sur l'investissement dans le monde, Repères et vue d'ensemble*, Nations Unis, New York, Genève.

Diemer A., de Souza Coelho P. I., Morales, E. (2017), Analyzing Symbiotic Relationships in Sustainable Cities – A Framework, Working Paper, Université d'Auvergne, October.

Diemer, A. (2018), *Principes d'économie politique*, Oeconomia, 2nd édition, 1st edition (2009).

Diemer, A. (2012), *Le développement durable vu par les économistes*, Editions Oeconomia.

Diemer, A., Dozolme, S. (2011), *Les enseignements de la crise des Subprime*, Clément Juglar.

Diemer, A. (2004), "Le développement durable et la dynamique des systèmes", *Working Paper n 2004/05*, HERMES, Université de Reims, 24 mai, p. 20.

Egner, J. (2009), "*Insight-Based Model Investigates the Housing Crisis*", June 23, https://blog.iseesystems.com.

Forrester, J.W. (1961), *Industrial Dynamics*, Waltham, MA, Pegasus Communications.

Forrester, J.W. (1967), "Market Growth as Influenced by Capital Investment", 9th Annual Paul 0. Converse Awards Symposium, University of Illinois, April 13, p. 23.

Forrester, J.W. (1968a), *Principles of Systems*, Waltham, MA, Pegasus Communications, p. 391.

Forrester, J.W. (1968b), "Industrial Dynamics: After the First Decade", *Management Science*, vol 14, n 7, March, pp. 398–415.

Forrester, J.W. (1969), *Urban Dynamics*, Waltham, MA, Pegasus Communications, p. 285.

Forrester, J.W. (1971a), *World Dynamics*, Waltham, MA, Pegasus Communications, p. 144.

Forrester, J.W. (1971b), "Counterintuitive Behavior of Social Systems", *Technology Review*, vol 73, n 3, January, pp. 52–68.

Forrester, J.W. (1975a), "A National Model for Understanding Social and Economic Change", *Simulation Today*, vol 33, pp. 129–133.

Forrester, J.W. (1975b), *Collected Papers of Jay W. Forrester*, Waltham, MA, Pegasus Communications, p. 284.

Forrester, J.W. (1976), "Business Structure, Economic Cycles and National Policy", *Futures*, vol 8, pp. 195–214.

Forrester, J.W. (1977), "Growth Cycles", *De Economist*, vol 125, pp. 525–543.

Forrester, J.W. (1979), "An Alternative Approach to Economic Policy: Macro Behavior from Microstructure", in Kamrany, N., Ray, R. (eds.), *Economic Issues of the Eighties*, Baltimore, John Hopkins University Press.

Forrester, J.W. (1980), "Information Sources for Modeling the National Economy", *Journal of the American Statistical Association*, vol 75, n 371, pp. 555–566.

Forrester, J.W. (1981), "Innovation and Economic Change", *Futures*, vol 13, pp. 323–331.

Forrester, J.W. (1987), "Nonlinearity in High Order Models of Social Systems", *European Journal of Operational Research*, vol 30, pp. 104–109.

Forrester J. W. (1989), The Beginning of System Dynamics, Banquet Talk, International Meeting of the System Dynamics Society, Stuttgart, Germany, July 13, http://web.mit.edu/sysdyn/sd-intro/D-4165-1.pdf

Forrester, J.W. (1991), *System Dynamics and the Lessons of 35 Years*, Sloan School of Management, MIT, April 29, p. 35.

Forrester, J.W. (1995), "The Beginning of System Dynamics", *McKinsey Quarterly*, November, p. 14.

Forrester, J.W. (2007), "System Dynamics: A Personal View of the First Fifty Years", *System Dynamics Review*, vol 23, n 2/3, pp. 345–357.

Forrester, J.W., Mass, N.J., Ryan, C.J. (1976), "The System Dynamics National Model: Understanding Socio-Economic Behavior and Policy Alternatives", *Technological Forecasting and Social Change*, vol 9, pp. 51–68.

Friedman, M. (1957), *The Theory of Consumption Function*, Princeton, NJ, Princeton University Press.

Goodman, M.R. (1974), *Study Notes in System Dynamics*, Cambridge, MA, MIT Press.

Goodwin, R. (1951), "The Nonlinear Accelerator and the Persistence of Business Cycles", *Econometrica*, vol 19, pp. 1–17.

Gordon, R.A. (1951), *Business Fluctuations*, New York, Harper and Row.

Hicks, J. (1950), *A Contribution to the Theory of the Trade Cycle*, Oxford, Clarendon Press.

Juglar, C. (1862), *Des crises commerciales et de leur retour périodique en France, en Angleterre et aux Etats Unis*, Paris, Guillaumin et Cie.

Kaldor, N. (1940), "A Model of Trade Cycle", *Economic Journal*, vol 50, pp. 78–92.

Kalecki, M. (1935), "A Macrodynamic Theory of Business Cycles", *Econometrica*, vol 3, n 3, July, pp. 327–344.

Kalecki, M. (1937), "A Theory of the Business Cycle", *The Review of Economic Studies*, 4.2 77–97.

Kitchin, J. (1923), "Cycles and Trends in Economic Factors", *Review of Economics and Statistics*, vol 5, n 1, pp. 10–16.

Kondratiev, N.D. (1935), "The Long Waves in Economic Life", *Review of Economic Statistics*, vol 17, pp. 105–115.

Kondratiev, N.D. (1928), *The Long Wave Cycle*, translation by G. Daniels, 1984, New York, Richardson and Snyder.

Kosow, H., Gassner, R. (2008), Methods of Future and Scenario Analysis: Overview, Assessment, and Selection Criteria. Bonn: Deutsches Institut für Entwicklungspolitik.

Kydland, F.E., Prescott, E.C. (1982), "Time to Build and Agregate Fluctuations", *Econometrica*, vol 50, n 6, pp. 1345–1370.

Lane D.C. (2008). "The Emergence and Use of Diagramming in System Dynamics: A Critical Account", *Systems Research and Behavioral Science* 25, 3–23.

Lane, D.C., Sterman, J.D. (2011), "Jay Wright Forrester, Chapter 20", in Gass, S., Asssad, A. (eds.), *Profiles in Operations Research: Pioneers and Innovators*, New York, Springer, pp. 363–386.

Low, G.W. ([1976] 1980), "The Multiplier: Accelerator Model of Business Cycles Interpreted from a System Dynamics Perspective", in Randers, J. (ed.).

Meadows, D.H., Meadows, D.L., Randers, J. (1972), *The Limits to Growth*, New York, Potomac Associates.

Meadows, D.L. (1970), *The Dynamics of Commodity Production Cycles*, Cambridge, MA, Wright Allen Press.

Meadows, D.L., Meadows, D.H. (1973), Toward Global Equilibrium, collected papers, Wright: Allen Press.

Meadows, D.L. (1976), "The avoidable a priori", in J. Randers (ed.), *Elements of the System Dynamics Method*, MIT Press, pp. 23–57.

Milsum, J.H. (1968), *Mutual Causality in General Systems: In Positive Feedback, a General Systems Approach to Positive Negative/Feedback and Mutual Causality*, Oxford, Pergamon Press.

Minsky, H.P. (1992), "The Financial Instability Hypothesis", *Working Paper n 74*, The Jerome Levy Institute of Bard College, May, p. 10.

Minsky, H.P. (1986), "Global Consequences of Financial Deregulation", *Working Paper n 96*, Department of Economics, Washington University, September, p. 62.

Morecroft, J.D.W. (1985), "Rationality in the Analysis of Behavioral Simulation Models", *Management Science*, vol 31, n 7, pp. 900–916.

Morecroft, J.D.W. (1982), "A Critical Review of Diagramming Tools for Conceptualizing System Dynamics Models", *Dynamica*, vol 8, n 1, pp. 20–29.

Mundell, R. (1963), "Inflation and Real Interest", *Journal of Political Economy*, vol 71, n 3, pp. 280–283.

Nerlove, M. (1958), "Adaptative Expectations and Cobweb Phenomena", *The Quaterly Journal of Economics, Oxford University Press*, vol 72, pp. 227-240.

OECD (2017), *Economic Outlook*, The Policy Challenge: Catalyse the Private Sector for Stronger and More Inclusive Growth, Paris, 28 November, p. 25.

Piketti, T. (2014), *Capital in the 21st Century*, Cambridge, MA: Harvard University Press.

Piketti, T. (2016), "2007–2015, une si longue récession", *Le Monde*, 8 janvier.

Pugh, A. (1963), *DYNAMO User's Manual*, Second Edition, Cambridge, MA, MIT Press.

Radzicki, M. (2011), "System Dynamics and İts Contribution to Economics and Economic Modeling", in Meyers, R.A. (ed.), *Complex Systems in Finance and Econometrics*, New York, Springer, pp. 727–738.

Radzicki, M. (2008), "Institutional Economics, Post Keynesian Economics, and System Dynamics: Three Strands of a Heterodox Economics Braid", in Harvey, J.T., Garnett, R.F.J. (eds.), *Future Directions for Heterodox Economics*, The University of Michigan Press.

Randers, J. ([1976] 1980), *Elements of the System Dynamic Method*, Cambridge, MA, MIT Press.

Roberts, N. (1975), *Dynamic Feedback Systems Diagram Kit*, Cambridge, MA, Pugh-Roberts Associates.

Samuelson, P.A. (1947), *Foundations of Economic Analysis*, Cambridge, MA, Harvard University Press.

Samuelson, P.A. (1939), "Interactions between the Multiplier Analysis and the Principle of Acceleration", *Review of Economic Statistics*, vol 21, pp. 75–78.

Schumpeter, J.A. (1939), *Business Cycles*, New York, McGraw-Hill.

Skraba, A., Kljajic, M., Kofjac, D., Bren, M., Mrkaic, M. (2006), *Cobweb Model in System Dynamics from Hyperincursive Perspective*, University de Maribor, Faculty of Organizational Sciences, Slovenia, p. 23.

Slate, D., Ferber, R. (1968), *Systems Analysis: Research and Implications for Marketing*, Urbana, IL, Bureau of Economic and Business, Research, University of Illinois.

Sterman, J.D. (2007), "Exploring the Next Frontier: System Dynamics at 50", *Special Issue of System Dynamics Review*, vol 23, n 2–3.

Sterman, J.D. (2000), *Business Dynamics: Systems Thinking and Modeling for a Complex World*, New York, Irwin, McGraw-Hill.

Sterman, J.D., Mosekilde, E. (1992), "Business Cycle and Long Waves: A Behavioral Disequilibrium Perspective", *MIT System Dynamics National Model Project*, D – 4308, December, p. 37.

Sterman, J.D. (1985), "A Behavioral Model of the Economic Long Wave", *Journal of Economic Behavior and Organization*, vol 6, n 1, pp. 17–53.

Tinbergen, J. (1937), *An Econometric Approach to Business Cycle Problems*, Paris, Herman and Cie.

United States. (2011). The Financial Crisis Inquiry Report: Final Report of the National Commission on the Causes of the Financial and Economic Crisis in the United States. New York, Public Affairs.

Wack P. (1985), Scenarios: Uncharted Waters Ahead, *Harvard Business Review*, vol 63 n 5, September–October, pp. 73–89.

Wolstenholme, E.F. (1985), "A Methodology for Qualitative System Dynamics", Proceedings of the 1985 International System Dynamics Conference, Keystone, Colorado, pp. 1035–1048.

Wolstenholme, E.F., Coyle, R.G. (1983), "The Development of System Dynamics as a Methodology for System Description and Qualitative Analysis", *Journal of the Operational Research Society*, vol 34, n 7, pp. 569–581.

Part II

Monetary and fiscal policies

Crisis and change

3 Changes in the ECB monetary policy approach during the crisis

Antonio Forte

Preface

The crises faced by the Western economies since 2007 have had an impact on the economic situation and on the behavior of the policymakers, as well. The extraordinary economic situation lived by enterprises and households and the consequences of this new structural economic condition have created the right background for rethinking the public intervention in the economy. In this respect, central banks have been the first policymakers to react against the crisis. Their response to the crisis has been twofold: on the one hand, they used all the standard tools to ease the monetary policy; on the other hand, given a so unexpected awful economic situation, they started to innovate the nature of their actions aiming at strengthening the monetary policy. In the euro area, the monetary policy has experienced a deep process of innovation as well.

This chapter analyzes the innovations that the European Central Bank (ECB) has introduced in its way of conduct the monetary policy of the euro area. This subject is interesting for many reasons. First, the ECB is a relatively newly constituted central bank, and so its board needed to be more cautious not to lose credibility. Indeed, during the first period of the crisis, innovations launched by the ECB have been closely analyzed by scholars, economists and financial markets, and the board of the ECB implemented such unconventional measures being aware of the collateral effects on its own reliability. As a consequence, the ECB was the last central bank to start the so-called quantitative easing since this measure could have affected its main objective – price stability – and its own credibility. Second, the ECB has a defined mandate, tighter than that of the US Federal Reserve, and so it has less autonomy. As a result, it is interesting to investigate how the ECB has been able to increase the efficacy of its intervention notwithstanding this more limited autonomy. Third, after a so long period of accommodative monetary policy, it is possible to shed some light on the effectiveness of these measures.

So, the fundamental aim of this chapter is to give an ample view of the ECB actions during the last decade and to analyze some critical features of its monetary policy. In so doing, the rest of the chapter will be organized as follows: the following section will highlight the innovations of the monetary policy and it will be divided into two subsections: the first will deal with the changes in refinancing operations, while the second section will investigate the new programs launched by the institution based in Frankfurt. The next section will focus on the public sector asset purchases, the so-called QE, showing both the results achieved by this program and some problematic features of this non-standard measure. Indeed, in this section I will show that almost two-thirds of the liquidity injected through the QE is unused and that only the remaining part of the liquidity is into the veins of the real economy. The next section contains a review of the literature on the efficacy of the non-standard monetary policy measures on the major economies. At the end, the final section will highlight some unsolved problems and providing a possible path that the ECB could follow to restore a standard monetary policy during the next years.

Innovations in the ECB monetary policy

The monetary policy has given a crucial contribution to solve the euro area crisis. It is important to underline that the mandate of the ECB is not so ample like, for example, that of the Federal Reserve in the US. This means that the ECB had to face operational limits that central banks operating in other jurisdictions do not have. Notwithstanding this scenario, the ECB has been reactive in changing many features of its monetary policy conduct from the very first months of the sub-prime crisis. With the development of the crisis, the Governing Council of the ECB deeply modified the monetary policy even adopting unconventional measures, following the actions of other central banks.

In order to extensively explain the innovations of the monetary policy in the euro area, this section is divided into two parts. In the first one, I will analyze the changes in the refinancing operations, while in the second I will examine the non-standard measures launched by the ECB, such as the Securities Markets Programme, the Outright Monetary Transactions and the Asset Purchase Programme. All these measures have been launched during the last decade in a crescendo, trying to support the euro area economy in the worst period of its still short existence.

Changes in refinancing operations

As known, a central bank provides to banks operating within its jurisdiction the liquidity they need. This relationship is crucial because in this way the banks can get the funds useful for their current business. Central banks usually organize periodic auctions in order to provide liquidity to banks. Obviously, even the ECB follows this approach using the so-called main refinancing operations (MROs) and longer-term refinancing operations (LTROs). The objective of these operations is different: "MROs serve to steer short-term interest rates, to manage the liquidity situation and to signal the monetary policy stance";[1] while LTROs provide additional liquidity to the financial sector.

Table 3.1 Features of MROs and LTROs before and during the crisis

Features	*Before the crisis*	*During the crisis*
Interest rate	Variable rate, established in the auction	Fixed rate
Amount	Fixed	Full allotment
Duration	One week, three months	One week, three months, six months, one year, three years, four years

The sub-prime crisis and the sovereign debt crisis have induced the ECB to deeply modify the nature of these operations. The first reason that pushed the ECB to innovate the operations was the drying up of the interbank loans markets in 2007 and 2008. The Frankfurt institution, in order to limit potential bank liquidity crises promoted a long series of innovations in MROs and LTROs to provide all the needed liquidity to banking systems. Table 3.1 synthesizes the transformations of the refinancing operations during the last decade.

The first two changes concern the interest rate of the operations and the amount of liquidity provided by the ECB during the same operations. As regards the interest rate, before the onset of turmoil, the interest rate was established in the auction based on the bids submitted by the banks. The ECB declared the minimum bid rate, and the banks competed to obtain the funds. In other words, the rate was variable. But, in a crisis period and with the frozen interbank funds market, there was the risk of an exceptional increase of the interest rates in the ECB's refinancing operations because banks could be forced by adverse circumstances to offer very high rates in order to obtain liquidity. So, the Governing Council of the ECB decided to change the auction procedure establishing a fixed interest rate to avoid any type of liquidity risk. By means of this adjustment, accidental and uncontrollable interest rate upward pressure during the auctions has been eliminated.

The second innovation has modified the amount of liquidity that the ECB provides during the auctions. Before the crisis, the amount of offered liquidity was established and communicated before the auctions. As a consequence, with such a procedure, in case of very high liquidity demand, banks could not get all the required funds. So, to avoid rationing and potential liquidity crises, at the beginning of the crisis, the ECB decided to provide all the liquidity demanded by the banks: operations with full allotment.

Given these innovations, the euro area banks participating in the operations have got all the demanded liquidity and have paid a fixed pre-established interest rate since 2008. These changes almost completely deleted a potential bank liquidity risk from the euro area scenario.

The third modification has been applied to the maturity of the operations. Before the crisis there were two operations: the seven-day MROs and the three-month LTROs. That is, from 1999 to 2007, the ECB lent funds to banks for a duration of seven days through the MRO and for three months through the LTROs. During the crisis, the ECB has progressively extended the maturity of the LTROs, launching operations with durations of six months, one year, three years and four years. This extension of the maturity has been useful in order to increase the strength of the monetary policy. Indeed, in this way the ECB has affected not only the very short-term portion of the interest rates curve, but also the longer-term section. Furthermore, with the longer-term operations, the ECB has provided liquidity to credit institutions not only for the current business. Indeed, especially the last LTROs, called Targeted LTROs (TLTROs) and launched in 2014, had the objective of easing credit conditions and stimulating bank lending to households and firms. These operations stimulated the demand of liquidity by offering attractive conditions. The last version of the TLTROs (TLTRO II) has established that the interest rate applied is linked to the bank lending. The more loans that participating banks issue to firms and households, the more attractive the interest rate (even negative) on TLTRO II becomes. So in this last case, the refinancing operations have had a more ample purpose: they have been useful not only for providing longer-term liquidity, but for directly stimulating the economic activity through the improvement of the credit conditions.

Figure 3.1 depicts the amount of the liquidity provided by the ECB from the onset of its activity. This figure shows liquidity injected through both the MROs and the LTROs. It is straightforward to note the increase of the liquidity amount during the worst periods of the last decades and the increased importance of the LTROs.

There is another valuable change that the ECB has adopted during the last decade. As well known, an interest rates corridor exists. Indeed, the interest rate on the MROs is the policy rate and guides the monetary policy, but there are other two important rates: the rate on the deposit facility (DF) and the rate on marginal lending facility (MLF). The DF interest rate lies below the MRO rate, while the MLF rate is above the MRO rate. These three interest rates shape the so-called interest rates corridor. Before the crisis the distance between the MLF rate and the DF rate was equal to 2%, with the MRO rate in the middle. For example, if the MRO rate was 4%, the DF rate was 3% and the MLF rate was equal to 5%. Even in this case, in order to reduce the volatility of the interbank market rates and to make the additional liquidity provided through the MLF more convenient, the amplitude of the corridor has been gradually reduced. After a long series of changes, now the distance between MLF rate and MRO rate is 25 basis points and the one between MRO rate and DF rate is equal to 40 basis points.

This section has described the innovations of the refinancing operations set up by the ECB in order to counteract the negative effect of the crisis. These measures are in the usual set of instruments that a central bank can put in place in an adverse scenario. The extraordinary fact is that the ECB has been forced to use all these instruments together and to use them until their limit, as, for example, proved by the zero level reached by the MRO rate. But the crisis of the euro area has been so dramatic to persuade the ECB that even non-standard

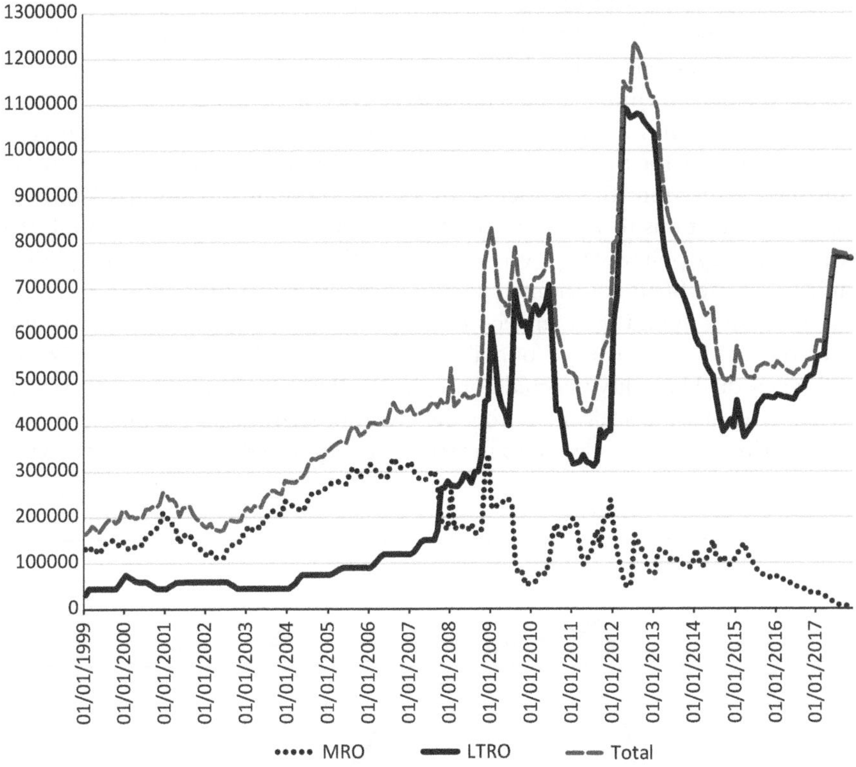

Figure 3.1 Liquidity provided by the Eurosystem through MROs and LTROs, million euros

Source: European Central Bank Statistical Data Warehouse, Internal Liquidity Management http://sdw.ecb.europa.eu.

measures were indispensable. The next subsection deals with the three most important non-standard tools put into effect by the ECB to tackle the crisis.

Non-standard measures

Among the various measures launched by the monetary authorities, it is worth describing three programs which can be considered an evolution: the Securities Markets Programme (SMP), the Outright Monetary Transactions (OMT) and the Asset Purchase Programme (APP).

The SMP, activated during the Jean Claude Trichet presidency of the ECB (2003–2011), aimed at reducing the sovereign spreads and ensuring depth and liquidity in those market segments that are dysfunctional. Through the SMP, the ECB bought the sovereign bonds of the euro area members that faced speculative attacks in 2010 and 2011. The SMP started to buy bonds in May 2010 with a focus on Irish and Greek bonds. More than one year later, in August

2011, it was reactivated to buy Portuguese, Spanish and Italian sovereign bonds that in the second half of that year started to face very strong speculation in financial markets. So, the SMP tried to limit the negative effects of speculation on interest rates, buying bonds that in 2010 and 2011 were losing value because of the financial turmoil. At the end of its activity, in September 2012, the stock of sovereign bonds bought by the SMP was almost equal to 220 billion euros (see Figure 3.2 for the source of the data). A clear limit of this program lied on the sterilization: the impact of these interventions was sterilized through specific operations to re-absorb the liquidity injected and thereby ensure that the monetary policy stance was not affected. As a consequence, the positive impact of the SMP was limited to the sovereign bond market and there was no increase in liquidity or any economic stimulus. It is important to remember that the ECB's Governing Council decided to suspend the weekly sterilization of the residual liquidity injected under the SMP in June 2014. The end of SMP sterilization has been decided, together with other measures launched during the Mario Draghi presidency, to increase liquidity into the markets and to avoid

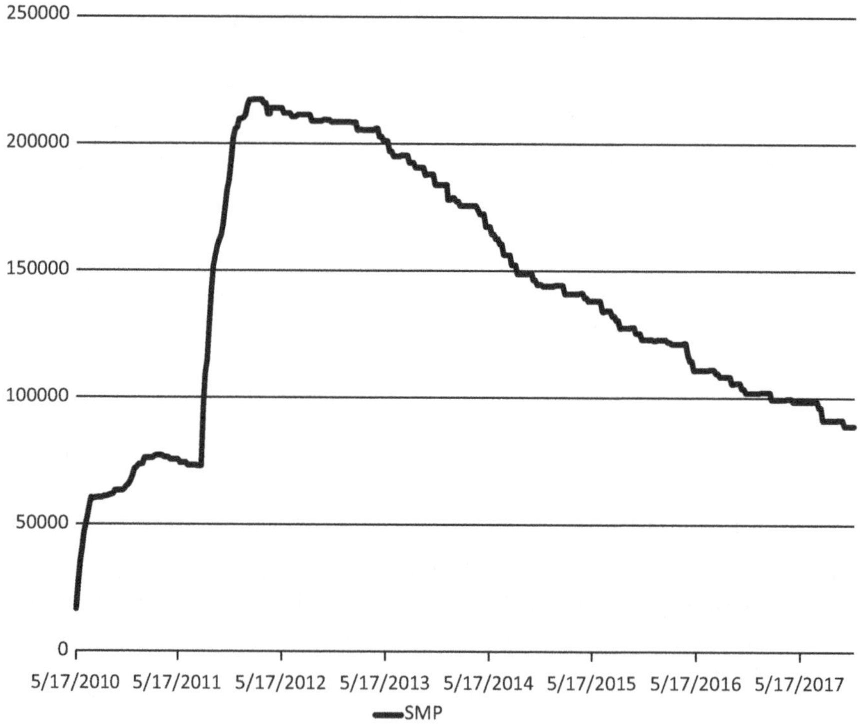

Figure 3.2 The Securities Markets Programme, million euros

Source: European Central Bank web site, Statistics – ECB/Eurosystem policy and exchange rates – Minimum reserves and liquidity (Note: The SMP was suspended in 2012. The actual amount represents the not-yet-matured bonds)

the risk of a prolonged deflationary period. Figure 3.2 shows the stock of the bonds bought under the SMP from the beginning of its activity. Obviously, Figure 3.2 shows a residual stock of sovereign bonds, because not all the bonds bought in 2010, 2011 and 2012 have already matured.

In September 2012, the Outright Monetary Transactions (OMTs) were launched and took the place of the SMP. This unconventional monetary policy instrument passed under the presidency of Mario Draghi. A very particular aspect of the OMTs is that they have never been activated. In this case, the building up of the instrument has been sufficient to mitigate the financial speculation and for changing the mood of the markets. Through this unconventional tool the ECB is ready to buy sovereign bonds with a duration from 1 to 3 years. A member state that needs this type of support has to ask the intervention of the European Union and sign an agreement about reforms to put in place within its jurisdiction. Indeed, the ECB can be involved only after the state signs an accord with the European institutions. In other words, the ECB support is conditional to a precise program of reforms. The OMT have been designed to complement the support of the European Stability Mechanism. It is fundamental to stress that the liquidity created through OMT will be fully sterilized. So, if the ECB will activate this instrument, it will be obliged to absorb from financial markets an amount of funds equal to that injected for buying sovereign bonds in secondary markets. This feature makes the OMT similar to the SMP. As said previously, this tool has never been used, so neither statistics nor inferences can be drawn. Nevertheless, the existence of this alternative instrument represents a shield against future dramatic speculative attacks.

At the end of a very long process paved of obstacles inside and outside the Frankfurt institution, the ECB finally decided to launch a tool without sterilization and conditionality: the so-called quantitative easing (QE). The ECB was the last central bank of the developed economies to initiate such a program. Indeed, the US Federal Reserve, the Bank of England and the Central Bank of Japan started to buy sovereign bonds some years before the ECB. Doubtless, the three mentioned central banks had to buy one type of sovereign bond and did not have to face the same restrictions provided by the ECB statute. Moreover, in the euro area there are different preferences about the role of the monetary policy, and this has blocked a more intense intervention of the ECB for a long time. So, only at the end of 2014 the ECB started the Asset Purchase Programme (APP), that is the official name of the QE in the euro area. During the very first months of its activity, the APP was devoted to the purchase of covered bond (CB) and of asset backed securities (ABS). Finally, in March 2015, the ECB extended the APP in order to buy sovereign bonds (EAPP). The fundamental reason that induced the ECB to launch the APP and the EAPP was the diffusion of deflationary alarms, as explained by Preat (2016). Indeed, during 2014, the increase in price started to slow and the inflation rate became very low or even negative in some countries. Table 3.2 shows the minimum level reached by the inflation rates in the major euro area economies during the last years.

Table 3.2 Minimum level of the inflation rates, harmonized index of consumer prices, 12-month rate of change, euro area and selected members

Nation	*Inflation rate*	*Period*
Germany	+0.1%	From Oct. 15 to Dec. 15, from April 16 to Aug. 16
France	+0.1%	From Sept. 15 to Jan. 16, from April 16 to July 16
Italy	−0.1%	From Sept. 16 to Dec. 16
Portugal	−0.2%	From Dec. 14 to Feb. 15
Ireland	−0.2%	From Oct. 16 to Feb. 17
Spain	−0.8%	From July 16 to Aug. 16
Greece	−1.6%	From Feb. 15 to Sept. 15
Euro area	0.0%	From Sept. 15 to Dec. 15 and July 16

Source: Eurostat web site, data-database-economy and finance-prices http://ec.europa.eu/eurostat/web/main/home

Given the mandate of the price stability, the ECB decided to inject new and additional funds in financial markets in order to avoid the risk of a persistent deflation in the euro area. Indeed, as known, the increase in liquidity stimulates (via credit) the demand and this should create inflationary pressure.

Figure 3.3 shows the monthly data of the APP. As one can note, the largest part of the APP is directed to the sovereign bond purchases. At the end of November 2017, the amount of public sector bonds was equal to 1842 billion euros, while the covered bonds and the ABS purchased by the ECB were equal to 239 billion and 25 billion euros, respectively. It is important to stress that in June 2016 the ECB started to buy corporate sector bonds as well and at the end of November 2017 their value was 128 billion euros.

Three features of the EAPP are also worth noting. The first one is the monthly amount of purchases. In the period that goes from March 2016 to December 2016, the ECB purchased 60 billion euros of ABS, CBs and sovereign bonds every month. This amount was increased to 80 billion euros per month in April 2016. After one year, in April 2017, the average monthly pace was reduced again to 60 billion euros, given the decline of the deflationary pressures. Moreover, originally the sovereign bonds purchased by the ECB must had a maturity range between two and 30 years. In December 2016, the Governing Council of the ECB decided to broaden the set of purchasable bonds, decreasing the minimum maturity from two years to one year. In October 2017, the Governing Council of the ECB announced a reduction of the monthly amount of purchases to 30 billion euros starting from January 2018 and the extension of the program until the end of September 2018.

The second important feature is the so-called "capital key." The ECB decided to divide the total amount of monthly sovereign bond purchases on the basis of the national central banks' share of the ECB capital. In other words, the capital key governs the proportion of bonds that the ECB can buy from each country. In this way, given that this share is linked to the country's share of the euro area GDP, the largest part of the purchases are directed to the German bonds. In second and third position, we find the French and the Italian sovereign bonds.

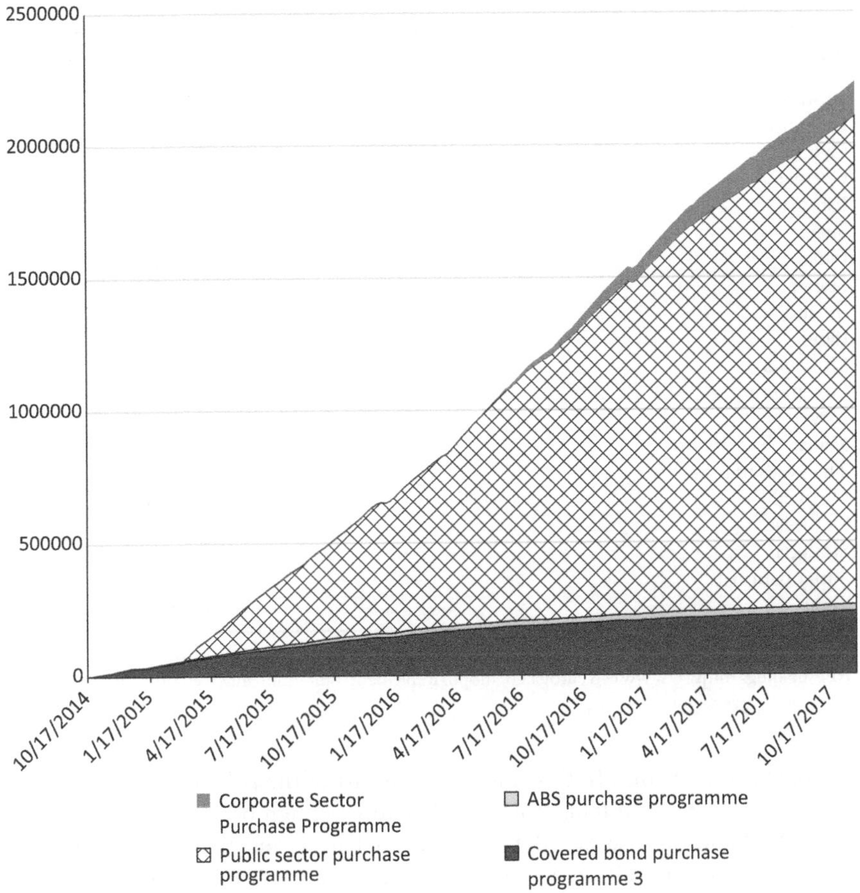

Figure 3.3 The Asset Purchase Programme, million euros

Source: European Central Bank web site, Statistics – ECB/Eurosystem policy and exchange rates – Minimum reserves and liquidity

A characteristic that must be stressed is that the Eurosystem did not purchase the Greek bonds under the EAPP. Indeed, these bonds were not eligible given the negative economic situation of the Greek economy. In order to provide data on the national purchases, Table 3.3 shows the stock of public sector bonds held by the Eurosystem at the end of November 2017 by nationality.

The last important feature of the EAPP is that the purchases are not made exclusively by the ECB. Indeed, in order not to share the risk of these purchases, the Governing Council of the ECB decided to divide purchases on a national base. For this purpose, the ECB directly buys the 8% of the total amount of the EAPP and limits its purchases to government bonds and agency securities across all eligible jurisdictions. The remaining 92% is purchased by

Table 3.3 Breakdown of debt securities under the Public Sector Purchase Programme, end of November 2017

Nation	*Million euros, book value*
Austria	50673
Belgium	63806
Cyprus	214
Germany	448657
Estonia	65
Spain	224296
Finland	28530
France	366545
Ireland	24589
Italy	318768
Lithuania	2842
Luxembourg	2312
Latvia	1737
Malta	1006
The Netherlands	100415
Portugal	30547
Slovenia	6671
Slovakia	10589
Supra nationals	202792
Total	1885054

Source: European Central Bank web site, Monetary Policy, Instruments, Asset purchase programmes, APP holdings. https://www.ecb.europa.eu/mopo/implement/omt/html/index.en.html#pspp

national central banks. In this way the large part of the risks are not shared. For example, the Banca d'Italia holds the Italian sovereign bonds purchased under the EAPP and, in case of a default of the Italian bonds, the loss will stand on the Banca d'Italia itself, remaining inside Italy. This was a tactic to get the support of northern member states that were (and still are) not so favorable to the risk sharing.

Notwithstanding some clear deficiencies, the APP has given an important contribution to reduce the risk premia in the euro area and to restore a quieter financial situation. Indeed, thanks to these monthly purchases, the interest rates on sovereign bonds went down, spreads among the sovereign bonds in the euro area have decreased and, thanks to the injected liquidity, the banking systems started to increase the lending to the real economy.

These two subsections have highlighted the most important innovations in the euro area monetary policy during the last decade. The crucial aspect is that the ECB has always tried to find a support for its unconventional tools inside the mandate of the price stability. This is the reason why some of the innovations have been launched late in comparison with what other central banks did. In other words, the ECB has had the opportunity to launch the QE only when the deflationary pressures appeared in the euro area. Before that moment, its mandate did not allow it to implement such an expansionary measure. Notwithstanding this indispensable equilibrium that slowed down the action of the ECB, it has been able to avoid the dissolution of the Monetary Union using both the conventional and unconventional monetary policy tools of a modern and innovative central bank.

Efficacy of the Public Sector Purchase Programme (PSPP)

In this section, I will examine the effects of the PSPP in order to provide a preliminary verdict on its efficacy. Three aspects will be analyzed: (1) the impact of the QE on the sovereign bonds interest rates, (2) the evolution of the credit flows to households and firms during recent years, and (3) the expansion of the liquidity deposited by the banks of the euro area on their current accounts.

Even if the main aim of the PSPP is to improve the monetary policy transmission and to avoid the risk of deflation, obviously the purchases of the sovereign bonds under the PSPP have an impact on their interest rates. The launch of the OMTs had already reduced the risk premium and fostered a lowering of the spreads among euro area sovereign bonds. The PSPP has strengthened this trend, as shown in Figure 3.4. The figure shows the yield of the 10-year German, Italian, Spanish, Ireland, Portuguese and Greek sovereign bonds. So, the figure depicts the movement of the interest rate of the key country of the euro area, Germany, and of the nations that have suffered the worst consequences of the crisis. As one can observe, the PSPP contributed to reduce the interest rates and the spreads during 2015 and the first half of 2016. Then, in the second part of 2016 the trend was reversed due to the international political tensions, the elections in some member states and the change in the Federal Reserve monetary policy. Notwithstanding these tensions, during 2017, the interest rate levels remained very low thanks to the PSPP. In this context, it is important to remember, as stressed earlier, that the Eurosystem has never purchased the Greek sovereign bonds under the PSPP because they were not eligible. So, the reduction of the interest rates of this nation is not directly linked to this program, but to the national and European improved background.

So, as regards the interest rates spreads, the PSPP has demonstrated a certain usefulness in limiting spread levels and volatility, even in turbulent periods (see Brexit, US and French presidential elections, Italian referendum vote).

The fundamental aim of the PSPP, together with the other non-standard measures, is to foster inflation. The mechanism to reach this aim is the following: the Eurosystem purchases bonds, in this way injecting new money in banking systems and, via credit, awakening inflation. Given this transmission mechanism, it is worthwhile to inspect the credit conditions in the euro area. More in detail, the attention will be focused on loans to households and non-financial corporations in the euro area and in some member states. As regards the euro area as a whole, data published by the ECB[2] show that the annual growth rate of loans to households was equal to 2.7% in October 2017 (the last available datum). During the 12 months before the onset of PSPP, from February 2014 to February 2015, the annual growth rate of loans to households

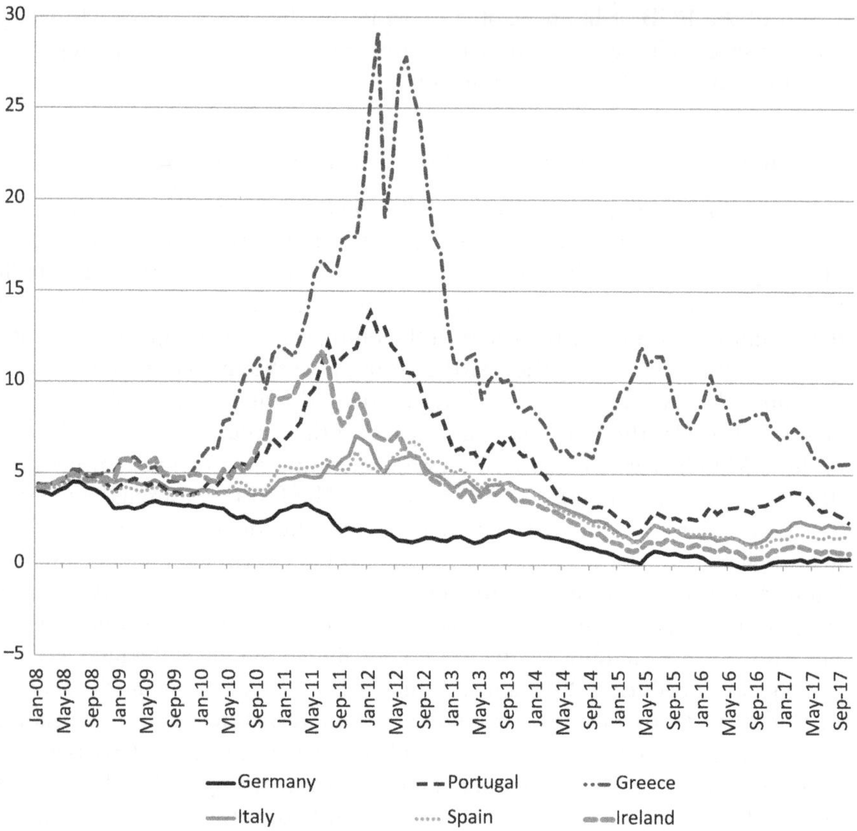

Figure 3.4 Ten-year sovereign bond yield

Source: Eurostat web site, Data-Database-Economy and finance-Interest rates http://ec.europa.eu/eurostat/web/main/home

was equal to −0.2%. As regards loans to non-financial corporations, the annual growth rate was 0.2% in October 2017, while in February 2015 there was a negative annual variation: −1.1%. So, considering the euro area as a whole, the evidence is quite positive. On the contrary, the situation in memberstates is mixed. In October 2017, the annual rate of change of loans to both households and non-financial corporations were positive in Germany, France, Austria and Belgium. In Italy, in the Netherlands and in Ireland, the annual rate of change was positive for loans to households but negative for loans to corporations. In the same period, the annual rate of change of loans to households and to non-financial corporations was still negative in Greece, Spain and Portugal. The rate of change of loans to household and corporations improved in all these countries, except Greece, during the PSPP period but, as data have shown, the credit expansion is not still widespread in all the member states.

Summing up, the PSPP, together with the other measures, has improved the credit conditions but in many member states a credit crunch is still in place – albeit milder in comparison with the previous years.

A possible explanation of a not-so-strong impact of the PSPP on credit expansion is proposed in the following original analysis. Figure 3.5 shows two lines: one represents the growth of the public sector purchases, and the other line represents the increase in deposited liquidity that is directly linked to this expansionary measure. The second line is built as follows: starting from 13 March 2015, the weekly change of the sum of deposit facility and of excess of reserves is offset by the change of open market operations (MROs and LTROs) and by the increase in covered bonds and ABS purchases. I disregarded the Corporate Sector Purchase Programme (CSPP) in this calculation because under this program, banks are not the most important counterpart of the Eurosystem. Indeed, under the CSPP, the Eurosystem can buy corporate bonds directly on primary and secondary markets. In other words, the liquidity injected under the CSPP does not directly and mandatorily go to the banking sector. So, the second line depicts the increase of unused liquidity. The result is that at the end of November 2017 only the 31.5% of the liquidity injected under the PSPP was in the veins of the real economy. Indeed, at the end of November, the purchases under the PSPP were equal to 1842 billion euros while the increase in unused liquidity was equal to 1262 billion euros. This analysis sheds more light on the usefulness of the PSPP and explains why the impact of this program has not been as wide and strong as expected. So, euro area banks continue to place a large amount of money with the ECB despite the interest rate they pay on the reserves in excess of the reserve requirement.

Do the non-standard measures work?

In order to inspect the effectiveness of the unconventional monetary policies put in place by the central banks, this section reviews the recent literature focused on this subject with a particular attention to the euro area case. First of all, it is important to cite some data on the effectiveness of the non-standard measures in the US and UK. Bernanke (2012) highlights that the first two rounds of the Federal Reserve large-scale asset purchases may have raised the level of output by almost 3% and the private payroll employment by more than 2 million jobs. Bernanke himself underlines that these estimates should be treated with prudence, but he stresses that the evidence of the literature supports the conclusion that central bank securities purchases have provided support to the economy and have mitigated deflationary risks. Moreover, Bonis et al. (2017) find that the effect of the asset purchases made by the Federal Reserve results in a reduction of about 100 basis points in the 10-year Treasury yield. Turning to the UK economy, Joyce et al. (2011) summarize a series of

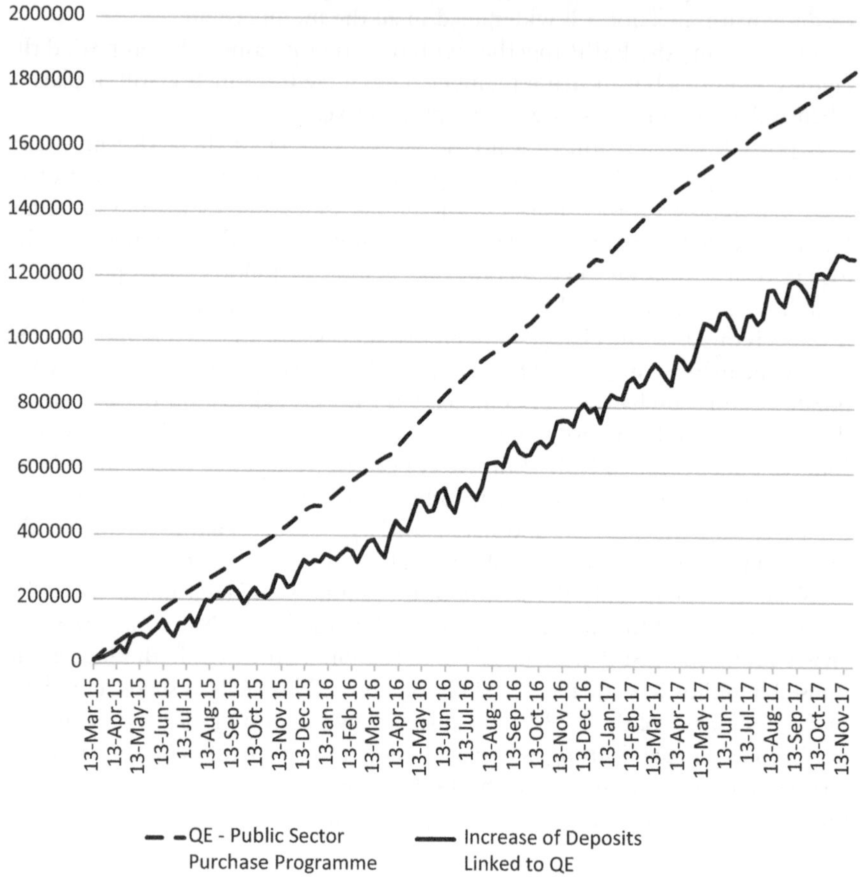

Figure 3.5 PSPP purchases and liquidity deposited by banks, million euros

Source: elaboration on data from the European Central Bank web site, Statistics – ECB/Eurosystem policy and exchange rates – Minimum reserves and liquidity

results of the effects of the Bank of England's quantitative easing and highlight an impact between 1% and 2% for real output and between 0.75% and 1.5% for inflation rate in the UK. Baumeister and Benati (2010) find that the unconventional monetary policies by the Federal Reserve and the Bank of England have avoided risks of deflation and deep economic downturn.

There are estimates on the effectiveness of the ECB's unconventional measures, as well. First of all, it is worth noting two papers published by the ECB. Andrade et al. (2016) find that the APP had different positive effects: it reduced sovereign yields on long-term bonds and increased the equity prices of banks that held a large amount of sovereign bonds in their portfolios. Moreover, using a model to assess the impact of the APP, they find that the APP contributed to support both inflation and output. Furthermore, the introduction of the APP increased the long-term inflation expectations toward the inflation objective. Summing up, according to this paper, the APP achieved al large variety of goals. In a more recent paper, Gambetti and Musso (2017), through an empirical analysis, find that the EAPP had a significant impact on both GDP and inflation. The impact on GDP was higher during the first quarters of 2015 and then it disappeared, while the impact on inflation was very small in the first quarter of 2015 but it increased until the last quarter of 2016. So, they also find that the APP was useful to support the economic activity and inflation.

Another interesting study is that proposed by Fielder et al. (2016). They summarize the results of many papers focused on the unconventional monetary policies. As they underline, there is a broad consensus in the economic literature on the facts that the unconventional monetary policy measures can have an important impact on financial markets and can stimulate economic activity. They also stress that the impact of expansionary measures decreases over time. It is now useful to cite some of the papers mentioned by Fielder et al. (2016). For example, Fratzscher et al. (2016), by using an event study approach, find that the announcement of the ECB measures had a significant impact on financial markets variables such us equity prices and bond spreads. The same result is highlighted by Gibson et al. (2016), who show that the implementation of unconventional policies produced a reduction in sovereign spreads and mitigated financial stress. But they also stress that the quantitative effects of the ECB unconventional measures were modest. Pattipeilohy et al. (2013) find that the LTRO interventions had a favorable effect on government bond yields and that the SMP had a downward effect on Italian and Spanish bond yields, but this effect disappeared after few weeks. Briciu and Lisi (2015) replicate the analysis by Fratzscher et al. (2016), including the announcement of the EAPP, and find similar results. The announcement of both the EAPP and the previous unconventional measures decreased the bond spreads. Another interesting result is found by Szczerbowicz (2015). She measures the impact of SMP, OMT, covered bond purchases and long-term refinancing operations on bank and government borrowing costs. She finds that SMP, OMT and covered bond purchases were successful in reducing the borrowing costs for banks and governments in the presence of high sovereign risk. Moreover, she finds that exceptional liquidity measures, like long-term refinancing operations, reduce money market tensions. Other papers focused on the economic activity effects of the unconventional measures. For example, Boeckx et al. (2017) study the macroeconomic effect of the ECB balance sheet measures. They find that these expansionary measures stimulate credit growth, stabilize financial markets and support output and inflation. But they also contribute to depreciate the currency and to lower sovereign bond spreads. Another recent paper finds similar results. Bernoth et al. (2016) study the effects of the ECB quantitative easing. On the one hand, they find that the announcement of the EAPP decreased bond yields and spreads in the euro area. On the other hand, they show that the EAPP increased economic activity up to 0.2% and the inflation of about 0.1%.

Summing up, this section has highlighted that there is widespread agreement on the fact that the unconventional monetary policy measures are effective in stimulating both the output and inflation and in reducing bond yields. Some studies underline that the impact of unconventional measures is weak, but it is unquestionable that the non-standard measures have helped the economies in recovering from the crisis.

Conclusion

In this chapter, I depicted the evolution of the monetary policy in the euro area through a very long series of innovations: on the one hand, the traditional tools of the ECB have been transformed in order to sustain the banking system and to avoid liquidity risk; on the other hand, unconventional measures have been launched to reactivate the monetary policy transmission mechanism, to avoid the risks of a prolonged period of deflation and to weed out the idea of the Eurozone disintegration. Undoubtedly, all these measures have rubbed out the worst scenario, that is the end of the Eurozone, but the analysis of their effectiveness has revealed that they probably have not had the expected impact.

Indeed, some problems are not yet vanquished. The rise of inflation during the first months of 2017 has been broadly linked to energy prices trend and not to the effects of the QE. This could lead to a future inflation decrease when this temporary effect will fade away. In addition, the interest rate spreads on sovereign bonds have increased from the second part of 2016 ahead, notwithstanding the strengthening of the EAPP. Moreover, a difference in the interest rate paid by firms in the different states of the euro area still exists, even if it is now reduced in comparison with two/three years ago. The ECB does not have to focus on such a problem, but it is not fair that, in a common market with a common currency, firms have to pay different interest rates not for their own riskiness, but for national problems or for deficiencies in the euro area framework. This is a problem that not only the ECB but also the European and national politicians have to face.

The last unsolved problem is the unused liquidity injected under the PSPP, described in Figure 3.5. Banks are paying an interest rate for the extraordinary excess liquidity they deposit with the ECB but, notwithstanding this, they continue to increase the stock of deposited money. This liquidity could be useful for feeding the economic recovery and for helping the inflation to be close to 2%. The ECB has not been capable of inducing the banks to use these funds, more than 1200 billion euros. The impact of the QE would have been certainly stronger if all this unused liquidity had been injected in the veins of the real economy.

The economic literature highlights that the non-standard measures have had an impact on the economy. The effect of this kind of intervention has been positive in the US, in the UK and in the euro area: in fact, they stimulated the economic growth, reduced the interest rates and pushed prices, avoiding any risks of deflation. So all in all, even if it is difficult to inspect the effectiveness of these policies, the economists underline the positive role of the extraordinary measures put in place by the central banks.

Looking ahead, it is possible to speculate about the path that the ECB will follow to gradually restore a conventional monetary policy. If the evolution of the inflation follows the current expected scenario, the first action will be the end of the EAPP, probably during the last quarter of 2018. Then the second step will be a very gradual increase of the policy rate, probably starting in 2019. In the following years, the ECB will widen the interest rates corridor and change the nature of the refinancing operations reestablishing a fixed amount of liquidity and a variable rate. Observing the Federal Reserve approach to monetary policy normalization, we can be sure that the ECB will be very cautious in the same way. Before increasing the interest rates, the ECB will observe a self-sustaining inflation rate below but close to 2%. So, probably in 2020, we will observe a gradual return of positive real interest rates. The last step will be the reduction of the stock of the assets purchased under the EAPP.

In conclusion, the last decade was very challenging for the central banks all around the globe and especially for the ECB, given its very short history and the complexity of the euro area. The lack of historical credibility did not affect the moves of the ECB, which has been fairly ready to approve the necessary measures for tackling the crisis. The results achieved by the ECB have been quite good: it contributed to rescue the euro area and to avoid the risk of deflation. However, we can be sure that the next decade will be as demanding as the past one, because the monetary policy will certainly face new and unexpected challenges along the path of normalization.

Notes

1 European Central Bank web site, Monetary Policy – Instruments – Open markets operations, https://www.ecb.europa.eu/mopo/implement/omo/html/index.en.html

2 European Central Bank Statistical Data Warehouse – Money, credit and banking – MFI aggregated balance sheet. http://sdw.ecb.europa.eu

References

Andrade, P., et al. (2016), The ECB's asset purchase programme: An early assessment. *ECB Working Paper Series*, No. 1956.

Baumeister, C. and L. Benati (2010), Unconventional monetary policy and the great recession: Estimating the impact of a compression in the yield spread at the zero lower bound. *ECB Working Paper Series*, No. 1258.

Bernanke, B. (2012), Monetary policy since the onset of the crisis. *Remarks at the Federal Reserve Bank of Kansas City Economic Symposium*, Jackson Hole, WY.

Bernoth, K., et al. (2016), Effectiveness of the ECB programme of asset purchases: Where do we stand? *DIW Berlin: Politikberatungkompakt*, No. 113.

Boeckx, J., et al. (2017), Effectiveness and transmission of the ECB's balance sheet policies. *International Journal of Central Banking*, 13(1): 297–333.

Bonis, B., et al. (2017), The effect of the Federal Reserve's securities holdings on longer-term interest rates. *FEDS Notes*, Board of Governors of the Federal Reserve System (U.S.).

Briciu, L. and G. Lisi (2015), An event-study analysis of ECB balance sheet policies since October 2008. *Economic and Financial Affairs*, Economic Brief 1.

Fielder, S., et al. (2016), Transmission channels of unconventional monetary policy in the euro area: Where do we stand? *European Parliament: Directorate-General for Internal Policies Monetary Dialogue*, Monetary Dialogue 28 November 2016.

Fratzscher, M., et al. (2016), ECB unconventional monetary policy: Market impact and international spillovers. *IMF Economic Review*, 64(1): 36–74.

Gambetti, L. and A. Musso. (2017), The macroeconomic impact of ECB's expanded asset purchase programme (APP). *ECB Working Paper Series*, No. 2075.

Gibson, H. D., et al. (2016), The effectiveness of the ECB's asset purchase programs of 2009 to 2012. *Journal of Macroeconomics*, 47: 45–57.

Joyce, M., et al. (2011), The United Kingdom's quantitative easing policy: Design, operation, and impact. *Bank of England Quarterly Bulletin*, September: 200–212.

Pattipeilohy, C., et al. (2013), Unconventional monetary policy of the ECB during the financial crisis: An assessment and new evidence. *De Nederlandsche Bank Working Paper*, No. 381.

Preat, P. (2016), The ECB's fight against low inflation: Reasons and consequences. *Speech at Luiss School of European Political Economy*, Rome, 4 April.

Szczerbowicz, U. (2015), The ECB unconventional monetary policies: Have they lowered market borrowing costs for banks and governments? *International Journal of Central Banking*, 11(4): 91–127.

4 From 1980s onwards, new emerging forms of money facing monetary theory

A revolution or evolution?

Nicolas Barbaroux

Introduction

> [T]he proposal in this Paper by Professor Hayek has moved from being "politically impossible" to being within our grasp. We should seize it.
>
> (Wood, *Preface* to third edition, in Hayek, 1990: 22)

In the aftermath of the great financial crisis (*GFC*), Paul Krugman (2011) not only blamed the economists for being blind to the crisis, but also for being unable to foresee what could have happened at that time. According to him, none of them even considered the possibility of a crisis. It is a tricky and unsolvable question to know to what extent economics *can* do precise forecasts for the future. However, for once in the history, one economist escapes to that ontological reproach under the person of Friedrich von Hayek. The 1974 Nobel Prize winner attracted renew of interests, quite recently, owing to the increasing development of the virtual currency, and especially concerning all the numerous debates that surrounded the bitcoin.

It is quite paradoxical to recall Hayek in the first front of the scene in the current state of the economy, as he was in favour of a weak degree of state intervention. Even though the 1980s were of great value for Hayek owing to the liberal wave that blew all around the world and enabled the financial globalization, the current period is in many respects in contradiction with the ideal economic functioning that Hayek had in mind: increasing central banks' power, strong fiscal weight following GFC, huge public debt and deficits for many of the G8 countries, quantitative easing policy, etc. It is right that we owe to the Austrian economists the due importance we set on interest rate management tools, but Hayek was a fervent opponent of whatever form of interest rate settings by central bankers, and he was more enthusiast with a self-regulation process by way of free market procedures.[1] By contrast, Hayek would have applauded the emergence of start-ups, the securization process, the increasing development of market derivatives and the development of (financial) market-based sources of financing for firms. If here is one sector in which Hayek would have been ready to stand up and applaud, it is without doubt what is occurring in the monetary field with the development of virtual currencies.

By challenging the state monopoly of money issue, the virtual currencies open a new world with new rules. Even though more than 750 virtual currencies exist, they all have in common being both cryptocurrencies and at the origin of a *decentralized* banking sector. Many libertarians dreamed for many decades, not to say a century, of such initiatives.

This chapter will be based on the pioneered work done by Hayek and especially on his book on "*Denationalization of Money*" originally published in 1976. As claimed in the quotation opening this chapter by Professor Geoffrey E. Wood in his preface to the third edition of Hayek's 1976 book, the actuality of Hayek's core message is eye-catching. In the introductive quotation, the "paper" mentioned by Prof. Wood referred to the *Hobart Papers* series from the Institute of Economic Affairs (IEA), a free market think-tank based in Westminster in the United Kingdom. Professor Hayek contributed to it between 1972 and 1978. Among those papers for the IEA, one of them supported the idea that the supply of money should be better place into the hands of the market rather than into those of human beings.[2]

Hayek's 1976 "*Denationalization of Money*" becomes a helpful contribution to "the most fascinating theoretical vistas" (Hayek, 1990: 13) which are occurring with the development of virtual currencies. If we enter into the hypothesis that "government should be deprived of its monopoly of the issue of money" (*ibid*), we are facing the "possibility of arrangements which have never been considered" (*ibid*) hitherto. The central message of the book is crystal clear. It aims at demonstrating to what extent "the price level stability can be achieved only by removing from national governments their monopoly of money creation" (Hayek, 1990: 19). In fact, Hayek was concerned by the (*in*)stability of prices while underlying their due effects on economic cycles (Hayek, 1933). Throughout his career, Hayek questioned the central banking system and its own ability to regulate the economy, but widely states' intervention in economics at large. Hayek's reluctance against states was not only due to the fact that states' interventions had proved to be inflationary, but more importantly, Hayek thought that the state was representative of what he called simulacra of knowledge. The latter refers to the pretended knowledge or ability to control something that we are unable to control or manage by definition. This concept applies to monetary phenomenon, but also to economic "rules of the games" at large. While being impressed by the scientific progress inherited from the Enlightenment of the 18th century, Hayek saw the world as too complex to be truly understood by human beings. Thus, he truly believed in the impossibility to make previsions in economics, which explained why he was influenced by Darwinism rather than by physics. We will not mislead the reader by advocating that Hayek was sceptical of the idea of understanding economics' phenomenon. It is exactly the reverse which applies. Among Hayek's motivations to study economics, the one of unwinding economics' wheels was overriding.

As financial (*free*) markets became a leading component of the type of capitalism that emerged from 1980s and owing to the increasing developments of virtual currencies which gave birth to a *decentralized* banking sector, it is worth considering how relevant is Hayek's practical proposition for today and onwards into the future. By entering into that question, we will be able to contribute to the thesis defended by Michael Woodford's (1999) historical paper on the macro family tree. He summarized macroeconomics as an endless movement between periods of (*theoretical*) *evolution* and *revolution*. To him, the first *revolution* dated back from the apparition of Keynesianism in the inter-war period. The following currents – such as Monetarism, New Classical Economics or Real Business Cycle Theory – can be understood as different waves of attack on Keynesian macroeconomics. In Woodford's sense of the word, they are just *evolutions* of macroeconomics. The latest macroeconomics *evolution* was linked to the development of the models in the 1980s which put a specific focus set on the role of different types of imperfections on the economic fluctuations, notably with New Keynesian and New Neoclassical Synthesis models. Is the Hayekian "*Denationalization of Money*" a new *revolution* in macro family tree? Or will it only be a simple *evolution* from preceding movements?

Throughout this chapter, we will analyze the development of the new (*private*) types of money alongside the monetary theory. More precisely, we will inquire to what extent the private types of money are theoretically founded, and especially to what extent the monetary theory inherited from Hayek's *Denationalization of Money* is a useful framework to understand the challenges caused by the development of private currencies.

The chapter will be structured as follows: the next section provides a brief description of the new types of money and their goals over the last 30 years. The following section will evaluate this evolution alongside the monetary theory, and especially the one developed by Hayek and his revolutionary program of "*Denationalization of Money*". The final section will conclude by providing some reflections and new challenges that central bankers will have to face onwards.

The types of money beyond banking

It is common ground to summarize the 1980s as the years of the "*financial big bang*", owing to the development of financial markets, and especially the derivatives ones. The *liberal* wave that hit many countries around the world – and notably with the elections of Margaret Thatcher in the United Kingdom and Ronald Reagan in the United States – facilitated that structural change. However, a new wave submerged Europe during the past decade with the development of new types of currency outside the banking sector. Those two *"waves"* have in common setting a world in which market forces took a leading place while escaping many forms of regulations and regulatory institutions.

The capital markets and the markets for derivatives

The increasing development of financial markets in the mid-1980s brings about two leading changes for the economic functioning: *first*, a disintermediation process; and *second*, the line of separation between money and financial assets has become unclear.

The European economies, as those of most English-speaking countries, were hit by the famous "3D revolution" by way of a threefold process of *deregulation, disintermediation* and *decompartmentalisation*. The logical consequences had been to weaken the banking sector in its duty of financing the economy to the benefits of the financial markets. The development of direct external funding enabled by the many types of capital markets, and their multiple assets, boosted the economy while structurally transforming the functioning of the banking sector. As most of the firms can easily finance their business by way of the issue of assets, the assets side of the bank's balance sheet substituted claims on credit by an increasing assets portfolio. Structurally, the global level of risks hedged by banks increased. However, it was not prejudicial to the economic stability, owing to the new facilities offered to the banks and financial institutions to externalize or hedge those risks. With the help of the new types of market, called the *derivatives markets*, the economy was supposed to be able to trade the risk worldwide while reducing risk costs at large. The development of those derivatives markets – especially the *futures* markets, the *forwards* markets and the ones on *options* – is the seminal feature set by the deregulation process of the 1980s. However, the derivatives markets quickly became speculative ones rather than a market for insurance. Moreover, as many new types of assets had been created by financial institutions (under the agreement of the appropriate institutions, both national and international), the distinction between a *monetary asset* and *financial assets* became unclear. For instance, convertible bonds in share had been created to reduce the liquidity constraint. The derivatives markets and the securization process created as well new possibilities (such as credit default swaps, interest rate swaps, assets-backed securities, mortgage-backed securities, collateralized debt obligation, etc.) to transform a risk (backed by pool of assets) into liquidity. In the end, the distinction between (*liquid*) money and (*illiquid*) financial assets is more complex.

One of the main consequences that the 1980s brought about for Europe was the systemic risk blindness, and the increasing discrepancy between the pre-supposed prudential rules and the true level of risks. The banking sector is still regulated by increasing prudential rules, as risk is more complex and difficult to foresee (*off*-balance sheet risk), but the stability of the economic system has been weakened, such as demonstrated by the GFC in September 2008. In the end, both the competitiveness of the banking – and financial – sectors and the financial stability were affected. Many commentators wonder to what extent financial stability should become the new official goal of central banks. If we move to that goal, a new series of questions quickly appears: Which type of *financial* risk should we focus? How can we measure financial instability? Which indicators are relevant and robust enough to see the risk?

At first sight, deregulation processes fit with Hayek's theory. If firms can find funds and capital in a free competitive and international market, the interest rate will be lower as the one set by whatever private banks (under the influence of the central bank's policy rate). However, Hayek was himself really sceptical about what occurred at that time. Even though the Thatcherian idea of "*rolling back the state*" was welcomed by Hayek, he was, thus, disappointed by the functioning of the markets as the deregulation was not complete. The freedom to intervene, to buy and sell on the supposed deregulated markets, was not real. The main point of departure was the presence of a "*lender in last resort*" duty in many central banks' institutional settings. Hayek truly believes in self-regulation and self-responsibility for the economics' agents. The deregulation process gave to banks, and mostly to private financial institutions, all the rights unless the one became bankrupt. Without any surprise, the "*too big to fail*" rule applies. The banks, the insurance companies and the financial institutions were induced to merge and create complex structures with deregulated subsidiaries out of the scope of many supervisory institutions. The roots of instability are also a subject in which Hayek was farsighted. The emergence of the GFC proved the Hayekian theory to be right. The Hayekian theory is mostly a theory against state intervention due to its effects on the business cycle. Hayek saw central banks as being responsible for the crisis by setting inappropriate interest rates, or by creating inflationary cycles due to the overwhelming public debt in many European countries.

A last question deserves to be asked: To what extent are the developments of capital and derivatives markets of specific concern for monetary theory? On that subject, Hayek's contribution is really helpful. In the 1970s, Hayek anticipated what we currently face by way of the decreasing discrepancy between money and non-money (namely, financial assets). Hayek pleads for a new definition of money. In his *Denationalization of Money*, he fully assumes that there is no clear difference between what money *is* and what it *is not*. Most of the dictionaries or textbooks defined money by its degree of "*liquidity*"; Hayek favoured defining money as an adjective – rather than as a noun – which describes "a property which different things could possess to varying degrees" (Hayek, 1990: 56). Thus, money and financial assets can be combined or mixed up as both serve the same goal: financing the economy.

Meanwhile, the financial and derivatives markets emerged, the economy saw the birth of two new "*types*" of currency: local currency and (crypto) virtual currencies. Both of them have in common opening wide the doors to question government's monopoly on the issuing of money.

Local currency and cryptocurrenies

By echoing the old monetary debates according to which money should be – or not – a sole media of exchange, the appearance of "*local currencies*" is an interesting evolution in a context of increasing globalization. The supply of local currency aims at boosting the local economy (within a limited area of exchange) by allowing a non-banking agent to issue its own currency on condition that this local currency will be convertible in the official currency (the one granted by legal tender). As the local currency has no legal tender, the holders of this type of money are induced to use it in a limited number of shops and stores (which agreed to sustainable development rules). By so doing, they will favour local shops at the expense of bigger companies or major (globalized) brands. The development of this new type of currency is interesting in two respects: *first*, money recovers its former duty, the one of boosting the circulation of good and services; *second*, non-banking agents (mostly local institutions or associations) get the power to issue money outside the scope of banks and central banks. The latter point is without impact for the price stability as those issuers of local currency convert official currency into a local currency; in neither case do they have the power to create new money. Even though local currencies enable non-banks to issue a type of money, the development of private cryptocurrencies differs from them as the latter created the foundation of a decentralized monetary system.

Cryptocurrency is the leading monetary initiative that has emerged since Hayek wrote. Following the Lehman's collapse, an unknown researcher, under the (fake) name of Satoshi Nakamoto, published in 2009 a nine-page article untitled "Bitcoin: A Peer-to-Peer Electronic Cash System" in which we can find the origin of the most popular virtual currency at the moment. The bitcoin is a networked virtual currency which exclusively circulates on the internet by way of e-business. It allows the settling of transactions without bank's involvement. It is called a *cryptocurrency* as the currency took the form of a complex series of codes with different types of digits, numbers and symbol. The basic (libertarian) idea of Nakamoto was to propose a new banking system *without banks*! In fact, thanks to a blockchain protocol, the article provides a new organization to make payments between individuals. The true motivation behind that monetary "*innovation*" is to prevent fraud and cheating caused by human beings at large, especially banks and governments. To Nakamoto, people will trust in that system because it is totally "*dehumanized*". Most of the people who hold bitcoin already buy it on a trading platform on internet. Another possibility is to participate in the functioning of the bitcoin system, which is commonly called "*mining*". In fact, what makes this currency unique is the particular way of issuing it since the system involves no third party, contrary to a traditional centralized banking system. (Nashibe, 2014: 50). Thanks to a complex system of a peer-to-peer network of computers, the human being is totally substituted by computers, which play the same role as the (*old*) banks: collecting payment orders, checking the information on both the buyer side and the seller side, debiting the account of the debtors, crediting the account of the creditors. The network supplies automatically the fixed quantity of bitcoin when a mining activity is completed; that is to say, when a computer – or a network of computers – performs the role of the banks (the one of collecting the information, paying out the money, etc.). For each mining activity, an award is given to the computer which did the job. This award (paid in bitcoin) is divided by two every four years. As a consequence, the rate of growth of the supply of bitcoin slows down, which partly explains why bitcoin's value increased recently.

When a payment is made, we never know the real "name" of the debtors (and he same for the creditors). Each transaction is anonymously made through the exchange of two types of "*keys*". To make a payment, the creditor should use his unique *private* key associated with a *public* key which is generated by the network itself (as soon as all the verification had been made during the mining activity). The amount of bitcoin is transferred from one account to the other as soon as the creditors unlocked the amount with his unique private key. For this reason, the system is safe since no one can steal any payment without this unique private key. The same is true concerning the supply of bitcoin. It is impossible to issue *fake* bitcoin – contrary to official currency – since each currency takes the form of a unique code. As soon as a similar code circulates within the network (during the checking period of mining before payment is made), the transaction is automatically cancelled and no one can unlock the payment.

The main advantage of bitcoin, while simultaneously also being its main disadvantage, is that it is a fully anonymous system. For that reason, bitcoin is the most popular currency in the darknet. As there is no possibility to track the holder of the bitcoin's account, it is easy to make payments and transactions when illicit activities are concerned. This is the leading motivation for central banks to regulate that currency. Money control is one of the main central banks' functions. By so doing, central banks indirectly wish to maintain their monopoly of issue.

In the end, European economies did not escape the global tendency of both the disintermediation process and increasing non-monetary assets that played the same role which money used to play. Fredrik Hayek would certainly have enjoyed the recent development of virtual and cryptocurrency, as they open wide the doors to a world *without* central banks.

The new forms of money facing monetary theory

Following the last three decades of the evolution of monetary forms, it is the economist's duty to analyze them. When the economic practices precede the theory, it is not a waste of time to return back to old books and theories so as to explain them. Hayek's *Denationalization of Money* enables us to wonder if the generalization of private money is a utopia or an incoming reality.

The Hayekian background: a libertarian criticism against the state

Friedrich von Hayek was an Austrian economist born in Vienna in 1899. He was raised by a family of scientific scholars, which explained his everlasting intellectual curiosity for science at large. He truly believed in science's power in order to understand the complexity of the world. He paid attention to economics as he thought it useful to solve the missing equation within the history of sciences; that is to say, decrypting the economic wheels that run the world. However, he quickly admitted that economics, contrary to hard sciences such as physics, is unable to make predictions. In that sense, the only method that matters is to look back in history and understand the fundamental mechanisms that occurred at that time. This is exactly what he did when studying the behaviour of the young Fed (US Federal Reserve Bank) during the "great depression" from the "*Black Thursday*" in 1929, October 24. Hayek blamed the Fed's rate policy at that time for disturbing the natural economic cycle. In fact, the central banks' rates that have been too low for too long[3] created an unprecedented speculative bubble which brought about an historic depression cycle for many countries in the 1930s.

Hayek saw many changes throughout his life. He was, thus, deeply affected by the rise of communism in Europe and its planned economy reforms. From that episode, he wrote one of his leading books, *The Road to Serfdom*, in 1944, from which he provides his strongest criticism against state intervention. The increasing power of State's intervention within the economy, especially following World War I and World War II, has to be understood as the willingness from the state to control people. In fact, managing the economy is a path to reduce individual freedoms. This libertarian thesis, which still finds echoes nowadays, mostly in the United States, enables us to understand Hayek's position on monetary phenomenon, both in theory and practice.

Without any surprise, the Hayekian theory became fashionable from the 1980s, particularly when Margaret Thatcher aimed at "*rolling back the state*" while quoting Hayek in different speeches. But, even now, Hayekian ideas are celebrated for two seminal changes: the development of unconventional monetary policy and the development of private (*virtual*) currencies in competition. On the first point, there is no doubt about the fact that though Hayek was not favourable with central banking at large, he would have welcomed the fact central bank substituted an "interest rate transmission mechanism" by a "non-banking agent's refinancing channel", usually called unconventional monetary policy (Artus, 2009: 1).[4] By so doing, central banks act directly where the need of liquidity has arisen and out of the banking sector. It is a paradox for central banks to behave outside the banking sector, but, by so doing, they implicitly admitted that setting interest rates is not relevant to managing economic cycles, as Hayek demonstrated all along his career and notably in his 1933 book *Monetary Theory and the Trade Cycle*. Concerning the second point, this is the seminal argument to revive Hayek's contribution to the modern European economy. In fact, Hayek's revolutionary ideas – or insane ideas (*according to his detractors*) – find thorough relevancy in the aftermath of the GFC. The publication of the "Bitcoin: a Peer to Peer Electronic Cash System" article by Satoshi Nakamoto in 2009 is an outstanding U-turn in the monetary history, as it opens wide doors to numerous private virtual currencies as Hayek dreamed in his 1976 book *Denationalization of Money*.

The Denationalization of Money *thesis*

If we want to understand Hayek's monetary theory, we need first, to consider his philosophical background. Hayek always put freedom at the forefront of debates. Throughout his life, he demonstrated that state interventions had always been both prejudicial and inefficient; Hayek was, first, motivated by raising the degree of freedom to individuals within the society at its maximum level. This applies to monetary phenomenon. If you aimed at "disillusioning the world", you need to fight against two monetary myths: the "mystique of legal tender" and "the Gresham Law". On the first myth, Hayek questioned the fact that legal tender law had been the *basis* of government monopoly. In fact, the expression "*legal tender*" only refers to the kind of objects or unit of account (*i.e.* either commodity or monetary units) which have to be accepted by creditors to settle the debt. But "that means neither all money need to be legal tender" (Hayek, 1990: 37).[5] On the second myth, Hayek concluded that Gresham law "applies only if a fixed rate of exchange between the different forms of money is enforced" (Hayek, 1990: 43).

The main ideas of the *Denationalization of Money* are fully based on a thorough historical analysis. The first seven chapters are mostly historical. Hayek started by demonstrating, by way of concrete examples, that: (1) economic instability and government growth are mostly caused by bad (*government's*) money, and (2) private initiatives, even in monetary and banking activities, had always proved to provide better results than those reached by a state's governance. One of the best arguments to illustrate these two ideas is the early days of paper money issued by the state. The dark episode of the French Assignats in the 18th century was one example among many others. Before the European Absolutism in the 15th century, many currencies circulated simultaneously, and the public came to prefer private money because government money was depreciating. In that time, private money outcompeted public money. Thus, in Hayek's mind, history can repeat itself and private money can outcompete public money once again.

The Hayekian revolutionary reform is to be found in chapters 8 and 9 of his 1976 book. At first, Hayek's monetary reform can be summarized as follows:

> It would therefore now be possible, if it were permitted, to have a variety of essentially different monies. They could represent not merely different quantities of the same metal, but also different abstract units fluctuating in their value relatively one with another.
>
> (Hayek, 1990: 32)

Table 4.1 summarizes the main elements of the *Denationalization of Money* schedule. The leading motivation behind his reform was to prevent governments to play with money and, by so doing, cause depressive business cycles.[6] By introducing competition in monetary field, Hayek considers that "the threat of the speedy loss of their (the one of the private enterprises) whole business . . . would provide a much stronger safeguard than any that could be devised against a government monopoly" (Hayek, 1990: 48).

Monetary management following Hayek's monetary reform

The expression "*monetary policy*" is misleading, as Hayek was in favour of the abolition of monetary policy such as we currently define it. However, each

Table 4.1 Hayek's monetary reform

	Content
Item 1 Supply of money	Private banks issue a non-interest-bearing certificates or notes(assuming it will be legally possible to do so).
Item 2 Currency's definition	The private currency is a commodity-based currency.
Item 3 Liquidity constraint	Obligation to redeem the notes and deposits on demand with other official money (or foreign currencies).
Item 4 Redemption value	Each private currency has a redemption value which is to be understood as a floor "below which the value of the unit could not fall" (Hayek, 1990: 46);
Item 5 Demand for currency	Each individual can demand the private currencies in two ways:"The certificates and notes would be made available to the public by short-term loans or sale against currencies" *(ibid).*
Item 6 Exchange between private currencies	As a corollary to the previous items, the private currency will be sold "at a premium above the value of any one of the currencies in which they were redeemable" (Hayek, 1990: 47); This item is justified by the preferences offered between the governmental currencies in which the private money can be redeemed.
Item 7 Competition between currencies	Money will be accepted and demand by individuals *only if* the real value would be kept constant.
Item 8 Discretionary power	The issuer is free to change the value definition of its own currency (after announcement to the public) "to alter the composition of the commodity standard as experience and the revealed preferences of the public suggested" (ibid).
Item 9 Quantitative monetary management	Competition will force each private issuer to regulate the quantity of its own money so as to make it acceptable to the public. The quantity regulation of each currency into circulation "constitute the best of all practical methods of regulating he quantity of media of exchange for all possible purposes" (Hayek, 1990: 52).
Item 10 Competitiveness between currencies	The success of the issuer will depend on "establishing the credibility and trust that the bank was able and determined to carry out its declared intentions" (Hayek, 1990: 51). Thus, the competition between the competing issuers of different currencies will rely on "the quality of the currencies they offered for loan and sale" *(ibid).*
Item 11 New form of Gresham's Law	Both official and private currencies are free to circulate within the economy. The market forces will select the best ones."Once the competing issuers had credibly demonstrated that they provided currencies more suitable to the needs of the public than government has ever provided, there would be no obstacle to their becoming generally accepted in preference to the governmental currency" *(ibid).* "The appearance and increasing use of the new currencies would, of course, decrease the demand for the existing national ones and, unless their volume was rapidly reduced, would lead to their depreciation. This is the process by which the unreliable currencies would gradually all be eliminated" (Hayek, 1990: 53).
Item 12 Press monitoring	Banks' transparency and press monitoring: "The competition between the issuing banks would be made very acute by the close scrutiny of their conduct by the press and at the currency exchange. . . .) all possible information would be supplied daily in the financial press, and have to be provided by the issuing banks themselves for the information of the public" *(ibid).*

bank of issue will have to manage an internal policy so as to keep its currency value stable as regard to its well-established standard (see Table 4.1, Items 2 and 4). There are two main consequences that we can discern from Hayek's monetary reform proposal. The first one concerns the value basis of the private money issued. On that point, Hayek refers to paper money history in Europe and elsewhere. As paper money has no intrinsic value, per se, the state does not have other choice than forcing people, by way of legal tender law, to accept it unless people will be punished.[7] He concludes as follows: "to be accepted as money they [i.e. pieces of paper or token of material itself] must at first derive their value from another source, such as the convertibility into another kind of money" (Hayek, 1990: 31).[8] However, all of that is preconditioned by the fact government's paper is *bad money*, meaning depreciating money, owing to the inflationary process engineered by government itself. In fact, Hayek doubts the state's ability to satisfactory manage paper money: "governments have become wholly inadequate for the task and, it can be said without qualifications, have incessantly and everywhere abused from their trust to defraud people" (Hayek, 1990: 30).

As a consequence, a system in which private banks can issue currencies in competition is a better system than a centralized one in which only (*bad*) official money circulates. The trust given by Hayek to private enterprises is related to the fact it is in their business interests to satisfactory manage the currency they issue.[9] Simultaneously, it has always been in the interests of the state to issue *depreciating* money as it diminishes the *real* value of its public debt.

If private currencies become available in the monetary system, what should be their value basis? Similarly as with paper money, private currencies have no intrinsic value, per se. Thus, the acceptability of the many private currencies relies on their ability to keep their value as nearly constant as possible; that is to say, it depends on their ability to be a good unit of account, means of payment and store of value. For those reasons, the credibility issue is the primary condition for the development of monetary system with private currencies in competition.

Concerning the second consequence, Hayek opens wide the doors to a new type of monetary policy with a decreasing power given to central banks as the official money will step by step depreciate and be eliminated. The final step will be the "abolition of central banks".[10] A new question appears: If central banks do not control anymore the value of money, how will private issuers manage to control the quantity of their own currency so as to keep their value (constant)? In other words, what would be a monetary policy *without* central banks?

To Hayek, the banks of issue will have to implement two different policies:

- i to buy and sell its currency against other currencies into circulation (with the possibility to accept securities, and possibly some commodities as well)
- ii to increase and contract its own credit activities

As noted in Item 12 of Table 4.1, the role played by the press is an important element for the implementation of the monetary management. The banks' policies rely on daily information gathered by computers, or in modern terms, "big-data" systems. The real-time information dataset will enable the bank's chairman and officers to react on a daily basis to the fluctuations of the commodity prices and more importantly to react on the fluctuations of the rate of exchange of the *others'* currencies in which the private currency of the bank is exchanged. In practice, a list of useful commodities (coffee, oil, corn, etc.) should be established so as to provide basic monetary information concerning the quantity of goods traded, the price of each commodity expressed in one of the currency at disposal (*billing currency*), the rate of exchange between the bank's own currency and the one of the billing currency. Based on that information, it will be the duty of the bank to conclude if prices of commodities increase or decrease, and to adapt its policy (*i.e.* expanding/contracting loans or selling/buying other currencies). As we already saw, the role played by daily press is important to implement and manage the currency within the economy. In a world featured by many ICT devices and real-time data, this characteristic should not be problematic unless the information becomes costly.

The crucial factor in that new policy is the demand for the currency that people are expected to hold. All of that depends on "the willingness of the public to hold the currency" instead of "the demand for borrowing" (Hayek, 1990: 62). As a consequence, an interest rate policy is not relevant for our purpose:

> The disappearance of what is called "interest policy" is wholly desirable. The rate of interest, like any other price, ought to record the aggregate effects of thousands of circumstances affecting the demand for and supply. . . . So long as each separate issue bank in its lending activity aimed at regulating the volume of its outstanding currency so as to keep its buying power constant, the rate of interest at which it could do so would be determined for it by market.
>
> (Hayek, 1990: 107)

Conversely, a quantitative policy issue with a specific focus set on credibility and transparency will be preferable. The constancy of the value of the currency demands to adopt the following "*never-never*" rule:

> [N]ever increase it [i.e. private currency] beyond the total the public is prepared to hold without increasing expenditure in it so as to drive up prices of the commodities in terms of it; . . . never reduce its supply below the total the public is prepared to hold without reducing expenditures in it and driving prices down. . . . The bank would therefore have to look to the effects of changes in its circulation, not so much directly on the prices of "other" commodities, but on the rates of exchange with the "currencies" against which they are chiefly traded.
>
> (Hayek, 1990: 59–60)[11]

If we follow Hayek's monetary schedule, one last point deserves to be debated: What will be the (*hypothetical*) future of central banks? The title of Hayek's chapter 18 is crystal clear in that respect: "Monetary policy neither desirable nor possible". If there is no doubt about the fact central banks should be abolished, as it should be made with the government monopoly of issue; however, it does not imply a total absence of any institution:

> One might conceive of some private bank assuming the function of a central bank and because it might be thought that, even without government's monopoly of issue, some of the classic functions of central banks, such as acting as "lender of last resort" or of "holder of the ultimate reserve" might still be required.
>
> (Hayek, 1990: 105)

In other words, Hayek has in mind that one private bank could act as a "*lender in last resort*" owing to the fact it is necessary to secure the elasticity of the circulation. According to Hayek's own words, "elasticity" of the monetary system is a "genuine problem" (Hayek, 1990: 106). However, what is the heart of the problem is not what we commonly called "*liquidity*" but rather "*purchasing power*". Faithful with the previous elements of Hayek's monetary reform, the relevancy of the monetary system – and its feasibility – mostly relies on the purchasing power embodied in the private currencies issued:

> What makes a currency a universally acceptable, that is really liquid, asset will be precisely that it is preferred to other asset because its buying power is expected to remain constant.
>
> (Hayek, 1990: 106)

All of that reminds us that the monetary system always turns around the credibility and transparency of the money issuers, while finding some internal arrangements to secure the system so as to guarantee the constant purchasing power of money. By assuming that, we can conclude that money, whatever the form it takes, is above all a medium of exchange for the services of the goods circulation (and to the services of the business cycle). To conclude, it is tempting to consider that the monetary management that Hayek has in mind seems to be closed to the one defended by Monetarist, as expressed by his chief and spokesman Milton Friedman. On that ground, Hayek agrees with the "demand-pull inflation" mechanism favoured by Monetarists, however, he strongly rejects the Quantity Theory of Money exclusiveness that Friedman assumed. The following quotation is crystal clear on that point:

> Keeping the quantity of money constant does not assure that the money stream will remain constant, and in order to make the volume of the money stream behave in a desired manner the supply of money must possess considerable elasticity.
>
> (Hayek, 1990: 59–81)[12]

Is it realistic to set up competition between different currencies? Is the bitcoin as a practical answer to Hayek's monetary reform?

Following Hayek's monetary reform in 12 items listed in Table 4.1, two main questions appear: First, is Hayek's monetary program realistic? To what extent is the reform achievable? Second, shall we consider the increasing development of virtual currencies, especially the bitcoin, as a practical application of Hayek's 1976 proposal?

On the first question, the answer is crystal clear. The answer is yes, as a system in which competition between different currencies already existed. Hayek referred to the Bimetallic system, but the currencies (both gold and silver coins) were managed by state rules. However, he also makes allusion to the early foundations of the banking sector in Amsterdam and elsewhere. At that time, the private merchants attempted to create their own money so as to secure their business. The initiative quickly collapsed due to "rising absolutism [which] soon suppressed all efforts to create non governmental currency"[13] (Hayek, 1990: 35). Thus, the state should make the first step by abolishing the legal tender of the official currency. By so doing, the official currency and the private currencies could simultaneously circulate, and it will be into the people's hands to make the choice according to the type of currency each individual entrusted the most confidence, namely the one which will be the most stable.

Concerning the second question, the European Central Bank has made a first step in 2012 when publishing a booklet on "*Virtual Currency Scheme*" in which it makes the bridge between the two. To the European Central Bank (ECB), the increasing development of virtual currencies, especially the bitcoin, can be viewed as a practical answer to Hayek's *Denationalization of Money* programme:

> The theoretical roots of Bitcoin can be found in the Austrian school of economics and its criticism of the current fiat money system and intervention undertaken by governments and other agencies, which in their view result in exacerbated business cycle and massive inflation.
>
> (ECB Publication, 2012: 23)

However, the schedule that Hayek has in mind is different than bitcoin in many respects: first, the bitcoin is not a commodity-based currency, nor does it derive its value from any anchoring to other foreign currencies; second, and most importantly, the quantity of issue of the bitcoin is fixed and limited to a maximum of 21 billion (which should be reached in 2140) (Böhme et al., 2015). Thus, no quantitative management policy can be implemented by its issuer, which is in total contradiction with Hayek's original *Denationalization of Money* programme. The bitcoin system is based on an automatic rule (which depends on the cryptography techniques used by that system) from which the supply of bitcoin (called mining) increases approximately every 10 minutes by a specific amount of bitcoin (which is divided by two every four years).[14] All of that explains why the bitcoin value exponentially expands (+120,331.67% between 2012 and 2017).[15] The later point demonstrates to what extent the bitcoin differs from Hayek's reform in which the constant value of the private currency is the sole condition for its own demand (as compared with the official currency or other private monies).[16] The only common point between bitcoin and Hayek's monetary programme is the stress given to trust and credibility as the sole conditions in bitcoin value. In fact, bitcoin's creator, Satoshi Nakamoto, clearly based the entire system on the total absence of intervention by a human third party. As a consequence, this *decentralized system* is judged more secure than the centralized system in which a human third party can corrupt or cheat the entire system. Hayek himself would have shared this opinion. The credibility issue relies on the blockchain's protocol which enables to guarantee the anonymity of people and the security of the entire system. Table 4.2 presents the two different frameworks inherited from a centralized or decentralized banking system.

Table 4.2 Decentralized versus centralized monetary systems

	Decentralized Monetary System (Hayek's Monetary Reform)	*Centralized Monetary System (Current Central Banking System)*
Competition structure	Free competition between private (bank) issuers	Monopoly of issuing of money
Supply of money	Private banks	Central bank
Demand of payment	Sales between private currencies; Short-term loans	Banking loans
Money value	Law of supply and demand	Legal tender law
Goal	Constant purchasing power	Price stability
Monetary functions	(1) Unit of accounts (2) Cash purchases (3) Holding reserve for future payments (4) Standard of deferred payments	(1) Unit of account (2) Medium of exchange (3) Store of value
(Internal) exchange rate	Fluctuating exchange rate according to the ability of the issuer to keep constant the purchasing power of its own currency	Not relevant Only one legal tender currency, so 1 euro is worth 1 euro *(1 for 1 rule)*
Monetary policy instruments	Selling and buying currency Short-term credit (quantitative monetary management by each issuer)	Conventional and unconventional monetary policy instruments; Mostly setting Interest rates (refinancing operations)
Monetary policy's indicators	Press Monitoring (daily data on exchange rates between private currencies, sales and purchases of currencies, price in commodities in different currencies' basis)	Price Index; Both monetary and non-monetary data (GDP, exchange rate, Investment rate, unemployment rate)

Conclusion

Quite surprisingly, economists have not discussed the subject of private competing currencies so far. The only one reason is to be found in the government's own prerogative to consider as its own right the privilege to issue currencies, whatever metallic ones or paper money. Hayek is a special case, as his pioneering work in 1976 questioned an unquestioned state of affairs: the existence of the state's monopoly of issue of money. For many scholars and academics, the centralization of money creation – under the establishment of a more or less independent central bank – is viewed as a better framework as the one of private currencies in competition.

The development of private currencies, and especially the bitcoin, enables us to wonder to what extent it could be a good candidate for being a new (*private*) money as opposed to the official one, the *euro*. The monetary reform proposal developed by Hayek provides a good framework to answer to this question. Four major arguments feature Hayek's monetary reform proposal: first, Hayek considered only private banks as issuer of currencies, and he never consider private firms; second, the private currencies in competition should be commodity-based currencies so as to guarantee a standard to evaluate its intrinsic value; third, and the most important argument, the supply of the currency should be *flexible* so as to guarantee its *constant* purchasing power (quantitative management policy by issuers); and last, the private currency should be able to serve as money – that is to say, to fulfil the four monetary functions (reliable unit of accounts, cash purchases, holding reserve for future payments and standard of deferred payments). One last point needs to be added. We should not mislead the reader by giving the impression that Hayek was only a free-banker and an unconditional supporter of competition. As we already mentioned, Hayek was against the state's control in monetary issue, but he recommended regulation in monetary "*management*" (as the term "*policy*" is inappropriate) through a private bank which could behave *as if* it were the central bank. All of that should made us remember that money is a *peculiar* good which cannot completely be managed as if it is a *traditional* one.

As regard to the four previous arguments, bitcoin does not satisfy any of them: it is not a bank nor a firm but a network; moreover, the supply of bitcoin is rigid, as it is set by the system itself to reach 21 billion in approximately 2140; the latter points prevent it from managing a quantitative policy so as to keep constant its value; and finally, as a consequence of these last three points, bitcoin is unable to keep its value stable, which prevents it from being a good currency.

In the introduction to this chapter, we asked if the private currencies are *theoretically* founded, and similarly to what extent the monetary theory inherited from Hayek's monetary reform is helpful to see clearer in the development of private types of money. Insofar as bitcoin is concerned, we will answer in the negative concerning its Hayekian foundation.

By opening wide the doors to a world *outside the banks' scope*, the last four decades gave us the impression that we are on the path to a more libertarian world. If we have a look at what's happening in Europe, we can say that many European countries – and the European Union itself – set up a globalized world while increasing regulations, especially prudential rules for banking and financial activities. The recent development of many virtual currencies will not change that tendency. A first step has been made with the new regulations imposed by the Directive on Payment Systems (DSP 2), adopted by the European Parliament in July 2013. As it is among the ECB's duties to fight the financing of terrorism, a more complex monitoring should be set up, especially on the trading platforms from which virtual currencies pass through and finance terrorism and other illicit activities. As Hayek anticipated, the globalization process from the 1980s has never created a world of total freedom such as the libertarian would have dreamed, but in contrast an *institutional-free* world.

Notes

1 The emergence of the Austrians' cycle theorists – Carl Menger and Eugen von Böhm-Bawerk, to name two – was of great value for the evolution, not to say revolution, in macroeconomics. In fact, by focusing on the roundabout process, the Austrians put emphasis on the interest rate mechanism to coordinate individual decisions.

2 Hayek, F. (1976), "*Choice in Currency*", Occasional Paper N 48, Feb., Institute of Economic Affairs, http://iea.org.uk/sites/default/files/publications/files/upldbook409.pdf.

3 Hayek (1933: 231).

4 The French economist Patrick Artus defined "unconventional monetary policies" as ones:

> that do not require bank liquidity and bank credit as a mechanism for the transmission of monetary policy. . . . These are therefore direct loans (or guarantees) from the Central Bank to private sector borrowers: the Central Bank injects liquidity into the accounts of "non-banks".
>
> (Artus, 2009: 1)

5 On that point, Hayek quoted several examples from court decisions which enable the acceptance of foreign currencies or commodities as official money to pay the claims.

6 "*[M]oney became more than ever before the plaything of politics*" (Hayek, 1990: 36).

7 Hayek quotes Arthur Nussbaum's 1950 book on *Money in the Lawn, National and International* to demonstrate to what extent history of money is an history of punishment:

> From Marco Polo we learn that in the 13th century Chinese law made the rejection of imperial paper punishable by death, and twenty years in chains or, in some cases death, was the penalty provided for the refusal to accept French assignats. Early English law punished repudiation as "lese majesty". At the time of the American revolution, non acceptance of Continental notes was treated as an enemy act and sometimes worked a forfeiture of the debt.
>
> (1950: 53)

8 The terms in brackets are mine.

9 "There is no reason to doubt that private enterprise whose business depended on succeeding in the attempt could be keep stable the value of money it issued" (Hayek, 1990: 36).

10 The expression refers to chapter 18 in Hayek (1976), in which he devoted an entire paragraph to that issue.

11 The words in brackets are mine.

12 It is not the purpose of that chapter to analyse the link between the Hayekian monetary theory and the one of Milton Friedman. The criticism developed by Hayek against

Monetarism is richer than the few lines we wrote on that subject. We advice the readers to have a look at Hayek's chapter 14 for a thorough analysis.

13 The term in bracket is mine.

14 For example, in 2017, the supply of bitcoin increases by 12.5 bitcoins every 10 minutes, which means that the supply of bitcoin increases by 3.9% in 2017. From 2020 to 2024, the increase in the supply of bitcoin will be diminished (the awards for mining, which is equivalent to the supply of bitcoin, will only be 6.75 bitcoin every 10 minutes).

15 Source: www.buybitcoinworldwide.com/fr/cours-bitcoin

16 For instance, on the morning of December 27, 2017, bitcoin was worth slightly more than $15,400 while being valued $969 on December 28, 2016, https://en.bitcoin.it/wiki/Controlled_supply

References

Artus, P. (2009): *Que sont les politiques monétaires non-conventionnelles?*, Special Report N 28, 6 Fevrier, Natixis.

Böhme, R., Christin, N., Edelman, B., & Moore, T. (April 01, 2015): Bitcoin: Economics, Technology, and Governance. *The Journal of Economic Perspectives*, 29, 2, 213–238.

ECB Publication (2012): *Virtual Currency Scheme*, ECB Publication, October.

Hayek, F. (1933): *Monetary Theory and the Trade Cycle*, Bedford series of economic handbooks, New York: Harcourt, Brace & Co.

Hayek, F. (1990 [1976]): *Denationalisation of Money*, Westminster, London: Institute of Economic Affairs, 3rd ed.

Krugman, P. (2011): The Profession and the Crisis, *Eastern Economic Journal*, 37: 307–312 (uploaded in December 2017), https://link.springer.com/article/10.1057/eej.2011.8.

Nakamoto, S. (2009), "Bitcoin: A Peer-to-Peer Electronic Cash System", https://bitcoin.org/bitcoin.pdf

Nishibe, M. (2014): *The Enigma of Money, Gold, Central Banknotes and Bitcoin*, Springer.

Nussbaum, A. (1950). *Money in the Law, National and International: A Comparative Study in the Borderline of Law and Economies*, Brooklyn: The Foundation Press.

Woodford, M. (1999): Revolution and Evolution in Twentieth Century Macroeconomics, Princeton University: Working Paper (uploaded in December 2017). www.columbia.edu/%7Emw2230/macro20C.pdf.

5 The limitations of national budgetary deficits and other Eurozone rules

The near-failures of their implementation and the excessive delays (20 years) in the introduction of a European budgetary stabilization mechanism

Maurice Baslé

Introduction

The euro area and the European Union are based on a system of laws, treaties, regulations and pacts, i.e. a rules-based system (RBS). An RBS generally has the strength of a standard and its implementation should be feasible, possibly with flexibility and without giving rise to too many disputes. If not, it is a standard without strength (Laïdi, 2005). In order to be introduced, an RBS has to be relevant and adapted to a specific context. It has to be implementable (targeting certain goals and succeeding). In addition, the rules and treaties being institutions, an RBS must also be adopted and followed by all the actors (by the virtue of a good acceptability and of simple honesty).

Here, the history of the Eurozone matters. The more or less hidden common objective was to experiment and proceed step by step, law by law, treaty by treaty, with a new "rules-based confederation" (RBC) that would be directed or supervised "one day" by a "European state actor" that should become a real stakeholder holding a piece of budgetary and fiscal sovereignty.

Let us recall that the founders' idea was that a process of institutionalization implemented in stages would enable the new EU to achieve success, based on an ever-closer union in the form of this RBC. Consequently, the Eurozone was founded without respecting the fundamentals of an optimal currency area.

The European Union (EU) should have been an innovative economic policy sphere working "as if" member states would share a common definitive meta-national objective later on. The economic policy agenda was based principally on this type of voluntarism for the future.

The initial choice for the RBS of the Eurozone reflected a minimal recourse to the budgetary instrument. The Budgetary Rules were an institutional arrangement with no federal treasury, so there was no European macroeconomic stabilization function. The European Commission, guardian of the treaties, and the

European Council (representing the member states' present interests) felt that it was too early to install this federal treasury.

Therefore, on the budgetary side, at an EU level, European fiscal resources and expenses were not, strictly speaking, constitutive of a confederal or federal anti-cycle budget. We could say that it rather resembled a cooperative fund, a jackpot, or a special endowment fund. Literally, the agreement said that there would be "contributions" from the member states' budgets (for France, see Baslé, 2015) for the core of the resources; and that, there would be "structural funds" and "subsidies" (when related to the Common Agriculture Policy) (Baslé, 2017) for the corresponding expenses. An administrative unit of the EU, the Directorate General DG Budget (European Commission), organizes a joint redistributive venture, and each country calculates its share of the "contributions" and the "recoveries" through this redistributive process. Since 1999, there was no actor for macroeconomic European stabilization and no European treasury!

In this chapter, we will explore why that specific historical construction (a cooperative, not a federal nor a confederal one, and a neglect for a stabilization function) was "understandable" in the 1990s. We will also observe how the EMU1 (European Monetary Union Phase 1) has functioned since the 1990s. After some preliminary drafts, the final Rules of the EMU1 introduced very specific Monetary and Budgetary Regulations (Alesina, Tabellini, 1987): the most important aspect was the absence of a federal treasury and, to counter the budgetary free-riders, the invention of specified budgetary constraints for member states. We will recall that the EMU Phase 1 was de facto in limbo, due to the fact that the European Union was not homogeneous in political ideas or economic traditions (meta-beliefs in the state, tax duty, money emission, social pact, debt creation etc.). So, in the treaties in the beginning, the "small" European Fund was simply considered as neutral in the macro-policy-mix. The Werner Report (Werner Report, 1970) was solely interested in national budgets. It stated the following first commandment that would be seminal from 1999 to 2017:

> The essential data of all public budgets, in particular, the change in their volumes, the size of balances and the financing methods or utilization of these are decided at EU level.
>
> (p. 12)

This chapter will focus only on the standard budgetary work of the EC, which was a type of monologue interpreted by the EC and constantly renewed: the respect of the public national budget equilibrium, a norm that was inserted in the first treaties and an insistence on the recommendations concerning the national budgets of member states.

In addition, this chapter discusses the initial choices and attributes them to the doctrinal influences in the two leading countries: Germany, where abandoning the Deutsche mark had to be compatible with an ever present ordoliberalist and selfish conservative agenda which was well-rooted in the minds of the elite (Solchani, 2015; Commun, 2016; Rabault, 2016; Schefold, 2002 Röpke [1942]; Young, 2012); and France, where the compromise over a "monnaie unique" (understand single currency and not common currency), as it was claimed, should be compatible with the respect for the sovereignty of the French central state (Eck, 2009; Modena, 2012; Aglietta, 2012; Légé, Marques Pereira, 2016).

Lastly, we will recall that, in both countries, the doctrines were hostile toward the creation of a federal treasury. This chapter will explain how, formally, each member state agreed to European supervision of *the golden norm* (golden rule) of a national public budget equilibrium. We will explain, this rather curious, amazing, almost incredible "bricolage institutionnel" (institutional tinkering) in a non-optimal monetary zone which was developed from the beginning. Since this unprecedented phase of improvisation and experimentation has lasted for more than 15 years, it will be important to observe and then assess the consequences of this initial weakness in the design of the European policy-mix. We will observe how the negative consequences have originated from the flaws of implementation.

The first section begins by discussing the initial budget deficit rules and presents the flaws in their implementation, their first evolutions in 2004–2005 toward the objective of a new public deficit norm with new possibilities of taking account of the countries' short-term difficulties and the desire not to aggravate the crises.

The second section will present a new phase of implementation of regulations that began after the 2008 crisis. The phase after 2008 has been characterized by the addition of new budgetary regulations and a supervision process. In this phase, the concept of "structural public budget deficit" was introduced in the treaties as a novelty (without saying that it had come from mainstream US economists many years before and that it should have been introduced in the initial treaties). In addition, the innovation introduced the principle that budgetary rules should be constitutionalized.

The third section will focus on the subsequent new "European semester process" implemented after 2012, and will recall their recurring flaw partly due to non-observance of rules by some major state members.

The fourth section will invoke the necessity of a new reform of the Eurozone policy-mix rules, advocating, as announced early in the 1970s and 1990s by the mainstream economic policy of the policy-mix, the introduction of a federal treasury in the institutional design of the Eurozone in 2017.

The conclusion will insist on the observed time shift (20 years) in the introduction of this treasury, which was soon a necessity in the 1990s for the mainstream economists, and was not settled due to a cultural gap between German and French ideas and those of the mainstream economists. Legal writings in the original treaties have introduced a naïve veil of ignorance on intelligent economic recommendations of this epoch (Kaldor, 1971, for example). This type of veil did not help to curb the initial contradictions of the EMU1.

The succession of flaws in their implementation exacerbated by the realities of the financial crisis in 2008–2011 finally ended up destroying such "EMU1 compromises", and finally persuaded five European presidents of the necessity of the implementation of the recommendations of the historical standard economic ideas of the Optimal Currency Area. In EMU1, de facto, member states had lost some of their general budgetary sovereignty.

Now, EMU2 should be managed with a different partial sharing of this fiscal sovereignty as Kaldor and other mainstream economists recommended in 1971. We dare say that, among other new institutions like a European monetary fund, the introduction of a European treasury should have been institutionally defended from the beginning, instead of claiming it as a fallacy like "rules, only rules especially for the others" (as said by Germans, French and Dutch governments). Sharing fiscal sovereignty is not abandoning sovereignty, neither in a federal state like Germany nor in a France with large territorial authorities and public finance centralization, nor in Italy with fiscal decentralization and recent fiscal consolidation (Piperno, 2012).

The European meta-rules concerning budgetary equilibria or deficit rules after the Amsterdam Council of 1997 and their inclusion in the so-specific policy-mix toolkit (EMU1 as a ruled-based Eurozone Phase 1)

Every European state has an individual history and path-dependent economic and social organization and mentality. However, post-World War II, a consensus arose in the West around the need to organize a real socio-economic development zone. The Cold War period (1945–1989) was characterized by confrontation between two types of organizations – planned economies and market economies. Western European leaders opted for a market economy system which was operationalized in each country in different ways. Germany's system was (among other factors) based on the ideological concept of "Soziale Marktwirtschaft" (social market economy) while, in France, it drew on the ideology of indicative planning to regulate the long term in a mixed-market economy.

Very early on, at the beginning of the 1950s, the French assumed leadership of a sectorial reconciliation between old enemies, in the form of the European Coal and Steel Community (the ECSC was established formally in 1951 by the Treaty of Paris). In 1957, six sovereign states founded the European Economic Community (EEC) as a supranational organization intended to deepen economic integration (including the Common Agricultural Policy and a common market) between West Germany, Belgium, France, Italy, Luxembourg and the Netherlands. The success of this cooperation led almost naturally to the idea of a larger union (extended to include some Central and Eastern European countries) at an appropriate time (after 1989). This idea was supported by the majority of member states. Relevant institutions emerged slowly.

We should recall that the European Union is based on the concept of genuine solidarity, through practical actions: the European Coal and Steel Community, the Treaty of Rome, EURATOM, the "currency snake", the European Currency Unit (a parallel currency), European Central Bank, etc. The founders' reports in favor of this European Solidarity were authored by French innovators like Jean Monnet, Robert Schumann, Robert Marjolin (the 1962 report), Jacques Delors (See Verdun, 1998; Dyson, Featherstone, 1999) and other non-French policy-makers (see for example the Werner Report of October 1970).

Later on, in the 1990s, measures were adopted to deepen cooperation with a view to creating an economic and monetary union (EMU) initially including 11 member states (in the early 2000s) and several years later (2016) 19 members.

The Euro was born on 1 January 1999 for bank accounts and financial products and concerned 11 countries. Euro notes and coins were introduced in 2002 as an inevitable product of previous treaties (Single European ACT 1986–1987, Maastricht Treaty 1992–1993, Amsterdam Treaty 1997–1999). The 1997 European Council held in Amsterdam represented the beginning of the first period of enactment of some general principles which had existed previously but were reinforced with the implementation of the Eurozone (EMU1).

The creation of this original EMU1 was unprecedented in world history

It did not emulate the birth and development of the American Economic and Monetary Union. None of the member states that ratified the EU constitution wanted to develop a European fiscal federalism. Subsequent European treaties (The Single European Act [SEA] 1986–1987, Maastricht Treaty 1992–1993, Amsterdam Treaty 1997–1999, the Stability and Growth Pact 1997, Nice Treaty 2001–2003, Lisbon Treaty 2007–2009) were intended to lay the foundations for an ever closer union. The objective was "a single international money".

The emphasis was more on the deficit control than on the organization of a European budgetary actor. In the 1990s, a large number of German, Italian and French theoretical publications contributed to the construction of the EMU with its monetary and budgetary rules. German ordoliberalism was attached to the principle of ruling not governing (Allen, 2005), and French elite civil servant policy-makers ("grands corps") and professionals played significant roles in not contesting this caution.

It could be said that the initial rules (the meta-cultural beliefs: Maes, 2002, 2004; Artis, 2002) reflected the cautious nature of the EMU1: in France, the choices of non-mainstream and irrelevant rules for a European policy-mix were justified by the need to totally respect each state's fiscal sovereignty, each state being in charge of smoothing the irregularities of the economic conjuncture (Baslé, 1975; Brunnermeier, James, Landau, 2016).

This attitude of procrastination revealed the existence of divergence between two different long-term national economic policy cultures in Germany and in France. These cultures and traditions could not be synthesized by a simple wave of a magic wand. Therefore, the EMU was not designed in 1997–1999 to meet the mainstream economists' conditions for having an optimal currency area:

> The participants in the UEM creation have bet that the benefits of the single currency would outweigh the disadvantages. In the famous phrase of Robert Mundell in 1961 they bet they constitute an optimal currency area.
>
> (Bénassy-Quéré, Coeuré, 2014)

The dominant laissez-faire ideology and the mistrust toward the member states were present in the initial rules: national budget deficits were considered as threats to the stability of the euro (Rochon, L.P. Rossi, S. p. 395). Each member state, with the euro, could allow its deficit to grow, become indebted and have a free-rider behavior. In a mainstream vision of the theory of the policy-mix (monetary and budgetary), the free-riders could hamper the work of the European Central Bank (ECB).

Due to this fear, but also due to cultural German fears of debt and deficits, it was decided that the agreement should set a juridical barrier to national public deficits and control Member States' discretionary budgetary behavior. French experts and politicians accepted this resolution. So, the initial RBS (rules-based system) contained no (European nor national) built-in stabilization mechanism in the case of the asymmetric shock of a member state (Allen, 2005; Bénassy-Quéré, Coeuré, Jacquet, Pisani-Ferry, 2012). The EMU1 Rules were centered on the supervision and control of national budgets.

The initial RBS demonstrate the distrust of the behaviors of member states. The EU decided to adhere to specific EMU1 budgetary rules, and to not trust the national governments. Thus, from the point of view of the mainstream economists (in the American Heller, Tobin and Mundell tradition), the EU invented an ad hoc economic policy-mix theory in the context of a new union of European nations (and for some, the desire to one day build a federal state). To be an optimal currency area, the EMU1 should have had from the beginning a true federal budget and should have had a European stabilization budgetary policy to compensate the shocks (Tobin, 1989). Political ideas and pre-scientific beliefs can explain this initial design and this initial phasing, which were really theoretically objectionable. Our explanation uses a reasoning issued from the research domain of the links between political ideas and economic policies (Kenis, Schneider, 1991).

The maturation of the transition to the optimal currency area would take a minimum of 20 years from the invention of the Stability and Growth Pact (SGP) in 1997. In fact, from the 1970s to the 1990s, starting with the Werner Committee and Werner Plan in 1970 (see Werner Report, 1970; Dyson, Featherstone, 1999; Herdengen, 1998; Verdun, A. 1998), we observed the rejection of the lessons from the policy-mix theory tested in the USA (Mundell, 1960; Heller, 1966; Friedman, Heller, 1969; Bordo, Jonung, 2000), and the rejection of the conditions of an optimal monetary area (Alesina, Tabellini, 1987).

Despite warnings from mainstream economists on the conditions required for an optimal currency zone, each member state voted for what could be described as "a wobbly building", and did so knowingly, hoping to avoid a non-common asymmetric shock which could be a potential barrier to the deepening of the European Union and the functioning of the EMU1.[1]

So, the EMU1 began as a purely voluntarist union project, dependent on past political ideas and influenced by faiths and ever present national and ideological traditions (in Germany and in France). EMU1 was implemented with no consideration for the needs of an optimal monetary area project. The initial trust in a norm EMU1 hides a weak initial cooperation, due to an anchor bias and to a fear about modern post-Schumpeterian and post-Keynesian political economic policy ideas (Laïdi, 2005, p. 59):

> la norme apparait alors comme une sorte de méta-valeur destinée à domestiquer des Etats indisciplinés.
>
> the norm then appears as a kind of meta-value intended to domesticate undisciplined States

What was the underlying budgetary doctrine? The initial national public deficit target was not, strictly speaking, a zero-deficit equilibrium, but "excessive deficits". A quasi-balanced budget reference – it was believed – provides a legal guarantee and could be designed to prevent free-rider behavior.[2]

The European budgetary deficit norm was not a structural public deficit

Structural deficit (OECD, 1995) is the level of deficit that exists independently of a bad or better economic conjuncture. However, the situation could have been different, because a new type of structural deficit norm had been previously introduced by US economists, following a long doctrinal debate about the stabilization work.

What was the recommendation from the American Council of Economic Advisers in the 1960s? At the time, this first approach called "neo-Keynesian" – short-term stabilization through enlarging the public expenses in recessions, was already obsolete. The debate no longer set demand-side economists and supply side economists against each other. The new smarter doctrine was a synthesis proposal made in the 1960s by Walter Heller, former president and activist in post-World War II Germany (Marshall Plan), and economist and influential adviser to President John F. Kennedy as chairman of the Council of Economic Advisers, 1961–1964. At the time, Heller recommended that a new fiscal policy be implemented as part of the economic policy in rich countries. Therefore, the mainstream recommendation was a policy-mix with a dominant fiscal policy (in the form of tax cuts and not cuts to public expenses) clearly oriented toward the mid-term stabilization of the cycle (Heller, 1966) and short-term tax cuts which should continue until the point of potential output is reached (a cyclical tax, Baslé, 1975). Note that, in Heller's new doctrine, yes, this discretionary or automatic behavior was a difficult task that required tact (Friedman, Heller, 1969), but as a general policy it was not irrelevant. In the

USA, to have a policy-mix taking account of automatic stabilizers was considered a golden rule. Surpluses could intervene in expansion phases and uncured deficits in bad recessions. That is the true concept of a structural deficit.

Advocated by Heller and then Tobin, this discretionary behavior for the policy-mix and the structural deficit norm had resisted the monetarist attacks. As Friedman noted (Friedman, Heller, 1969), monetary policy was not considered relevant. Heller explained that, in the federalist American Union with a huge federal budget, the critical information was the "potential output gap" and the dominant instrument was fiscal policy. What mattered were full-employment surplus or deficits and not the quantity of money (Friedman, Heller, 1969, p. 39):

> Key number: full employment surplus. Fine tuning the economy works . . . official economic forecasts have correctly led the President's economic advisors to urge expansionary action the early 1961 to the first half of 1965; to urge restrictive fiscal-monetary policy in 1966; to urge a roller-coaster policy in 1967, consisting of (a) fiscal-monetary ease early in the year to avert recession and then (b) a call for the surtax after mid-year to help ward off resurgent inflation; and to urge, with ever greater intensity, prompt enactment of the surtax in 1968.

James Tobin, of the Council of Economic Advisors, set forth the "principles" that should guide policy (Tobin, 1974):

> The "new economics" sought to liberate federal fiscal policy from restrictive guidelines unrelated to the performance of the economy.
>
> The Council sought to liberate monetary policy to focus it squarely on the same macroeconomic objectives that should guide fiscal policy.
>
> That´s just another way of saying that the "policy mix" should contemplate expansionary fiscal (tax cuts) sanctioned by a monetary policy that kept the interest rate "low".

In France, Germany and elsewhere, some said that these "Keynesian practices" were failing (Allen, 2005). This served as an excuse to avoid following the example of the USA's monetary union.

So, the German and French economic traditions did not try to import the lessons from the policy-mix in the USA, nor did they import the concept of structural deficit in the EMU1 Rules. This was rather paradoxical for France, which used the concept in its domestic economic policy (Baslé, 1975).

The first flaws in the implementation of the initial rules and the creation of a public deficit target "with some accommodations for some governments"

As announced by the European parliament in November 2003, France and Germany were, at the beginning, permanently above the maximum public deficit level allowed of 3% of GDP. The application of this rule should have led to the scolding and sanction of Germany and France. France and Germany, by requesting the suspension of the warnings on their own accounts, diminished the credibility of the pact. The Commission appealed to the Court of Justice of the European Communities (now Court of Justice of the European Union) which, in a judgment on 16 July 2004, annulled the decision of the Council to suspend the excessive deficit procedure against France and Germany. However, the Council could not "change [the recommendations] without a new impetus to the Commission, which has a right of initiative in the context of the excessive deficit procedure". Following this judgment and on the request of member states, the European Commission presented its proposals for a strengthening of the budgetary rules of the Stability and Growth Pact.[3]

Consequently, in June 2004, the European Council noted the need to strengthen and clarify the implementation of the initial Stability and Growth Pact (SGP).[4] The time had come to create a public deficit *target*, and to create a measure that would take us away from the rule of strict budgetary balance, and introduce some accommodations for some governments. This change responded to the pro-cyclic criticism of the SGP (decision to diminish public expenses in recessions).

Given the increasing economic diversification in an EU comprising 25 member states, uniform objectives for all countries seemed inappropriate and lacked economic rationale.

> In a European Union of 25 countries, characterized by considerable heterogeneity and diversity and given the experience of 5 years in EMU, an enriched common framework with a stronger emphasis on the economic rationale of its rules would allow to better cater for differences in economic situations across the EU. The objective is therefore to enhance the economic underpinnings of the existing framework and thus strengthen credibility and enforcement. The aim is not to increase the rigidity or flexibility of current rules but rather to make them more effective.

The European commission said that it was important to take into account the:

> [e]conomic circumstances and developments in the implementation of the Excessive Deficit Procedure.

And:

> This could be done mainly in two aspects of the procedure: – Catering for prolonged periods of sluggish growth through the "exceptional circumstances clause". Allowing for country-specific elements in the enforcement of the correction of excessive deficits (the adjustment path).

Following this, the European Council endorsed the report of the Council of Ministers of Finance (ECOFIN) dated 20 March 2005 entitled "Improving the implementation of the Stability and Growth Pact" and approved its findings and proposals. The report updated and complemented the Stability and Growth Pact, which consisted of the European Council Resolution of Amsterdam and Council Regulations Nos. 1466/97 and 1467/97. The Commission was invited to speed up the proposals for amending the Council Regulations.

Note that, from the outset, budgetary rules always have an implementation scheme. Now, the guideline is contained in a pact. The Stability and Growth Pact (SGP's *preventative* rules) entered into force in 1999. Some additional SGP *corrective* rules entered into force in 2005.[5] Article 126(12) of the Treaty on the Functioning of the European Union (TFEU) explained that there is a gradation in the surveillance process. We could summarize it in the following terms: a phase of observation of excessive public deficit (in percentage of GDP) and/or excessive public debt ratio (in percentage of GDP), a complementary observation of the evolution of these ratios and other relevant information, the writing of an internal report by the European Commission, the diffusion process of this Public Report, the delivering of public sermons, the implementation of a compulsory non-interest-bearing deposit and restrictions from the European Investment Bank, and last, fines (sticks).[6]

2011 and after the crisis: new budgetary flaws and general flaws of implementation of the macroeconomic imbalances rules

In spite of the reform of 2005, new flaws intervened after the financial crisis of 2008–2010. The European Parliament said (Source: idem):

> Despite this reform, the Stability Pact is not complied with in 2010 by most Member States. They know indeed a fiscal deficit well above 3%, 8.2% in France, 6% for Germany and 6.9% for the average of the euro area.
>
> Moreover, the revelations of the New Greek government in autumn 2009 on the state of the Greek accounts have shown the weaknesses of monitoring by Eurostat, since the figures that were submitted were false. In this situation, and although the offense States pledged to back down below the 3% mark, the need for a thorough reform of the Pact has emerged. Still in negotiations, this reform is loud because it is far from unanimous in particular the European Parliament.

New Rules in November 2011 should have been radically innovative on the budgetary side. However, they did not take into account the situation in Greece (which had lied about its figures), nor Spain (which had a surplus). Better supervising was needed. Therefore, there was an extension in the number of targets (indicators of macroeconomic imbalances) and an extension in the number of relevant indicators. The tool became a yearly cycle for reviewing member states' budgetary lives. Correlatively to an extension of the geographical perimeter of the control of macroeconomic imbalances (the EU is larger than the Eurozone), the European Union, set up a yearly cycle of economic policy coordination and supervision for each member state, called the European Semester that was launched in November 2011 (Official journal of the European Union, 2011).

The novelty is that budgetary rules are now inserted in an overview of new rules for monitoring the macroeconomic imbalances within the whole European Union area. For the functioning of the EMU, a more complete Six-Pack Treaty entered into force on 13 December 2011. It contains five regulations and one directive (that is why it is called a six-pack). It constituted a secondary general EU law which applies to member states and adds some specific rules for other euro area member states, especially regarding financial sanctions in case of disrespect of the different targets or thresholds.

> Each year, the Commission undertakes a detailed analysis of EU Member States' plans of budgetary, macroeconomic and structural reforms and provides them with country-specific recommendations (CSR) for the next 12–18 months.[7]

The bureaucratic process was strengthened further so that, in October 2015 the Commission decided to streamline the European Semester even more. It will theoretically include meta-objectives, and more political general objectives for the policy-mix:

> Employment and social performance, enhanced democratic dialogue, promoting convergence by benchmarking and pursuing best practices, and the support to reforms from European Structural and Investment Funds and technical assistance.

More realist rules but still a heavy monitoring of national budgets: the national public structural deficit 0.5% rule and budgetary rules should be constitutionalized as a golden rule

Since 2011, the six-pack reinforces both the preventive and the corrective arm of the pact, i.e. the Excessive Deficit Procedure (EDP), which applies to member states that have breached either the deficit or the debt criterion. The text of this new treaty (new meta-rule), signed on 2 March 2012 by the Heads of State and Government, entered into force on 1 January 2013. The Treaty on Stability, Coordination and Governance (TSCG) is a strict intergovernmental budgetary mechanism which has been signed by 25 of the 28 member states of the European Union on the convergence in the euro area.

Now, the norm is a small structural deficit: 0.5% of GNP. Moreover, the structural deficit may amount to 1% of GDP if the debt of the member state concerned is below 60% of GDP (if the deficit does not increase its debt). Financial sanctions for euro area member states are now imposed gradually, from the preventive arm to the latest stages of the EDP.

This was a first concession to the group of mainstream economists, but this realist attitude had some limitations. The six-pack wanted a stricter enforcement of these budgetary deficit rules by quantitatively defining what a "significant deviation" from the Mid-term orientations (MTO) was or the adjustment path toward it.

Moreover, the six-pack operationalizes the debt criterion so that an EDP may also be launched on the basis of a debt ratio above 60% of GDP, which would not diminish toward the treaty reference value at a satisfactory pace (and not only be launched on the basis of a single criterion of a deficit above 3% of GDP, which had been the case so far). The six-pack introduces reverse qualified majority voting (RQMV) for most sanctions, therefore increasing the likelihood of their implementation against euro area member states. (RQMV implies that a recommendation or a proposal of the Commission is considered adopted by the Council unless a qualified majority of member states votes against it.) Future euro area members agree to do so once they adopt the common currency.

Correlatively, the TSCG has set guidelines for a reinforced surveillance and coordination of economic policies, with ex ante coordination of debt issuance plans (among contracting parties and economic partnership programs for member states in EDP) and monitoring of structural public deficits. It also introduced the necessity of a meta-rule by constitutionalisation: Compliance with the rule should be monitored by independent institutions. These budget rules shall be implemented in national law through provisions of "binding force and permanent character, preferably constitutional". European Court of Justice (CoJ) may impose financial sanction (0.1% of GDP) if a country does not properly implement the new budget rules in national law and fails to comply with a CoJ ruling that requires it to do so. In the case of euro-area Member States, sanctions would be channeled to the ESM, in the case of "non-euro-area Member States", the money would be attributed to the EU budget. Compliance with the rule implementing the MTO in national law will also be monitored at the national level by independent institutions.

And a complement of the "Two-Pack" regulations

Sharing the budgetary deficit responsibilities[8] and acceptance of close surveillance, is a de facto loss of overall fiscal sovereignty. In order to strengthen the economic pillar of the Economic and Monetary Union, member states of the euro area could have been satisfied with the "six-pack" budgetary legislation adopted in 2011. However, the economic and fiscal policies that led these States obviously produced some negative ripples in other countries in the common currency area (Mourlon-Druol, 2012).

In good economic times, this interdependence could be the source of great prosperity. When the situation is worse, it implies more risk sharing. Currently, with the Two-Pack regulation, this risk sharing should be accompanied by shared responsibility, which requires a deepening of the exchange of information and coordination, as well as the application of a more fluid procedure to deal with any eventuality, including the use of financial support mechanisms.

As part of a common budgetary timeline, euro area member states should submit their draft budgetary plan for the following year to the Commission and the Eurogroup before 15 October, along with the independent macroeconomic forecast on which they are based. This obeys the Stability and Growth Pact (SGP), under which member states present the main characteristics of their medium-term public finance plans to the Commission and the Council in the spring (in Stability or Convergence Programs) (Heipertz, Verdun, 2010; Sawyer, 2012).

The Commission analyzes if the draft budget is in line with the SGP and the recommendations from the European Semester (which the country will have received in May/June). If the Commission assesses that the draft budgetary plan shows serious non-compliance with the SGP, the Commission can request a revised draft budgetary plan. Otherwise, it may address an opinion to the member states concerned, which would also be discussed by the Eurogroup. This regulation therefore complements the preventive arm of the SGP, by ensuring appropriate integration of EU policy recommendations in national budgetary preparations and increasing peer pressure in the Eurogroup.

Through this regulation, states should now be equipped with an independent opinion on their national budgetary plans; namely, the opinion of the Commission. In addition, for euro area member states in the EDP, the regulation introduces a system of graduated monitoring in order to secure a timely and durable correction of excessive deficits. This would allow the early detection of the risk that a member state will not correct its excessive deficit in the deadline set by the Council, and should permit them to take action accordingly. The co-legislators, together with the Commission, are aiming at incorporating elements of the TSCG in this regulation: in particular, the requirement to set up independent institutions in charge of monitoring budgetary rules which should implement the MTO at the national level; and also of ex ante coordination of debt issuance plans and economic partnership programs detailing structural reforms necessary to ensure an effective and durable correction of the EDP.

Thus, as independent observers, we can note the perpetual insistence, independent of the conjuncture and the crisis and after-crisis context, to control the public budgetary behavior of member states in the European policy-mix for EMU1 through rules.

The European Semester procedure and the macroeconomic imbalances procedure: a new rule with little success

A review of the implementations of the budgetary rules and of the Six-Pack and Two-Pack rules requires a lot of patience.[9] Many sources can be considered, and each member state should be analyzed.[10]

The best survey came from the European Commission. The EC undertook for its own guidance a review of the observance of the rules. The conclusions are clear and without appeal, especially in the case of the more recent rules.

The only moderation introduced by the critics in the report on the Six-Pack and the Two-Pack was the following:

> The ability to draw conclusions on the effectiveness of the regulations is limited by the short experience of their operation, with the six-pack entering into force in end-2011 and the two pack only in mid-2013. Not only is this time period short, but it has also been characterized by a severe economic crisis. This leaves the rules untested in normal economic times.[11]

An independent synthesis and a critical analysis of the EMU1 rules supplemented the critical diagnosis in November 2015 (Darvas, Alvaro, 2015).[12] The conclusions are that the effectiveness of budgetary rules has been poor, and the semester procedure and the macroeconomic imbalances procedure are unsuccessful. The report established small indexes of success in the following of the EC recommendations saying that in spite of the efforts made to improve the European Semester in recent years the implementation index steadily fell to 29 percent by 2014.

Concerning the SGP, the success rate is assessed to be of 44%:

> Even though SGP recommendations have the strongest legal basis, the average 44 percent implementation rate cannot be regarded as large, while the EIP implementation rate is even lower, suggesting that the European Semester is not particularly effective in enforcing the EU's fiscal and macroeconomic imbalance rules.
>
> (p. 2)

The comparison with the results of the OCDE recommendations is not favorable to the EC:

> Despite huge efforts by European institutions to coordinate economic policies within the European Semester, the rate of implementation of these recommendations is not higher than the rate of implementation of the OECD's unilateral recommendations. Overlaps between the European Semester and OECD recommendations only partly explain this similarity. OECD reform responsiveness rates were practically the same in 2013–14 and in 2007–08, suggesting that reform efforts have not increased compared to the pre-crisis period
>
> (p. 2).

The implementation rate is more satisfactory in countries which benefit from a financial assistance program.

> Countries tend to undertake more reforms when they are under a financial assistance program, experience market pressure or face high unemployment. Yet even in those countries, reform momentum fades once the

> situation normalizes . . . the 2015 euro-area recommendations with tangible economic goals are not well reflected in the recommendations issued to member states (with the exception of reforming services markets).
>
> (p. 2)

In 2016, a final attempt was made using new country-specific recommendations, the results of which have still not been corrected. These new country-specific recommendations provide another policy framework for action at national level. The Commission supports dialogue with member states, social partners and stakeholders at all levels to support the exchange of experience, to facilitate the follow-up, to ensure close monitoring and review performance. The European Commission has routinely undertaken to follow the steps detailed in the 2016 European Semester cycle. The package included:

> Country-specific recommendations (CSRs) for 27 Member States (excluding Greece, which is currently under a stability support program). The recommendations call for national actions to implement reforms and pursue responsible fiscal policies with a view to re-launch investment, create jobs and stimulate growth. Recommendations to the Council to abrogate the Excessive Deficit Procedures (EDP) (under Article 126(12) of Treaty on the Functioning of the European Union (TFEU)) for Cyprus, Ireland and Slovenia as these countries have brought their deficits below the 3% of GDP Treaty reference value and are forecast to remain below this level in 2016 and 2017. Reports on Belgium, Finland and Italy under Article 126(3) TFEU, in which it reviews their compliance with the debt criterion of the Treaty. Confirmation of the Commission decision on 8th March 2016 that Croatia and Portugal are to be considered to be experiencing excessive imbalances, but stepping up the Macroeconomic Imbalances Procedure (MIP) is not warranted.

After 2015, *the game was over*. To bet on a better economic situation is always tempting, but the lack of respect for the rules is evidence of the chess game of the European semester (on the budgetary side). In the case of France, the 2016 autumn pack considered that the targets were reached. Nevertheless, the economic context is still not a source of optimism:

> Unemployment is decreasing and investment is growing again. However, there is no room for complacency. Some of the tailwinds that have supported the recovery so far are fading. The legacies of the crisis, notably the social impact, high levels of public and private debt, and the share of non-performing loans, are still far-reaching.
>
> The Commission therefore calls on Member States to redouble their efforts along the principles of the "virtuous triangle" of boosting investment, pursuing structural reforms and ensuring responsible fiscal policies,

and in doing so, to put the focus on social fairness and delivering more inclusive growth.[13]

Flaws and neglect of the rules causes imbalances

More puzzling: a lot of experts have found evidence of disrespectful behavior on other imbalances rules (external balances rules) (Artus, 2015, 2016). For example, the Bruegel Institute said of the EC recommendations of investment behavior of some member states:

> Fostering investment is a key goal mentioned in two euro-area recommendations, but Country Specific Recommendations (CSRs) to the five largest euro-area countries are not consistent with this goal
>
> (Darvas, Alvaro Bruegel 2015, p. 3)

The preamble of the 2015 Council recommendation for the euro area also recognized that external imbalances do not conform to the rules. However, huge external surpluses are regularly observed for Germany and the Netherlands. So, now, the political question is either to completely reform rules that are not enforced (perhaps because they are not applicable, or not applicable at least in the context of the Eurozone) or to abandon this philosophical appeal to Rules and to change the model of the budgetary sovereignty devolution (Arestis, Sawyer, 2012, January 9). Substantial thought exists in favor of the second solution.

Thinking now about the reform of the budget rules and the other imbalances rules implemented through the project of the institutionalization of a real European treasury or a federal mechanism of stabilization

With the increasing flaws of implementations and the unpopularity of many governments in the Eurozone, there is an opportunity to introduce the first incremental modifications of the European semester procedure and, more largely, to infuse a new institutional design: the introduction of a "quasi-revolutionary actor", the actor that should have been initially expected in an optimal currency area, a "European treasury" in a non-federalist Union.

Last attempts of incremental reforms as the swan song in 2016

First of all, the Commission has made a number of changes to the 2016 European Semester cycle and in respect to the CSRs:[14]

- Better integration of the euro area and national dimensions, with the adoption of the recommendations for the euro area in November, ahead of the country specific recommendations. The earlier presentation of the euro area recommendation gives member states the possibility to focus on the euro area dimension when shaping their national policies.

- More focused country-specific recommendations, setting the policy objectives for the next 18 months, while the Commission will continue to monitor a wide range of economic policy developments.
- A stronger macroeconomic imbalances procedure, including the streamlining and stabilization of the categories of macroeconomic imbalances from six to four (no imbalance, imbalances, excessive imbalances, and excessive imbalances with corrective action).

A new internal project from the Five Presidents for a Eurozone Phase 2 (EMU2)

With a growing consensus on the conclusion that the previous rules became a routine that did not bring solutions for a better growth and more employment in the Eurozone, new thinking has been making its way into the political ideas. The resolution of controversies by a new institutional design seems to have happened.

Early in December 2012, the EU's four Presidents – the European Council President in collaboration with the presidents of the Commission, the Eurogroup and the ECB – produced their "final report on genuine economic and monetary union". The document was very ambitious in its new "federalist" and integrationist proposals: it suggested an increasing degree of common decision-making on national budgets and an enhanced coordination of economic policies, in particular in the field of taxation and employment, building on the member states' national job plans. In the long term (beyond 5 years), the dream was a full banking union and a full fiscal and economic union.

Note that this report was not at the outset largely communicated nor diffused by the media, but it is seminal.

In the wake of this previous report in June 2015, five presidents (with the addition of the European parliament president) accepted to sign the Five Presidents' Report which proposed to open a new phase of the Eurozone organization. The immediate reactions to the Five Presidents' Report were also weak.

For the UK Parliament, prevention of budgetary risks is the most important element (UK Parliament, 2015):[15]

> Common deposit insurance, common stabilization policies and other forms of risk-sharing are more likely to be accepted if there is a balancing insistence on mitigating the risks in the first place.

For some commentators, these propositions were a "flop". However, the report is not only voluntarist. It insists on the complementarity between monetary and budgetary instruments of stabilization, it explains the resistant difficulties of implementations of treaties when shocks intervene, it diagnoses a now significant divergence across the euro area and very fruitfully, it proposes that organizational European progress must happen on four fronts: economic, financial, fiscal and political.

The calendar of these innovations on the organizational side in the Eurozone was extremely precise: the Stage 1 should be from1 July 2015 to 30 June 2017. In this first stage ("deepening by doing"), the EU institutions and euro area member states would build on existing instruments and make the best possible use of the existing treaties. In a nutshell, this entails boosting competitiveness and structural convergence, completing the financial union, achieving and maintaining responsible fiscal policies at national and euro area level, and enhancing democratic accountability. In the second stage ("completing EMU"), concrete measures of a more far-reaching nature would be agreed in order to complete EMU's economic and institutional architecture. Specifically, during this stage, the convergence process would be made more binding through a set of commonly agreed benchmarks for convergence that could be given a legal nature. Significant progress toward these standards – and continued adherence to them once they are reached – would be among the conditions for each euro area member state to participate in a shock absorption mechanism during this second stage. There was a final stage (by 2025 at the latest): at the end of Stage 2, and once all the steps are fully in place, a deep and genuine EMU2 would provide a stable and prosperous place for all citizens of the EU member states that share the euro as a single currency, the euro beginning to be more attractive for other EU member states, inciting them to join if they are ready to do so (European Commisssion, 2015b).[16]

The principal innovation: a budgetary European actor

Historically, a lot of member states in the Eurozone defended maintaining their full budgetary sovereignty. De facto, from the strengthening of the surveillance by the Commission, this full budgetary sovereignty is a myth. The Eurozone must mutate but there is a political risk to imposing a solution against states' wishes. In the contents of the reform, we found that in international relations, there was only one representative from the IMF institution. On the internal side, for the budgetary coordination procedure, the evaluation is clear: a simplification is urgent: many "packages", "pacts", "procedures" and multiple reporting requirements have weakened its rationale and effectiveness. The innovation suggested is not incremental: the Five Presidents' Report endorses the idea of the responsibility to have a euro area-wide fiscal stabilization function with a quasi-new institution: a genuine fiscal union.[17]

> In case of a very severe crisis, national budgets can become overwhelmed, as was the case in some countries in recent years. In such situations, national fiscal stabilizers might not be enough to absorb the shock and provide the optimal level of economic stabilization, which in turn can harm the whole euro area. For this reason, it would be important to create in the longer term a euro area-wide fiscal stabilization function.

From the beginning (1999), as we have mentioned, mainstream economists recalled that a genuine fiscal union will require more joint decision-making on fiscal policy. Initial fears were undoubtedly justified, but, the experimentation with a wobbly Eurozone is over, even for experts from the French Treasury (Trésor, 2013; Bénassy-Quéré, Ragot, 2015).

The recommendation of a positive budgetary orientation in the EMU2

In November and December 2016, new orientations for the European semester were announced in the 2017 European semester autumn package. The focus is on the "need for a positive fiscal stance for the euro area". Facing the risk that the positive orientation declined in 2017, the recommendation is a global positive budgetary impulsion.

The target is a sum of budgetary positions leading to a global budgetary orientation of 0.5% of GDP. The task is dedicated to a group of member states that have a surplus (DE, EE, LU, LV, MT or NL), not to states which are in a more difficult situations (BE, ES, IE, FI, FR, IT, SI and PT). (For the model assessing the impact of fiscal expansion in surplus countries, see Veld, 2016).

> However, at the current juncture, with zero interest rates, multipliers and spillovers effects are larger. In the case of high efficiency of public investment, in line with other studies on infrastructure investment, additional government investment of 1% of GDP in Germany and the Netherlands, sustained over 10 years, could raise domestic GDP by 1.1 and 0.9 per cent, respectively. There is a somewhat smaller positive GDP effect for the Netherlands, as the country is characterised by larger trade openness, which implies stronger demand leakage to imports. Over the 10-year horizon, real GDP in Germany and the Netherlands would increase by more than 2 per cent. Long-term GDP effects exceed the short-term impact because government investment raises the productivity of private capital and labour over a sustained period of time (positive supply effect). In this scenario, the real GDP in other euro area regions (France, Italy, Spain and the rest of the euro area) would increase by around a range of 0.3–0.5 percentage points already after one year. The spillovers derive from the direct trade effect (more exports to Germany and the Netherlands) and some depreciation of the exchange rate (more exports also to the rest of the world) (European Commission, 2016).

This new positive orientation[18] is a first step toward a stabilizing function at the level of the euro area.

This new orientation has not yet been adopted by the Ecofin meeting of 5 December 2016. The discussion in the Council at least allowed us to put on the table the notion of a common budgetary stance and the principle that states with room for maneuvering should pursue policies favoring the increase in their domestic demand. In the press release of the Eurogroup, there is a sentence that goes exactly in this direction. Afterwards, on the questions of quantification of the effort, indeed, the figure of 0.5 for the structural deficit, nor whatever number elsewhere, has not survived. The reasons given are based on the idea that the euro area would have outgrown its growth potential! This raises the issue of measuring this potential growth rate again. And the issue of too heterogeneous economic situations in the euro area. As said by France-Stratégie (France Stratégie, 2016, p. 4):

> The effects of a fiscal stimulus of the partner countries on the economic situation of a country affected by a shock are indirect and extent been persistent controversy, which makes the problem coordination. That is why it is probably not possible to ignore a central budget or a common borrowing capacity.

Conclusion

We have agreed with the historical diagnosis of Nicolas Kaldor ([1971], 1978, p. 205): a full monetary and economic union was "unattainable without a political union", which presupposed "fiscal integration, and not just fiscal harmonization" (fiscal harmonization being recommended by the French Plan Commission). However, it should have required the creation of a "*Community Government and Parliament*" which would have "responsibility for at least the major part of the expenditure now provided by national governments" and would have been financed "by taxes raised at uniform rates throughout the Community" (Kaldor, [1971], 1978, p. 205).

A European Budgetary and anti-cyclical actor was for the majority of economists the piece lacking in the institutional puzzle of the EMU1 since 1999. At this time, political ideas and pre-conceptions and feelings in economic policy installed a confinement in misconceptions of the public budget deficit. This has led to the non-choice of a European anti-cycle Budget. However, now, as De Grauwe said(:

> in the long run the monetary union will have to be embedded in a significant fiscal union. This is probably the hardest part of the process to make the Eurozone sustainable in the long run, as the willingness to transfer significant spending and taxing powers to European institutions is very limited. It remains a necessary part, though. Without significant steps towards fiscal union there is no future for the euro. I have highlighted a number of small steps that can be taken now and that create a signal about the political commitment to move forward on the road to more integration. These steps have to be taken now as they act as signals of the resolve of the Eurozone countries that the union is here to stay.
>
> (p. 29)

The creation of a Budgetary European Anti-cycle actor should really be a carrier seed of a new future and there are "numerous ways to conceive such budget, based on quasi-automatic rules or discretion, aimed at stabilising idiosyncratic or symmetric shocks, targeting all shocks or only large shocks, etc." (Bénassy-Quéré, 2015).

As recommended by the Nobel Prize winner Joseph Stiglitz, this could be a solution for the pooling of debt and for providing more fiscal space for countries to have expansionary fiscal policies (Stiglitz, 2013, 2014, see also: Cripps, F. Duwicquet, Mazier, 2013; Devoluy, 2012, 2015).

> While there are many factors contributing to Europe's travails, there is one underlying mistake: the creation of the single currency, the euro. Or, more precisely, the creation of a single currency without establishing a set of institutions that enabled a region of Europe's diversity to function effectively.
>
> (Stiglitz, 2016)

The Five Presidents' Reports (including the President of the Eurogroup, who takes account of the needs of the European Central Bank and of the necessity of coordination) are really powerful and credible commitments. Curiously, the reactions to the messages contained in these reports by national public opinion were weak, very weak. The same treatment has been reserved for a similar new project of a Treaty for the Eurozone by Andrew Duff (Duff, 2016)[19] or in the "Fourth scenario for the Eurozone" by Rodrigues, M.J. (Rodrigues, 2012).

The stake is really a political one: in the past, a European anti-cycle budget could still be seen as a privation of sovereignty. However, the economic theory of the policy-mix in the current union has swayed in favor of this solution since the 1990s. The lessons of the flaws of implementation of non-economics based rules are so clear today that nobody could still hope for a lack of political support on a national level for a European actor for stabilization.

This definitely would not mean a definitive centralization of all aspects of revenue and expenditure policy. Euro area member states would continue to decide on taxation and the allocation of budgetary expenditures according to national preferences and political choices. However, as the euro area evolves toward a genuine EMU, some decisions will increasingly need to be shared collectively while ensuring democratic accountability and legitimacy. A future euro area treasury could be the place for such cooperative decision-making for European resources and public federal expenses. The Eurozone, as France Stratégie design it in its option three, has to "combine, on the one hand, the will to strengthen fiscal sovereignty at national level – not constrained by European rules – and the need, on the other hand, to create a zone-wide stabilization function" (France Stratégie, 2016).

The non-acceptance of national audiences, the return to the old national cultures of ordoliberalism or budgetary nationalism would be a definite obstacle to the future of EMU2. After long delays due to sighs and alterations of national interest groups, EMU2, with a stabilization function, should be proof of the concept of a European Union that cannot simply be a single market. A European budget sharing of part of the fiscal sovereignty and dedicated

European budgetary resources are today the key factors for the success and the method of financing the true urgent European policies (efficacy of migrations policies, fighting climatic change) that are required today by a consensus of the major States (Germany, France, Italy and so on) (Baslé, 2017) and even more so tomorrow, in the event of a new financial crisis. They are the price to be paid for guaranteeing the status of the euro as an international currency (this primarily concerns the Eurozone) and for guaranteeing the European Union's power in the world economic and financial world (and this concerns the 27 countries that identify themselves, with more or less popular enthusiasm, with the Union's future).

Those who follow this EMU2 strategy will be the winners: the Eurozone will be more optimal, the banking union will allow for better separation of risks and the European Monetary Fund will be the new institution that will act as an internal firefighter for the zone, which will therefore be stronger in the event of a new (and unwanted) international financial shock. And, contrary to the opinion propagated by conservatives or nationalists, the sharing of fiscal sovereignty between several levels of sovereignty (local or regional, national, supranational) will not be the abandonment of its national content. History is rich in successful experiences of fiscal federalism. It is not because a seemingly unionist European state would today endow itself with 2% of GDP that all the national states budgets are *hara kiri* (or bloodless): on the contrary, they can find themselves more vigorous after organizing a system of three categories of sovereignty (local or regional, national and European). The well-understood interest of Germany, France and other members of the euro area is to do better than before in overall macroeconomic management. It is the price to pay to keep the euro as an international currency and retain its benefits in the near future. An EMU2 will then have to reflect quickly on the level of intra-zone inequalities that will be tolerable in the future, failing which the European elections of May 2019 will provide a critical feedback on all the new European institutions. The time will no longer be right for general macroeconomic policy debates, and there will be a return to sub-optimal solutions of nationalism and do-it-yourself.

Notes

1 ECON 104. Parlement européen, PE 167.739 1998–2001, ajustement aux chocs asymétriques. www.europarl.europa.eu/workingpapers/econ/pdf/104_fr.pdf

2 Textually, the Article 104C TEC (Treaty on European Union, signed at Maastricht on 7 February 1992) stated that:

> 1. Member States shall avoid excessive government deficits. 2. The Commission shall monitor the development of the budgetary situation and of the stock of government debt in the Member States with a view to identifying gross errors. In particular it shall examine compliance with budgetary discipline on the basis of the following two criteria: (a) whether the ratio of the planned or actual government deficit to gross domestic product exceeds a reference value, unless: – either the ratio has declined substantially and continuously and reached a level that comes close to

the reference value, – or, alternatively, the excess over the reference value is only exceptional and temporary and the ratio remains close to the reference value.

3 Yet despite these recommendations, the reform that was adopted in 2005 following the Spring European Council (22–23 March) will, under the leadership of France and Germany in lead to? A relaxation of the rule. Source: (http://europarlement.touteleurope.eu/comprenez/grands-dossiers/quel-avenir-pour-le-pacte-de-stabilite-et-de-croissance/print.html).
4 See Council of the European Union 12197/04 ECOFIN 296 UEM 150 and Regulations (EC) No 1055/2005 and (EC) No 1056/2005, respectively. In addition, the Council Report dated 20 March 2005 on "Improving the implementation of the Stability and Growth Pact". Source: (http://europarlement.touteleurope.eu/comprenez/grands-dossiers/quel-avenir-pour-le-pacte-de-stabilite-et-de-croissance/print.html).
5 For the completed text see: http://ec.europa.eu/economy_finance/economic_governance/sgp/index_en.ht; for the completed text, see European commission site: https://ec.europa.eu/info/business-economy-euro/economic-and-fiscal-policy-coordination/eu-economic-governance-monitoring-prevention-correction/stability-and-growth-pact_en
6 See consolidated versions of the Treaty on European Union and the Treaty on the Functioning of the European Union – Consolidated version of the Treaty on the Functioning of the European Union – Protocols – Annexes – Declarations annexed to the Final Act of the Intergovernmental Conference which adopted the Treaty of Lisbon, signed on 13 December 2007. Official Journal: C 326, 26/10/2012 P. 0001–0390.
7 See: http://ec.europa.eu/europe2020/making-it-happen/index_en.htm
8 Regulation No 472/2013. Regulation No 473/2013. http://ec.europa.eu/economy_finance/articles/governance/2012-03-14_six_pack_en.htm
9 See: Communication from the Commission to the European Parliament, the Council, the European Central Bank, the European Economic and Social Committee and the Comity of Regions. Economic Governance Review Report on the application of Regulations (EU) n° 1173/2011, 1174/2011, 1175/2011, 1176/2011, 1177/2011, 472/2013 and 473/2013.
10 See the publications by the European Commission.
11 See note 9.
12 See Bruegel policy contribution (2015)/19, November, on the implementation of recommendations of the European semester procedure. See Darvas, Z., Leandro, A. (2015).
13 European Semester 2016 Autumn Package explained. Brussels, 16 November 2016
14 See: European Semester 2016 Spring Package explained. Brussels, 18 May 2016 (country-specific recommendations, European Semester 2016 Spring Package).
15 www.publications.parliament.uk/pa/ld201516/ldselect/ldeucom/143/14306.htm
16 See also: European Commission, "Completing Europe's Economic and Monetary Union: Commission takes concrete steps to strengthen EMU", 21 October 2015; European Commission, "A Deeper and Fairer Economic and Monetary Union: Combining stability with fairness and democratic accountability", a Commission priority, October 2015; and Devoluy, M. (2015).
17 See also: Duff (2016)
18 But it is still done indirectly. It is not yet an active European policy dedicated to financing anything other than national expenditure; for example, a common policy for migrants and refugees.
19 See Article 16, which adapts the excessive deficit procedure in Article 126 TFEU to the new situation. It introduces the budgetary and economic partnership programs that will apply to Eurozone states subject to the excessive deficit procedure. The programs will be laws voted in the normal way and will enhance the power of the European Parliament in terms of any revision to the Protocol on the debt and deficit targets. Lastly, they will protect the Court of Justice from having to judge on the existence of an excessive deficit.

Bibliography

Aglietta, M. (2012): *Zone euro: éclatement ou fédération*. Paris. Michalon.

Ahmad, E., Brosio, G., in Association with the International Monetary Fund (IMF) (2006): *Handbook of Fiscal Federalism*. Cheltenham. Edward Elgar Publishing.

Alesina, A., Ardagna, S. (2010): Large Changes in Fiscal Policy: Taxes versus Spending. *Tax Policy and the Economy*. NBER Working Paper No. 15438.

Alesina, A., Tabellini, G. (1987): Rules and Discretion with Non-Coordinated Monetary and Fiscal Policies. *Economic Inquiry*. Vol. 25, pp. 619–630.

Allen, C.S. (2005): Ordo Liberalism Trumps Keynesianism: Economic Policy in the Federal Republic of Germany and the EU. In B. H. Moss (Eds.), *Monetary Union in Crisis: The European Union as a Neo-Liberal Construction*. New York. Palgrave Macmillan.

Andrews, D.M. (2003): *Command and Control in the Committee of Governors: Leadership, Staff and Preparations for EMU*. European University Institute.

Arestis, P., McCauley, K., Sawyer, M. (2001): An Alternative Stability and Growth Pact for the European Union. *Cambridge Journal of Economics*. Vol. 25, No. 1, pp. 113–130.

Arestis, P., Sawyer, M. (2012, 9 January): The 'Fiscal Compact' Has Not Solved the Euro Crisis, *Triple Crisis*. http://triplecrisis.com/the-fiscal-compact-has-not-solved-the-euro-crisis/

Arestis, P., Sawyer, M. (2016): Triple Crisis Blog: Global Perspectives on Finance. Development and Environment.

Artis, M.J. (2002): The Stability and Growth Pact: Fiscal Policy in the EMU. In F. Breuss, G. Fink, S. Griller (Eds.), *Institutional, Legal and Economic Aspects of the EMU*. Wien-New York. Springer.

Artus, P. (2015): Que penser de l'excédent extérieur de l'Allemagne? *Flash économie*. Recherche économique. N°245.

Artus, P. (2016): Si les Allemands ne changent pas, la zone euro va vers une nouvelle crise. *La Tribune*. 22 February.

Baslé, M. (1975): Serisette ou Stoleruine: les heurs et malheurs du principe d'une taxe conjoncturelle. *Revue de science financière*. Paris: LGDJ. Vol. 67, No. 4, pp. 853–903.

Baslé, M. (2015): *Le budget de l'Etat*. Collection Repères. Paris. Editions La Découverte.

Baslé, M. (2017): Les finances publiques françaises dans le contexte du budget européen et des engagements de la France. Une solution non durable. In *Abécédaire de Droit de l'Union européenne*. Presses universitaires de Rennes.

Bénassy-Quéré, A. (2015): Maastricht Flaws and Remedies. In R. Baldwin, F. Giavazzi (Eds.), *The Eurozone Crisis: A Consensus View of the Causes and a Few Possible Solutions*. CEPR e-book.

Bénassy-Quéré, A., Coeuré, B. (2014): *Economie de l'euro*. Collection repères. Third edition. Editions La Découverte.

Bénassy-Quéré, A., Coeuré, B., Jacquet, P., Pisani-Ferry, J. (2012): *Politique économique*. Third edition. Ouvertures économiques. De Boeck.

Bénassy-Quéré, A., Ragot, X. (2015): A Policy Mix for the Euro Area: French Council of Economic Analysis. *Les notes du conseil d'analyse économique*, No. 21 (Mar.)

Bibow, J. (2005): Germany in Crisis: The Unification Challenge, Macroeconomic Policy Shocks and Traditions, and EMU. *International Review of Applied Economics*. Vol. 19, No. 1, pp. 29–50.

Blanchard, O. (2012): preface. In A. Bénassy-Quéré et al., *Politique économique*. Third edition. Ouvertures économiques. De Boeck.

Bordo, M.D., Jonung, L. (2000): *Lessons for EMU from the History of Monetary Unions*. London. Institute of Economic Affairs.

Brunnermeier, M.K., James, H., Landau, J.P. (2016): *The Euro and the Battle of Ideas*. Princeton, NJ. Princeton University Press.

Clapham, R. (2004): Entstehung und Entwicklung des Konzepts der Sozialen Marktwirtschaft. In A. Uwe (dir.), *Soziale Marktwirtschaft – eine Einführung* (pp. 12–33). Schwalbach. Wochenschau Verlag.

Coddington, A. (1976): Keynesian Economics: The Search for First Principles. *The Journal of Economic Literature*. Vol. 14, No. 4, December, pp. 1258–1273.

Commun, P. (2016): *Les Ordolibéraux: Histoire d'un libéralisme à l'allemande*. Paris. Les Belles Lettres, 418 pages.

Cripps, F., Duwicquet, V., Mazier, J. (2013): Les scénarios européens. In *L'économie mondiale en 2030: ruptures et continuité*. Paris. Editions Economica.

Darvas, Z., Leandro, A. (2015): The limitations of policy coordination in the euro area under the European semester. Bruegel policy contribution. No. 19. November.

De Grauwe, P. (2013): Design Failures in the Eurozone: Can They Be Fixed? *LSE 'Europe in Question' Discussion Paper Series*. LEQS Paper. No. 57, February.

Devoluy, M. (2012): *L'euro est-il un échec ?*. 2e éd. Paris. La Documentation française.

Devoluy, M. (2015): L'ordo libéralisme et l'avenir de l'Europe monétaire. *Bulletin de l'Observatoire des politiques économiques en Europe*. Hiver, No. 33.

Duff, A. (2016): *The Protocol of Frankfurt*. A New Treaty for the Eurozone. See: www.epc.eu/documents/uploads/pub_6229_protocol_of_frankfurt.pdf

Dyson, K., Featherstone, K. (1999): *The Road to Maastricht: Negotiating Economic and Monetary Union*. Oxford. Oxford University Press.

Eck, J.-F. (2009): *Histoire de l'économie française: De la crise de 1929 à l'euro*. Paris. Armand Colin.

European Commission (2015a): *Five President's Report* (July). Completing Europe's Economic and Monetary Union. Report by: Juncker, J.C. in close cooperation with Tusk, D., Jeroen, D., Draghi, M., Schulz, M.

European Commission (2015b), *Completing Europe's Economic and Monetary Union: Commission takes concrete steps to strengthen EMU*. 21 October 2015.

European Commission (2016). Towards a positive fiscal stance for the European area. COM(2016). 727 final. Annex 2.

France Stratégie (2016): *Quelle architecture pour la zone euro?* By Gouardo, C. Aussilloux, V. Décembre.

Friedman, M., Heller, W. (1969): *Monetary versus Fiscal Policy*. New York. Norton and Cie.

Heipertz, M., Verdun, A. (2010): *Ruling Europe: The Politics of the Stability and Growth Pact*. Cambridge. Cambridge University Press.

Heller, W. (1966): *New Dimensions of Political Economy*. Cambridge, MA. Harvard University Press.

Herdengen, M. (1998): Price Stability and Budgetary Restraints in the EMU: The Law as Guardian of Economic Wisdom. *Common Market Law Review*. Vol. 35, pp. 9–32.

Kaldor, N. ([1971] 1978): *New Statesman*, 12 March. In *Further Essays on Applied Economics*. Volume 6 of the Collected Economic Essays Series of Nicholas Kaldor. New York. Holmes et Meier.

Kenis, P.N., Schneider, V. (1991): Policy Networks and Policy Analysis: Scrutinizing a New Analytical Toolbox. In B. Martin, R. Mayntz (Eds.), *Empirical Evidence and Theoretical Considerations* (pp. 25–59). University of Tilburg, Westview Press.

Laïdi, Z. (2005): *La norme sans la force. L'énigme de la puissance européenne*. Paris. Les presses de Sciences Po.

Légé, P., Marques Pereira, J. (2016): Les hésitations de la parole autorisée durant la crise de la zone euro. *Revue de la régulation*. Vol. 19. http://journals.openedition.org/regulation/11814

Maes, I. (2002): *Economic Thought and the Making of the European Monetary Union*. Cheltenham. Edward Elgar Publishing.

Maes, I. (2004): On the Origins of the Franco-German EMU Controversies. *European Journal of Law and Economics*. Vol. 17, pp. 21–39. Kluwer Academic Publishers.

Modena, S. (2012): Le débat institutionnel français lors du passage à l'Euro: 1998–2002 Analyse du discours et argumentation. *Doctorat*. Paris-Est-Creteil.

Mourlon-Druol, E. (2012): *A Europe Made of Money: The Emergence of the European Monetary System*. Collection Cornell Studies in Money. Ithaca, NY. Cornell University Press.

Mundell, R. (1960): The Monetary Dynamics of International Adjustment under Fixed and Flexible Exchange Rates. *Quarterly Journal of Economics*. Vol. 74.

OECD (1995): Potential Output, Output Gaps and Structural Budget Balances. Report from Claude Giorno, Pete Richardson, Deborah Roseveare and Paul van den Noord, *Economic Studies*. No. 24, p. 1.

Official Journal of the European Union (2011, 16 November): Regulation (EU) No 1176/2011 of the European Parliament and the Council. *On the Prevention and Correction of Macroeconomic Imbalances*.

Piperno, S. (2012): Implementing Fiscal Decentralization in Italy between Crisis and Austerity: Challenges Ahead. *Perspectives on Federalism*. Vol. 4, No. 3.

Rabault, V. (2016): Rapport d'information Assemblée Nationale, Commission des Finances, de l'économie générale et contrôle budgétaire préalable au débat d'orientation des finances publiques en France.

Rochon, L.P., Rossi, S. (2016): *An Introduction to MacroEconomics: A Heterodox Approach to Economic Analysis*. Cheltenham. Edward Elgar Publishing.

Rodrigues, M.J. (2012): Quels scénarios pour l'avenir de la zone euro? *Analyse politique internationale*. Juin. Friedrich Ebert Stiftung.

Sawyer, M. (2012): The Contradictions of Balanced Structural Government Budget. In H. Herr alii. (Eds.), *From Crisis to Growth? The Challenge of Imbalances and Debt*. Marburg. Metropolis Verlag.

Schefold, B. Edr. (2002 Röpke [1942]): *Vademecum zu einem Klasiker der Ordnungstheorie, Kommentarband zum Repr. von Wilhelm Röpke*: Die Gesellschaftskrisis der gegenwart. Dusseldorf. Verlag Wirtschaft unf Finanzen [Erlenbach-Zürich, 1942].

Solchani, J. (2015): *Wilhelm Röpke, l'autre Hayek. Aux origines du néo-libéralisme*. Paris. Publications de la Sorbonne.

Stiglitz, J. (2013): An Agenda to Save the Euro. *Project Syndicate*. 16 December.

Stiglitz, J. (2014): Can the Euro Be Saved? An Analysis of the Future of the Currency Union. Rome. Conference. www.rivistapoliticaeconomica.it/pdf/vii_ix_Stiglitz.pdf

Stiglitz, J. (2016): *The Euro: How a Common Currency Threatens the Future of Europe*. New York. W.W. Norton.

Tavera, C. (Edr.) (1999): *La convergence des économies européennes*. Paris. Editions Economica.

Tobin, J. (1974): *The New Economics One Decade Older*. Princeton Legacy Library.

Tobin, J. (1989): *Policies for Prosperity: Essays in a Keynesian Mode*. Cambridge, MA. MIT Press.

Trésor (2013): A Budget for the Euro Area. *Tresor-Economics*. No. 120, October.

United Kingdom Parliament (2015): European Union Committee "Whatever It Takes": The Five Presidents' Report on completing Economic and Monetary Union 13th Report of Session 2015–16 – published 12 May 2016.

Veld, J. (2016): Public Investment Stimulus in Surplus Countries and Their Euro Area Spillovers, *Economic Brief* 16 August.

Verdun, A. (1998): *The Role of the Delors Committee in the Creation of EMU: An Epistemic Community?* European University Institute, Working Paper RSC 98/44.

Werner Report (1970): Report to the Council and the Commission on the Realization by Stages of the Economic and Monetary Union in the Community. *Council-Commission of the European Communities: Supplement to Bulletin*. No. 11.

Young, B. (2012): *The Power of German Ordo Liberals as Agenda Setters in the Euro Crisis*. Institute for Society and Globalisation. Roskilde, November 27.

Zsolt D., Leandro, A. (2015): Bruegel Policy Contribution: The Limitations of Policy Coordination in the Euro Area under the European Semester.

6 Social spending as a driver of economic growth

Has the theoretical consensus of the 1980s led to successful economic policies?

Sandrine Michel

Social spending: what are we talking about?

Since the emergence of social spending at the end of the 19th century, the question of how it affects economic growth has been considered from two angles. First of all, *why* does it increase? The causality from social spending to economic growth gives priority to arguments such as population structure (Monnier 2006), the conflictual nature of social relations and the adoption of social protection standards based on renewed income distribution (André 2002) or the institutional context, whereby social spending would stem from typified, historically defined social arrangements (Esping-Andersen 1990; Castel 2003). Conversely, the causal relationship from growth to social spending emphasises the latter's contribution to lessening the effects of declining income when economic conditions are unfavourable (Myrdal 1960), but also the burden such expenditures can represent for capital accumulation (Mazier et al. 1999).

A second question deals with *when* social spending increases. On this issue, and without looking for (nonexistent) consensus, the literature nonetheless indicates that its peak periods occur during economic crises and that once there is a return to growth, its long-term trend shows that it is maintained at roughly the level reached during the preceding crisis (Wagner 1883; Michel 2017). As an offshoot of economic conditions, social spending is thus a result of crises and growth alike, a kind of by-product that has taken dizzying proportions and that macroeconomic policies everywhere attempt to contain (Barbier 2013).

The present period of generalised economic crisis sheds light, in a specific context, on the long-standing dilemma that social spending constitutes for the economy. Indeed, it is argued on the one hand that these expenditures permit investments that are necessary for the future but which the market cannot identify as such, and also, through income-based contributions, the creation of safety nets to protect against the social risks tied to a more complex growth (Atkinson 2005). But on the other hand, it is maintained that these safety nets act as a disincentive, for both the individuals funding them and those benefiting from them (Nervole et al. 1993); they would thus generate inequities while their cost would constitute a threat to growth (Razin and Sadka 2005). Throughout Europe, 'austerity plans' attempt to rationalise social spending, whether by limiting the means allocated (for public services and protection against social risks alike) or by limiting the entitlements provided (retirement pensions).

This highly polarised debate was punctuated by a singular episode in the late 1980s, when advocates of two extremely different theoretical positions – the theory of endogenous growth (Lucas 1988) and *régulation* theory (Fontvieille 1990) – formulated the same hypothesis, namely that social spending had become an economic growth engine. This hypothesis suggests that social spending might no longer result from growth, whether because of crises or the relative ratchet effects following them, but rather, would generate it. Consequently, its conceptualisation in economic policies might be completely turned around so as to raise the question of sustaining it, rather than that of constantly seeking to reduce it.

This article aims to reconstitute the factors that led to formulating such a hypothesis and then consider how they have been put to the test by economic crisis. To that end, we rely on a diachronic reading of social spending in Europe, which is usually defined by social protection expenditures but which we have also taken to include those for education. In other words, we have opted for a human development approach (Ranis et al. 2000).

A hypothesis formulated simultaneously within two highly different theoretical approaches

In the late 1980s, the hypothesis of social spending as a growth engine was thus advanced in a context whereby the question of controlling public expenditures and social spending was already well established in macroeconomic debate. This hypothesis was singular in two respects. First of all, it reversed the most frequent terms of the political economy debate. But in addition, it was set out in two very different bodies of theoretical literature.

Endogenous growth: the role of human capital and public expenditures in long-term self-sustained growth

Endogenous growth theories improved the standard theory of growth (Solow 1956) in several respects: a theoretical representation of growth more consistent with international dynamics, as supported by the conditional end of constant returns to scale, and an endogenous technological advance made possible in particular by the ability to accumulate human capital, which is the qualitative component of labour.

In his model, Lucas (1988) bases his reasoning on a two-sector economy. In each period, the human capital stock is allocated to the production sector and the human capital production sector in the form of working time, along with the labour and capital factors. The proportion of human capital assigned to one or the other functions as a kind of investment rate for each person because the time devoted to human capital serves to increase future production. The marginal return in human capital production is positive. Over the long term, it is constant and therefore guarantees self-sustained growth. In addition, however, the returns of the human capital production system improve with time. Indeed, at every point in time, the knowledge transmitted is better than that of the earlier periods, which increases the productivity gaps between different generations. Even if the average level of human capital production is constant over time, the human capital stock might thus grow to the point of influencing the growth rate.

Lucas also insists on the fact that individual choices in the allocation of time between the two sectors affect not only the individuals themselves but the economy as a whole because of the spread of human capital. This externality has no effect on the growth rate of human capital based on individual decisions, which is always positive. However, the scope of these external effects permits the justification of public funding for educational policy. In the end, for Lucas, the human capital growth rate determines economic growth over the long term.

Romer (1986) had already shown that human capital plays an essential role in the production of new ideas. He demonstrates that innovation increases the stock of knowledge and that this increase will have a beneficial effect not only for the company generating it but for the firms as a whole (positive externality), which will stimulate growth. As a result, in his view, even an occasional increase, and not a general one as in the case of Lucas, leads to an acceleration of the growth rate.

Endogenous growth theories permit a new understanding of the appropriateness of public policies, which are envisaged differently insofar as they involve subsidising the growth factors or internalising the externalities. Thus, the impact of public funding on growth will be even less negative because it will be obtained through a levy on factors that do not generate externalities, such as physical capital, whereby an increase in efficiency is systematically sought in order to finance, for example, education (Glomm and Ravikumar 1997).

Régulation ***theory: in an unstable long-term accumulation process, increased social spending leads to structural change***[1]

Régulationist studies periodise structural changes in long-term growth by analysing its instability in terms of accumulation regimes (Labrousse and Michel 2017) and their crises (Aglietta 2000; Jessop and Sum 2006; Boyer 2015). Each accumulation regime is characterised by a historically contextualised arrangement of five institutional forms, or fundamental social relations: the *wage-labour nexus* (capital-labour relations), the *forms of competition*, the *financial/monetary regime*, the *relationship between state and economy* and the nature of *integration in the international regime*. The mode of *régulation* coordinates the linking of institutional forms through the production of regularities that ensure economic growth. By its very nature, this linking process is antagonistic because is intended to make largely incompatible economic decisions compatible within the accumulation regime. When the mode of *régulation* no longer allows the conflicts to be maintained, the economy plunges into a structural crisis during which its institutional architecture undergoes radical change.

In these studies, social spending appears first of all in research on the historical regimes of the development of wage labour, which is the dominant form of the wage-labour nexus (Boyer 1979). From the beginning of the 19th century to the Great Depression between the two World Wars, the rise of wage labour was considered competitive insofar as the buying and selling of labour power were determined by the fluctuating conditions of extensive accumulation, with employment level and wage rate functioning as adjustment variables. Wages constituted a cost to be permanently combated (Boyer 1979). After the end of World War II, a so-called monopolistic wage regime emerged owing to the decreased flexibility of the wage rate (Boyer 1979). The factors involved in the reproduction of labour power were integrated into the circuit of capital. This form of wage labour depended on the spread of a reproduction of labour power based on a norm of the broadest possible private commodity consumption and on collective consumption based on deferred wages (healthcare and retirement pensions) (Aglietta 2000).

Within *régulation* theory, an early group of studies maintained that, in a critical phase, the spending attributed to the deferred wage contributed to decreasing the profitability of capital and as such, constituted an obstacle to accumulation (Mazier et al. 1999). The commodification of the public services covered by social spending was therefore considered as a possible solution to the sharp increase in such expenditures. But this was not the case (Billaudot et al. 1979; Moulier-Boutang 2011).

As a result, this initial interpretation has come to be modified by a more recent group of studies. The analysis of the historical pace of the rise in social spending led to the hypothesis that when this spending attains a certain level, it can be considered an engine for long-term growth. This research shows that the increase in social spending is neither continuous nor proportionate to growth. Nor is it random. This has been demonstrated, in the French case, by a study of social spending over the long term, from 1850 to the present (Michel and Vallade 2007, 2010). Similar results have been observed empirically for other developed countries such as Germany (Diebolt 1997) and the UK (Carpentier 2003).

The evolution of social spending is marked by two salient features. First, all categories of these expenditures – education, health, retirement pensions – fluctuate in an identical way, with the same phases of accelerated and reduced growth. Second, their fluctuations in relation to the gross domestic product (GDP) are significant. Historically, they assume two different relationships to the long waves. From the mid-19th century to 1945, their growth is countercyclical. Each of their expansion phases corresponds to the long depression phases of the GDP (1873–1890 and 1928–1939). The justification for this expansion must therefore be sought in the causes of barriers to growth. The expenditures are funded by the devalorisation of over-accumulated capital (Marx 1894; Harvey 1982; Fontvieille 1999; Boccara 2013). After 1945, their fluctuations become procyclical, which signifies, beyond the sector-based contributions of each of these expenditures, their joint action within the mode of *régulation*. The synchronous fluctuations of all of these expenditures over the long-term economic cycle allows us to characterise them as human development. In fact, they constitute various solutions for social problems. However, the reversal of the direction of their fluctuations relative to the GDP after World War II also indicates a lasting change in accumulation, which now depends on social spending. This observation permits the hypothesis that social spending has become a growth engine.

Régulationist research explains the sharp rise in social spending by the fact that these collective services, including education, lead to a differentiation between individuals in the labour market. The standardisation of these expenditures by the public authorities then ensures the social cohesion of wage societies through a political process (Aglietta and Brender 1984; Amable 2017).

Common points and differences within the shared hypothesis

In their respective formulations of the hypothesis of social spending as a growth engine, the two theoretical approaches under consideration here manifest a number of common points. First of all, these expenditures are tied to the production of workforce quality as a factor for increasing the productivity of labour and capital. Second, time contributes to this production by improving the level of the initial stock before any general or targeted productive activity. Social spending thus develops a principle of self-accumulation that can be apprehended in the quality of the population. Last of all, this accumulation process is analysed as a levy on the resources available for capital accumulation.

At the same time, certain differences must be singled out. Endogenous growth theories reason in terms of a time frame differentiated solely by the quality of the human capital stock in each period, while *régulation* theory associates time with an ability to generate structural change through long-term transformations of the accumulation regimes and their institutional architecture. In this context, social spending depends on two distinct time frames, that of the business cycle for questions of capital accumulation and distribution and that of the long waves for structural changes, which are defined in terms of accumulation regimes and modes of *régulation*.

The rise of social spending in Europe

The empirical trajectory of social spending in the European countries has given rise to several theoretical interpretations (see Table 6.1).

Table 6.1 Increased social spending in empirical terms

Periods of social spending development		*What kind of social spending?*	*Causes*	*Pace (rhythm)*
1880–1930 Very slow take-off [from 0.5% to 2% of GDP] (Lindert 2004)		From poor relief to education, emerging social risk	1. Ageing 2. GDP growth 3. Voice	Expansion during depression phase of the business cycle (stabilisers)
After WWII	Accelerated growth after WWII[from 10% to 29% of GDP] (Lindert 2004)	Broad-based	1. Voice 2. GDP growth 3. Quality of working population 4. Ageing	Mixed: permanence of business cycle fluctuations but with a changing structure over the long-term: changing dynamics (large increases during economic growth)(Michel and Vallade 2010)
	Since the end of the 1980s: social spending in an in-between	Broad-based social spending still increasing	1. Ageing 2. GDP growth 3. Inequalities 4. Voice	Return of the single business cycle (Darby and Melitz 2008) but with the emerging notion of acyclicality (Arze del Granado et al. 2010; Afonso and Jalles 2013; d'Addio 2015)

Source: Author synthesis based on sources cited

An empirical view

There is no consensus concerning the pace of increases in social spending, insofar as it has long been associated with the business cycle in a countercyclical approach. These expenditures are then essentially conceived on the basis of income stabilisers in the Keynesian sense, which are made automatic by economic policies instituted in the European social model. Such an approach has been reinforced by studies over the long term, which bring out the fact that the dynamics tied to the business cycles are integrated into longer-term dynamics that are close to the long waves. Since the end of the 1980s – and thus during the extended depression phase of the present long wave – the business cycle is once again relevant for characterising the rhythm of social spending but this time, it is associated with fluctuations that are acyclical and not only countercyclical. Consequently, in the recent period, the long-term dynamics associating social spending with a possible structural change can be examined in terms of the transitions affecting shorter dynamics.

Theoretical views

Insofar as social spending was initially introduced as an income correction vector during phases of economic hardship, the redistribution factor predominates when we consider the long term. And for this reason, debates over the relations between social spending and economic growth go back to the 19th century. Thus, Wagner (1883) maintained that increasingly sophisticated economic growth necessitated greater public expenditures in order to provide national economies with collective infrastructures and meet the population's needs for better-quality goods. The debates persist since that time, and far from reaching any consensus, they continue to oppose different visions of the impact of the relationship between social spending and growth and that of the direction it takes.

Social spending as a by-product of growth

Key studies carried out in the mid-20th century have shown that the historical increase in public spending followed a particular model alternating periodic increases and ratchet effects (Peacock and Wiseman 1961). In order the explain this growth pattern, the authors advanced the hypothesis of a displacement effect whereby wars and economic crises would lead to accepting a higher tax level in order to finance the increase in new public expenditures needed to stimulate growth and then stabilise it. As a result, public spending was seen as a burden for economic growth. This ambivalence towards the impact of public spending on growth can be seen in Peacock and Wiseman's concept of 'public expenditure limit' (1961: 25) and, more recently, the search for the appropriate size of sustainable government (Flavin et al. 2014; Bakija et al. 2016). At all events, in this context, the structure of public spending is as important as its volume; historically, transfer expenditures have risen more quickly than all the other spending categories (Rowley and Tollison 1994).

More broadly, in the view of standard economists today, redistributive policies now result in net losses in terms of the community's well-being and/or a decline in growth which are accepted because of the lasting gains they are expected to promote in terms of equity. Population ageing (Nagarajan et al. 2017), the slowdown in the rise of per capita income for the lowest incomes (Dabla-Norris et al. 2015) and the increasing taxation and social competition associated with the present form of globalisation (Escudero and Lopez Mourelo 2017) all lead to an unsustainable rise in social costs and an increasingly inequitable distribution of expenditure. Consequently, the protection from economic instability provided by the social systems is no longer viewed as an adequate reason for postponing structural reforms in a system pressured by a public sector held to be ineffective (Karabarbounis and Neiman 2014).

Beyond social spending as a by-product of growth: alternative historical approaches

Several historical interpretations have contradicted the idea that the development of social systems essentially constitutes a burden on economic growth. These studies bring out the cumulative nature of social spending and its low sensitivity to setbacks in the economic situation. In *Growing Public*, Lindert (2004) shows that social spending has zero cost for growth: over the long term, the costs of social transfers and the gains they permit are equivalent, making social spending a 'free lunch' for the community. Indeed, as costly as this spending may be for growth, it permits labour productivity gains (education, health, etc.) and provides social support for workers excluded from the production system (retirement pensions, unemployment compensation). Lindert also considers the development of social spending as the result of the increase in political participation. He identifies a 'Robin Hood paradox' (Lindert 2004 I: 19) illustrated by the fact that social spending had historically grown when wealth has increased the most (i.e., industrial society) and where the political voice was most active.

Régulation theory has advanced another historical argument against 'public expenditure limit' (Peacock and Wiseman 1961: 25) by showing that public spending on social development contributes to the dynamics of crisis recovery (Fontvieille 1990). In the developed countries, from the Industrial Revolution to 1945, each long period of economic depression coincided with the transfer of a share of over-accumulated capital to the funding of social spending through taxation or voluntary contributions, which thus helped to create a new growth regime. Following each of these long depression phases, increased social expenditures supported more complex social activities (healthcare, retirement pensions, education, family, etc.) that were integrated into the growth regime. Initially countercyclical, this relationship becomes procyclical after 1945. Such a reversal reflects the increasing autonomy of social spending in relation to growth, thus supporting the hypothesis of the transformation of these expenditures into a growth engine (Michel 1999).

These historical approaches show that the cost of social spending for growth does not suffice to account for the economic phenomenon it represents. Indeed, its cost must be considered in relation to the growth of productivity it permits, for labour and capital alike, as well as the new social arrangements it allows, whether within the employment sphere (education, healthcare, etc.) or outside of it (retirement pensions, unemployment). By highlighting the economic contribution of social spending, these approaches provide arguments against the decline of the redistribution system (Atkinson 2016) and the welfare state (Barr 1992; Barbier 2013) and in favour of social innovation (Nolan 2013).

The historical analyses also single out the recurrences of social spending in the advanced economies and thus shed further light on its role in past growth regimes and the roles it could assume in the future. In this respect, these recurrences constitute a powerful incentive for debating the way social development influences the nature of growth.

European social spending today

Since the hypothesis of social spending as a growth engine was formulated at the end of the 1980s, these expenditures have continued to grow, in all countries and economic areas, whatever the economic situation. Europe is no exception (see Figure 6.1).

Aggregate social spending

In 21 countries of the European Union, the evolution of the share of aggregate social protection expenditures alone indicates that the welfare state has expanded there during the past 50 years (Adema et al. 2011), whether the

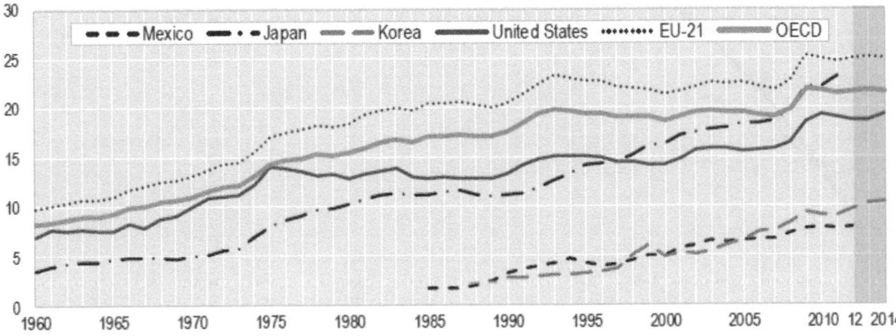

Figure 6.1 Aggregate social spending in percentage of GDP

Source: OECD (2014), 'Social Expenditure Update – Social spending is falling in some countries, but in many others it remains at historically high levels', available at www.oecd.org/els/soc/OECD2014-SocialExpenditure_Update19Nov_Rev.pdf

context is one of economic growth or one of crisis. During the structural crisis that emerged in the beginning of the 1970s, the European countries maintained the programmes set up in the 1960s. New programmes were subsequently added, including active employment policies and social policies targeting new publics or specific social risks such as retirement (because of the retirement of the post-World War II baby-boom generation (Monnier 2006). The activation of automatic stabilisers in response to the 2007 financial crisis constituted a final cause of rising social expenditures.

As of the 1980s, the general trend towards increased social spending developed in successive stages. The persistence of ratchet effects following the depression phases of the business cycle contradicts the theoretical hypothesis of social spending as a growth engine.

For a more complete picture of social spending that is open to the conceptualisation of human development, it is necessary to add expenditures for education. The theoretical justification for this argument is based on the concept of not limiting the analysis to the types of economic policies sustained by social spending, but rather reversing the perspective by associating these expenditures with the population quality they produce.

Careful attention must be paid to the data used. The time series presented in Figure 6.2 is derived from the merger of two series, both of which are reprocessed from the non-market GDP in order to control serial correlation biases.

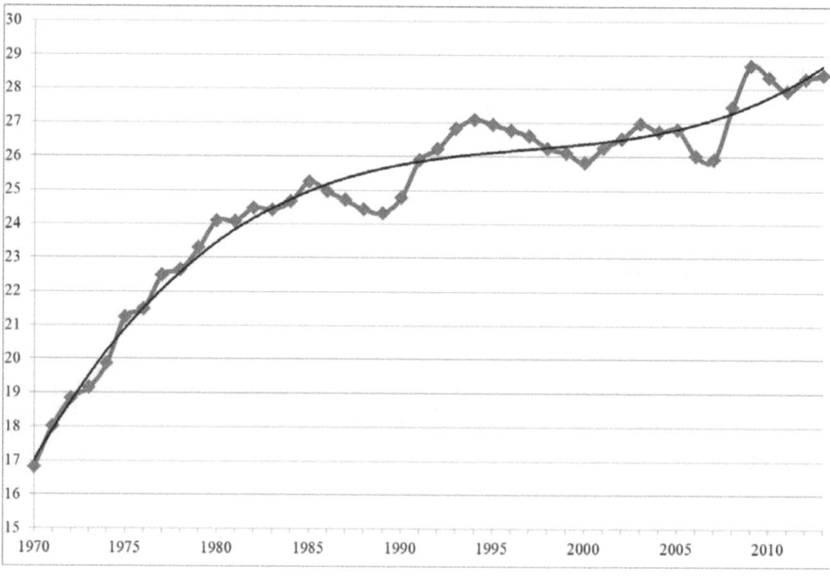

Figure 6.2 EU-21 – Total social spending for human development 1970–2013 – percentage of market GDP – R^2 = 0.97

Source: Author, based on OECD SocX and the World Bank Education database

- The market GDP was obtained from total GDP values less expenditures for social protection and education.
- Social protection expenditures are net values, corrected for taxation, drawn from the OECD SocX base (retrieved on 10 October 2017). Twenty-one EU countries are included, but the data provided does not cover identical periods. Missing variables have been reconstituted from country-specific trends. In order to evaluate the quality of the data, the series obtained has been compared to that obtained by Eurostat. The trends converge, although some significant variations cannot be overlooked.
- For the same EU-21 countries, the education expenditures used are drawn from the World Bank database (retrieved 10 October 2017).

According to this definition of human development, the behaviour of aggregate social spending remains heavily marked by the business cycle. All the episodes of business cycle depression in Europe are represented. The hypothesis attributing the increase in the share of social spending within the GDP during the depressive phases to fluctuations of the GDP alone must be rejected (Bird 1972). On the contrary, social spending increases in real terms between 1989 and 1993, and between 2007 and 2009.

The periodisation of the business cycles brings out the following points (see Figure 6.3):

Figure 6.3 Total social spending as a percentage of market GDP 1970–2013 – deviation around the trend

Source: Idem, processing by the author

- The crises in international oil prices during the 1973–1980 period. The rise in social spending is stable while the growth of the GDP declines.
- The crisis related to the extend of inflation, leading to the beginning of financial deregulation in the mid-1980s. There is a simultaneous slowdown in the growth of social spending and that of the GDP.
- With the bursting of the technology bubble in 2000–2004, the rise in social spending compensates for the slowdown in the growth of the GDP and its effects on household income, but subsequently converge once again with that of the GDP.
- The 2007 financial crisis spurs an immediate rise in social spending, while the EU shows a negative GDP growth rate in 2008 and 2009. During the years that follow, both the GDP and social spending stagnate.

Fluctuations in social spending relative to the GDP can be cyclical, countercyclical or stabilised by ratchet effects. These findings do not support the hypothesis advanced at the end of the 1980s, but rather appear to indicate the sensitivity of aggregate social spending behaviour to the severity of the crisis, as expressed by a return to pure countercyclicality at the very end of the period. But the period observed also indicates that social spending might occasionally experience procyclical growth, which is contrary to the strict historical knowledge of their behaviour over business cycles.

Consequently, if social spending does not seem to have become a growth engine, the fact remains that its overall contribution to growth does not strictly reproduce historical contingencies either. This in-between scenario calls for further investigation.

Sector-by-sector evolution of social spending

In order to establish a typology of the fluctuations proper to the different social expenditures, we assume that each one represents a particular function. We calculate their respective trends and the deviation around this trend over time. The difference of the deviations between each sector's social expenditure is then divided by the deviation around the aggregate social spending trend, over time as well.

In the case of the short-term fluctuations, the sector-based social expenditures do not all show the same behaviours. Two groups can be distinguished. The first includes social expenditures that clearly function countercyclically, while the second escapes this countercyclicality and can be characterised by an acyclicality.

Figure 6.4 brings together social expenditures for protection against a risk of income loss tied to the economic context. The preserve their countercyclical nature by substituting, at least partially, public coverage of the loss of income related to economic developments. When these expenditures are considered in relation to the business cycle, they are immediate (i.e., either compensation for job loss or the struggle against social exclusion). Unemployment-related

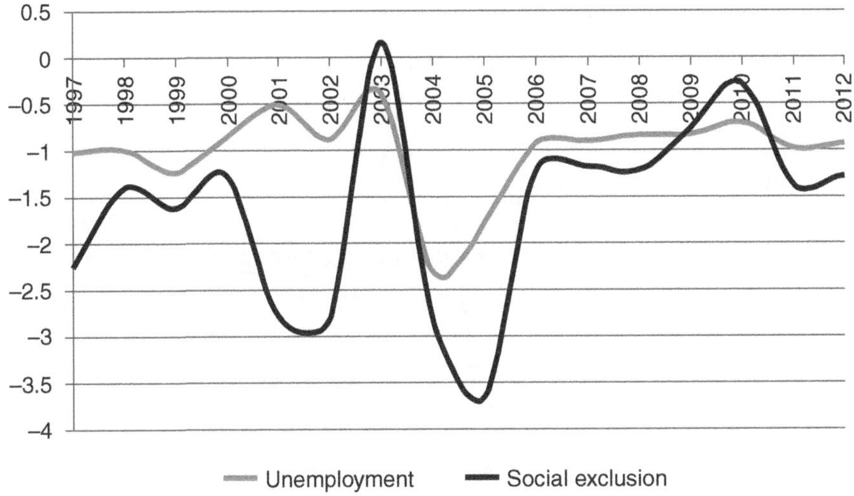

Figure 6.4 Group 1 – Countercyclical social expenditures

Source: Idem, processing by the author

expenditures are engaged over increasingly short time periods, which underscores a choice in favour of labour market mechanisms. There is nevertheless a gap between them, indicating that the second may well be substituted for the first once the cyclical peak is over. They are both likely to decline during cyclical upturns.

Historically, these expenditures are the closest to the welfare-related spending introduced throughout the 19th century. Institutionalised during the 20th century in response to business cycle risk, they support the overall demand function through the so-called automatic household income stabilisers. This function, which is inherently countercyclical, has persisted in the recent period. Today, these expenditures represent the long-term stratification of income inequalities and the growing relative poverty in the EU countries.

A second group of social expenditures has also emerged, however (Figure 6.5). Their behaviour is essentially acyclical in the sense that the effort in their favour is largely maintained across the different cycles.

These social expenditures operate over the long term in the sense that they have delayed effects. Education or health expenditures depend on a production apparatus – the education system or the health system – which is funded immediately, but the effects of these expenditures are accumulated by the individuals benefiting from them throughout their entire lifespans. Over the long term, these are the expenditures that sustain the post-World War II reversal (i.e., the shift from a countercyclical development of social spending relative to the long-term economic situation from the mid-19th century to 1945 to a procyclical development after that date). Their present relationship to the economic

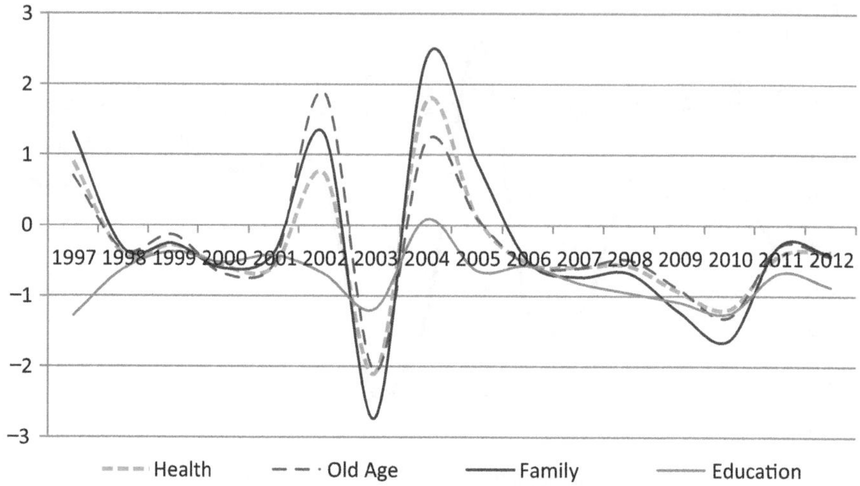

Figure 6.5 Group 2 – Acyclical social expenditures

Source: Idem., processing by the author

situation is characterised by a certain desynchronisation, brought out by their acyclical behaviour.

These social expenditures assist structural changes in the labour market, such as women's employment or the increasing qualification level of the workforce. They also reflect demographic changes, insofar as population ageing has led to the growth of spending for old-age care, which is the largest social expenditure category at the European level.

In economic terms, these social expenditures are tied to the production of the quality of the population. Their increasingly acyclical nature attests to their insensitivity to business cycle fluctuations. This acyclicality probably indicates their growing importance in the efficiency of both labour and capital, through their productive combinations. It can be connected with the many questions now being raised about the limitations of growth measurement indicators (INSEE 2009; Jany-Catrice and Méda 2013). Thus, standard measures of the productivity of the labour essentially based on time, are unable to reflect the productive effects of its quality. Present measures of capital performance are also relatively incapable of accounting for its growing efficiency in relation to the increase in the quality of labour. In addition, these expenditures integrate the quality of social life as well, through spending on retirement pensions or family assistance, which are not included in standard measures of wealth creation.

Findings and conclusion

Before assessing the hypothesis advanced in the late 1980s by both the theory of endogenous growth and *régulation* theory, namely that social spending can be a growth engine, it is necessary to recall that a certain degree of caution is required concerning the data. Much remains to be done in order to compare the available databases, which are generally designed by separating expenditures related to social protection on the one hand, and education on the other. In both cases, moreover, the country effects are often neglected despite the fact that welfare states, which are themselves always distinctive, emerge from the nations and their singular histories. The nature of national financing, whether public, private or mixed, also affects the dynamics of funding in a given economic context, but this is not adequately taken into account by the international databases.

That said, the results obtained support a certain number of observations concerning the evolution of social spending over business cycles. Trends in the rise of social expenditures remain sensitive to business cycle variations, and countercyclicality is still the characteristic principle of the evolution during short-term economically adverse contexts. Social expenditures thus play their full role in income stabilisation through public transfer policies.

Since the 1980s, however, new trends have somewhat modified the historically accumulated findings on business cycles. First, while the countercyclicality of social expenditures during phases of business-cycle slowdown is still confirmed, it now intervenes over shorter periods. More rapid cuts in income support programmes during crisis phases reflect faster recourse to the labour market to maintain the income of the populations and limit the time frame of the social effort.

Second, the emergence of the acyclical behaviour of certain social expenditures supports the hypothesis formulated in the late 1980s. Two of these expenditures, education and healthcare, are particularly insensitive to the fluctuations in activity manifested by the business cycle. On this point, the temporality of the business cycle converges with that of the long period. This convergence lends substance to the hypothesis advanced by the endogenous growth and *régulation* theories that social spending assumes an increasing role in economic growth and performance through the qualitative development of the labour force and thus also promotes this quality through better living standards. In the European countries, in spite of considerable national differences, these expenditures remain far from a market regulation. Their organisation as a growth engine thus reflects the fact that they cannot be separated from the institutional arrangements permitting their organisation and the fact that they stem from the democratic vitality of the social compromises which have historically shaped them.

The hypothesis advanced at the end of the 1980s has not been completely verified in that social expenditures as a whole cannot be assimilated to a growth engine. It must be recognised, nevertheless, that some of them – in particular, education and healthcare – support that hypothesis, as well as the fact that the growth of the advanced economies now depends on them. Consequently, the question of improvements in the efficiency of the institutional mechanisms through which these expenditures are organised and contribute to growth remains part of debates on the ways social spending influences growth.

Note

1 The French term *régulation* as used here does not refer to politico-legal 'regulation' in the English sense, but rather the 'regularisation' or 'normalisation' of economic activities through economic and extra-economic mechanisms (Jessop and Sum 2006: 4). Following the English translation of Robert Boyer and Yves Saillard's overview, *Régulation Theory: The State of the Art* (Boyer and Saillard 2002), we have left *régulation* in French to indicate the original term.

References

Adema, W., Fron, P. and Ladaique, M. (2011): Is the European Welfare State Really More Expensive? Indicators on Social Spending, 1980–2012 and a Manual to the *OECD Social Expenditure Database* (SOCX). *OECD Social, Employment and Migration Working Papers*, No. 124. http://dx.doi.org/10.1787/5kg2d2d4pbf0-en.

Afonso, A. and Jalles, J. T. (2013): The Cyclicality of Education, Health and Social Security Government Spending. *Applied Economics Letters*, 20 (7): 669–672.

Aglietta, M. (2000 [1976]): *A Theory of Capitalist Regulation: The US Experience*. London: Verso Classics.

Aglietta, M. and Brender, A. (1984): *Les métamorphoses de la société salariale*. Paris: Calmann-Lévy.

Amable, B. (2017): *Structural Crisis and Institutional Change in Modern Capitalism: French Capitalism in Transition*. Oxford: Oxford University Press.

André, C. (2002): The Welfare State and the Institutional Compromises: From Origins to Contemporary Crisis. In: *Regulation Theory: The State of the Art*, edited by R. Boyer and Y. Saillard. London and New York: Routledge, 94–100.

Arze del Granado, J., Gupta, S. and Hajdenberg, A. (2010): Is Social Spending Pro-Cyclical? *International Monetary Fund*, WP/10/234, Fiscal Affairs Department.

Atkinson, T. (2005): *Improvements in the Methodology for Measuring Government Output*. London: Office for National Statistics.

Atkinson, T. (2016): *Inequality*. Cambridge, MA: Harvard University Press.

Bakija, J., Kenworthy, L., Lindert, P. and Madrick, J. (2016): *How Big Should Our Government Be?* Oakland: University of California Press.

Barbier, J.-C. (2013): *The Road to Social Europe*. London and New York: Routledge.

Barr, N. (1992): Economic Theory and the Welfare State: A Survey and Interpretation. *Journal of Economic Literature*, 30 (2): 741–803.

Billaudot, B., Granou, A. and Baron, Y. (1979): *Croissance et crise*. Paris: Maspéro.

Bird, R. M. (1972): The Displacement Effect: A Critical Note, *Finanzarchiv*, 30 (3): 454–463.

Boccara, P. (2013): *Théories sur les crises. La suraccumulation et la dévalorisation du capital*, Vol. 1. Paris: Delga.

Boyer, R. (1979): Wage Formation in Historical Perspective: The French Experience. *Cambridge Journal of Economics*, 3 (2): 99–118.

Boyer, R. (1990 [1986]): *The Regulation School: A Critical Introduction*. New York: Columbia University Press.

Boyer, R. and Saillard, Y. (2002): *Regulation Theory: The State of the Art*. London and New York: Routledge.

Boyer, R. (2015): *Economie politique des capitalismes: Théorie de la régulation et des crises*. Paris: La Découverte, Grands Repères.

Carpentier, V. (2003): Public Expenditure on Education and Economic Growth in the UK, 1833–2000. *History of Education*, 32 (1): 1–15.

Castel, R. (2003): *From Manual Workers to Wage Laborers: Transformation of the Social Question*. New Brunswick, NJ: Transaction Publishers.

Dabla-Norris, E., Kochhar, K., Suphaphiphat, N., Frantisek Ricka, F. and Tsounta, E. (2015): *Causes and Consequences of Income Inequality: A Global Perspective*. IMF Staff Discussion Note: SND/15/13, International Monetary Fund, June.

d'Addio, A. C. (2015): The Dynamics of Social Expenditures over the Cycle: A Comparison across OECD Countries. *OECD Journal: Economic Studies*, 2015/1. http://dx.doi.org/10.1787/eco_studies-2015-5jrs63lpkmxr.

Darby, J. and Melitz, J. (2008): Social Spending and Automatic Stabilizers in the OECD. *Economic Policy*, October: 715–756.

Diebolt, C. (1997): L'évolution de longue période du système éducatif Allemand XIXème et XXème siècles. *Economies et Sociétés*, Série AF, 23: 2–305.

Escudero, V. and Lopez Mourelo, E. (2017): The Employment Effect of Changes in the Composition of Fiscal Consolidations. *International Review of Applied Economics*, 31 (1). http://dx.doi.org/10.1080/02692171.2016.1221388.

Esping-Andersen, G. (1990): *The Three Worlds of Welfare Capitalism*. Cambridge: Polity Press and Princeton, NJ: Princeton University Press.

Flavin, P., Pacek, A. and Radcliff, B. (2014): Assessing the Impact of the Size and Scope of Government on Human Well-Being. *Social Forces*, 92 (4): 1241–1258. https://doi.org/10.1093/sf/sou010.

Fontvieille, L. (1990): Education, Growth and Long Cycles: The Case of France in the 19th and 20th Centuries. In: *Education and Economic Development since the Industrial Revolution*, edited by G. Tortella. Valencia: Generalitat Valenciana, 317–335.

Fontvieille, L. (1999): Long Cycle Theory: Dialectical and Historical Analysis. In *The Foundation of Long Waves Theory*, edited by F. Louçà and J. Reijnders. Cheltenham: Edward Elgar Publishing, 314–342.

Glomm, G. and Ravikumar, B. (1997): Productive Government Expenditures and Long-Run Growth. *Journal of Economic Dynamics and Control*, 21: 183–204.

Harvey, D. (1982): *The Limits to Capital*. Oxford: Basil Blackwell.

INSEE. (2009): *Survey of Existing Approaches to Measuring Socio-Economic Progress*. www.insee.fr/fr/publications-et-services/dossiers_web/stiglitz/doccommission/Survey_of_Existing_Approaches_to_Measuring_Socio-Economic_Progress.pdf.

Jany-Catrice, F. and Méda, D. (2013): Well-Being and the Wealth of Nations. How Are They to Be Defined? *Review of Political Economy*, 25 (3): 444–460.

Jessop, B. and Sum, N. (2006): *Beyond the Regulation Approach: Putting Capitalist Economies in Their Place*. Cheltenham: Edward Elgar.

Karabarbounis, L. and Neiman, B. (2014): The Global Decline of the Labor Share. *The Quarterly Journal of Economics*, 129 (1): 61–103.

Labrousse, A. and Michel, S. (2017): Accumulation Regimes. In *Routledge Handbook of Heterodox Economics*, edited by T.-H. Jo, L. Chester and C. D'Ippoliti. London and New York: Routledge, 54–69.

Lindert, P. H. (2004): *Growing Public: Social Spending and Economic Growth since the Eighteenth Century*. Cambridge: Cambridge University Press.

Lucas, R. (1988): On the Mechanics of Economic Development. *Journal of Monetary Economics*, 22: 3–42.

Marx, K. (1894): *Capital*, 3. www.marxists.org/archive/marx/works/download/pdf/Capital-Volume-III.pdf, accessed 15 January 2016.

Mazier, X., Baslé, M. and Vidal, D. (1999): *When Economic Crises Endure*. New York: Sharpe.

Michel, S. (1999): *Education et croissance économique en longue période*. Paris: L'Harmattan.

Michel, S. (2017): Social Spending: Its Role in Recovery Processes and beyond: Arguments from the 19th to Mid-20th Centuries. In *Business Cycles in Economic Thought*, edited by A. Alcouffe, M. Poettinger and B. Shefold. London and New York: Routledge, 129–142.

Michel, S. and Vallade, D. (2007): Une Analyse de long terme des dépenses sociales. *Revue de la Régulation*, 1, June, http://regulation.revues.org/1507.

Michel, S. and Vallade, D. (2010): Financement des dépenses sociales: les apports d'une analyse de long terme. *Economie Appliquée*, 63 (3): 73–114.

Monnier, A. (2006): *Démographie contemporaine de l'Europe*. Paris: Armand Colin: Collection U.

Moulier-Boutang, Y. (2011): *Cognitive Capitalism*. Cambridge, UK: Polity Press.

Myrdal, G. (1960): *Beyond the Welfare State*. London: Gerald Duckworth & Co.

Nagarajan, R., Teixeira, A. and Silva, S. (2017): The Impact of Population Ageing on Economic Growth: A Bibliometric Survey. *The Singapore Economic Review*, 62 (2). https://doi.org/10.1142/S021759081550068X.

Nervole, M., Razin, A., Sadka, E. and Von Weizsacher, R. (1993): Comprehensive Income Taxation, Investments in Human Capital, and Productivity. *Journal of Public Economics*, 50: 397–406.

Nolan, B. (2013): What Use Is 'Social Investment'? *Journal of European Social Policy*, 23 (5): 459–468.

OECD. (2014): 'Social Expenditure Update – Social spending is falling in some countries, but in many others it remains at historically high levels', available at www.oecd.org/els/soc/OECD2014-SocialExpenditure_Update19Nov_Rev.pdf.

Peacock, A. T. and Wiseman, J. (1961): *The Growth of Public Expenditure in the United Kingdom*. NBER, General Series no. 72. Princeton, NJ: Princeton University Press. www.nber.org/chapters/c2302

Ranis, G., Stewart, F. and Ramirez, F. (2000): Economic Growth and Human Development. *World Development*, 28 (2): 197–219.

Razin, A. and Sadka, E. (2005): *The Decline of the Welfare State*. Cambridge, MA: MIT Press.

Romer, P. (1986): Increasing Returns and Long-Run Growth. *Journal of Political Economy*, 94 (5): 1002–1037.

Rowley, C. K and Tollison, R. D. (1994): Peacock and Wiseman on the Growth of Public Expenditure. *Public Choice*, 19: 125–128.

Solow, R. (1956): A Contribution to the Theory of Economic Growth. *The Quarterly Journal of Economics*, 70 (1): 65–94.

Wagner, A. (1883): Three Extracts on Public Finance. In (1958) *Classics in the Theory of Public Finance*, edited by R. A. Musgrave and A. T. Peacock. London: Macmillan, 1–15.

Part III

Economic thought and political confrontation

7 The influence of ordoliberalism in the European integration processes, with the Eurozone crisis as a case

Peter Nedergaard

Introduction

Are there any linkages between ordoliberalism and how the Eurozone crisis evolved and was tackled by decision-makers? This is the overarching question addressed in this chapter. In the scholarly literature, ordoliberalism (OL) and the Freiburg School[1] are generally recognized as a powerful economic philosophy framing the thought of post-World War II German political decision-makers (Berghahn and Young 2013; Bonefeld 2012; Feld et al. 2015; Goldschmidt and Rauchenschwandtner 2007; Vanberg 2004; Walters and Haahr 2005).

More recently, OL would appear to have acquired renewed relevance stemming from a postulated relationship between OL and the politics of the Eurozone crisis in the European Union (EU). Reference was made to OL to explain the apparent rigorism of the German-led crisis policy (Beck and Kotz 2017b; Biebricher and Vogelmann 2017a; Blyth 2013; Nedergaard and Snaith 2015). At the same time, the research community has also been warned against exaggerating the influence of OL in the European integration processes in general and in the Eurozone crisis in particular (Feld et al. 2017; Joerges 2017; Oksala 2017). The more precise aim of this chapter is therefore to provide a nuanced account of how the Eurozone crisis evolved and the attempts to solve it by European decision-makers, with Germany in the lead and with OL as a theoretical prism in order to determine whether this prism makes the developments and initiatives more understandable. In this regard, as in social constructivist philosophy, I assume that all types of policies are always embedded in certain ideas. Political facts and ideational factors are thus inseparable.

One could argue that if and when traces of OL are found, they are merely signs of German influence resulting from it probably being the most powerful EU member state (at least in recent years). This might be true even though (as shown in the following) there is far from a 1:1 correspondence between the actual German government positions and the normative recommendations of OL. Despite the fact that potential German interest promotion is largely what I find, I will argue that such interest promotion is hardly distinguishable from the influence of OL due to the fact that, according to German decision-makers, OL as a solution to the Eurozone crisis was and is in theory (but as already mentioned – not always in practice) in the interest of both Germany as well as Europe as a whole (Nedergaard and Snaith 2015). A possible consequence of this view is that there is no difference between the economic well-being of Germany and that of the Eurozone if and when they apply OL; whether this view is the whole truth is another matter.

In other accounts of the Eurozone crisis, it is either postulated that OL has hardly had any influence at all on the development of and attempts to solve the crisis due to it being all about German interests (Feld et al. 2017; Young 2017b), or that OL has had strong, detrimental influence on the crisis, causing austerity in the southern EU member states (Blyth 2013; Schmidt 2017). My position is somewhere in the middle. I agree that OL is an integrated part of the belief system of German decision-makers and, as such, has had significant influence on the attempts to solve the Eurozone crisis; however, the evolution of the Eurozone crisis and subsequent austerity is not the result of too much OL influence but rather too little (with some caveats) due to the fact that insufficient emphasis was invested in the efforts to bring about comprehensive compliance with OL recommendations as a result of inadequate support from Germany itself.

A second section analysing the ideational framework of OL is presented, followed by a third section analysing OL in relation to European integration processes in which the Eurozone is an integrated part. The fourth section is an analysis of OL in relation to the Eurozone crisis, and the conclusions are presented in the final section.

The ideational framework of OL

Two groups of principles are involved in OL: the fundamental constitutive principles concerning the polity of society, and the day-to-day regulative principles concerning policies of society. In both cases, the main instrument is law, but not only law. The constitutive principles (should) consist of a constitution of the economic order that was the basic framework of all of the economic activities of society. The regulative principles consist of the maintenance of the functioning of the competitive order and process, ensuring that the economic order functions with a workable price system (Eucken 1952). The original idea in OL is the specific relationship between these two sets of principles. Later in the chapter, I will analyse how this relationship is played out in relation to the Eurozone crisis.

History is important to OL. It needs to be mentioned that OL is a theoretical school of German origin, the most prominent representative of which is the late professor of economics, Walter Eucken (1891–1950) (Hutchinson 1981). The first generation of OL scholars also included Franz Böhm, Hans Grossmann-Doerth, Alexander Rüstow, and Wilhelm Röpke, who together formed the core personnel who created the ordoliberal tradition. They claimed that in OL only interdisciplinary science is capable of developing an accurate analysis of modern society. At the same time, according to OL, social science must be practical in the sense of a responsibility to inform political decision-making (Biebricher and Vogelmann 2017b).

According to Praet (2017, p. 80), '[t]he influence of ordoeconomics on Germany's post-war economic order, its social market economy and monetary stability, can hardly be exaggerated'. The influence of OL on contemporary top German decision-makers was also confirmed in a series of interviews conducted in 2014 (see Nedergaard and Snaith 2015), even though this was often a crude version of OL (Wyplotz 2017). Still others describe OL as a strong policy preference in Germany (Burda 2017). This is not to say, however, that other economic schools (e.g. Keynesianism) are not present and have influence in German academia and among economic experts (Feld et al. 2017). On the contrary, the German Council of Economic Experts (which advises German governments) explicitly takes Keynesian views into account (Schmidt 2017).

This chapter focusses on the impact of OL. In the ideal OL world, the state never intrudes directly into economic processes; it merely adjusts the so-called economic constitution (Biebricher and Vogelmann 2017b). OL is a profoundly rules-based economic philosophy reconstructed in a concrete economic constitution. There are significant differences between economic and political constitutions. The technical aspects of an economic constitution are proportionally far larger than in a political constitution, which is much more moral in character (Böhm 1937). The basic idea set out in the 'birth certificate' of OL – the Ordo Manifesto of 1936 (Eucken et al. 1936) – was that OL was to be established as a common interdisciplinary agenda of analysis of the totality of society (later labelled the 'interdependence' of economic, legal, political, and social orders).

The theoretical background of OL was the so-called *Methodenstreit* between historical-inductive and abstractive-deductive approaches in the social sciences. The manifesto almost exclusively chides historicism for its inability to generate general and robust knowledge and was criticized for relativism. The OL scholars insisted on principled thinking, whereas the National Socialist regime (1933–1945) viewed historicism rather favourably. A result hereof was the discretionary arbitrariness of the National Socialist economic policy (see Figure 7.1).

OL was also against the theoretical fatalism of Marxism, whereby techno-economic development was the sole determinant of historical progress. OL saw this as a sign of weakness on the part of certain intellectuals. Instead, OL emphasized the role of science in the policy process to secure the objective judgement independent of immediate economic interests of the actors in the actual political decision-making (Eucken et al. 1936). At the same time, it is important to be mindful of how, according to Eucken (in the OL's economic policy Bible: *Grundsätze der Wirtschaftspolitik*, i.e. Principles of the Economic Policy), economic policy can never be divorced from the historical context of individual nations.

OL also appears to be an essentially German 'invention'. Not many direct influences from other sources can be discerned in early OL, aside from minor influences from the Austrian School of Economics (with Ludwig van Mises and Friedrich A. von Hayek as leading figures) (Vanberg 2004). Ludwig Erhard, the father of the German *Wirtschaftswunder* and former minister of finance, Bundeskanzler, and economics professor, was an explicit proponent of the original OL framework (Hutchinson 1981).

At the same time, OL as a German economic philosophy has evolved over the years since its foundation and been influenced by other ideas. In recent decades, OL has been in dialogue with constitutional economics á la James Buchanan (Beck and Kotz 2017b), public choice theory (Wyplotz 2017), supply side economics (Burda 2017) and monetarism (Young 2017b). At least in Germany itself, the assumption is that the excellent economic performance and position of Germany since World War II have given weight to the ideas behind OL in terms of how various EU policies were constructed and have developed (Dullien and Guérot 2012; Goldschmidt and Rauchenschwandtner 2007; Vanberg 2004; Winkler 2017). While OL has always represented a broad liberal persuasion in political terms, its influence in Germany extends beyond the liberal-conservative political parties (e.g. FDP, CSU, CDU); according to Dullien and Guérot (2012), social democratic SPD and the Green Party are also influenced by OL.

It is of crucial importance that result in the economic constitution through the so-called 'politics of ordering' (a translation of a concept not so easy to translate): *Ordnungspolitik*[2] does not intervene explicitly into markets but must only be directed at market frameworks. The general maxim of an active Ordnungspolitik is to restore and safeguard the price system in the competitive order and process at all levels and in all areas of the economic constitution (Biebricher and Vogelmann 2017b).[3] Ordnungspolitik is (or should be) related to an economic constitution in the sense that it is the basis upon which Ordnungspolitik establishes a new political order.

To use football (or soccer) metaphors: The economic constitution is the rules of the game (the length of the field, dimensions of the goals, definition of off-side, duration of the game, etc.). These are the constitutive principles. The politics of ordering is how the teams play the game (offensive, defensive, 4–2–3–1 system, etc.) as decided by the coach (i.e. politicians and experts) within the frame of the constitutive principles. The overall objective is to be able to rely on matches being played in the long term according to the rules and based on fair play; that is, in accordance with the competitive order and process that are the decisions concerning regulative principles taken by the referee. The strong state of OL (cf. ahead) implies national and international football federations strong enough to sanction violations of both constitutive and regulative principles.

OL is both an analytical theory and a political programme (Vanberg 2004) (i.e. contains both the rules of the game as well as recommendations concerning strategy). It is strongly focused on explicit and rigorous rules as the preferred technique of economic governance and warns against discretionary initiatives. The preferred perspective of OL is the long term.

As mentioned, the primary result of Eucken's system of constitutive principles is the construction of a proper market with a well-functioning price system (Eucken 1952; Feld et al. 2017). The market is defined by its institutional set-up and, as such, subject to the choices made by potential decision-makers. In other words, an economic order based on an economic constitution is subject to human design and decision-making (i.e. an economic constitution can be changed). This anti-naturalistic assumption regarding the market is normally in contrast to laissez-faire liberals, for whom the market often seems to be an (almost) natural economic reality (Walters and Haahr 2005). Conversely, according to OL, decision-makers are responsible for actively creating conditions in the form of economic constitutions under which the proverbial 'invisible hand' can be expected to function (Vanberg 2004).

At the level of regulative principles, monetary policy decisions in accordance with Ordnungspolitik are concerned with initiatives to secure price stability[4] and central bank independence (Dyson 2009). These are key elements in establishing order in the monetary field (Dullien and Guérot 2012). According to Eucken, the constitutive and regulative principles are interconnected in this regard because an independent central bank should have a mandate for which price stability is dominant (Feld et al. 2017).

Here, one might imagine that specific German historical experience with hyperinflation was the sole reason for Germany's anti-inflationary policy as opposed to being the ideational influence of OL. However, many other European countries, including Greece, Italy, and Austria (countries without a rules-based economic-philosophical tradition, á la OL), have experienced hyperinflation but do not traditionally share the intense German fear of inflation (Dullien and Guérot 2012). This falsifies the hypothesis that the specific German historical context is the sole explanation of the German position on EU economic policies and strengthens the hypothesis that ideational frames are also at play.

As mentioned, OL is critical of laissez-faire liberalism. Eucken generally considered laissez-faire economic liberalism to be incompatible with the rule of law (*Rechtsstaat*), as this form of liberalism is without order and therefore always potentially threatens to harm society as a whole (e.g. via cartels and monopolies) (Hutchinson 1981). On the other end of the spectrum, interventionism also contradicts the principle of the rule of law, as it does not see the market as a common ground where actors can meet on an equal basis (see also Figure 7.1).

Consequently, Eucken was also highly critical of Keynesian interventionism and its notion that expansionary macroeconomic fiscal policy should solve the economic crises and achieve full employment. He regarded Keynesianism as a theory without Ordnungspolitik in the sense that it set no limits on how expansionary fiscal policy could be (Eucken 1940). Thus, there was always a serious risk of Keynesianism entailing permanent public deficits, as per custom in the National Socialist regime.[5] According to Eucken, the state should never be responsible for ensuring full employment, as such. Through stable and predictable economic policy, however, political decision-makers should provide the framework to make full employment attainable (Eucken 1952).

As already mentioned, according to OL, a free market is not simply that which one would find in the absence of government. According to OL, free market forces require careful 'cultivation' and maintenance to function properly (Vanberg 2004) (cf. previous about the construction of markets). Ordoliberals therefore use a gardening metaphor for what political decision-makers should do vis-à-vis the market: They should control undesired growth (Böhm 1937). In contrast, laissez-faire liberals typically used the night watchman metaphor (i.e. political decision-makers should only light up the night). In turn, interventionist state theorists typically refer to an engineering metaphor (cf. the concept of social engineering). There is almost an implicit Hegelian schema involved in the OL reasoning about this development: thesis (laissez-faire), anti-thesis (interventionism), and synthesis (OL) (see Figure 7.1).

At the level of regulative principles, according to Eucken, Ordnungspolitik first and foremost implies a policy aimed at securing a competitive order and process that works to the benefit of consumer interests. It should always pursue consumer sovereignty to the greatest possible extent (Vanberg 2004), because the consumer is a representative of the common interest in the ordoliberal philosophy, to which the OL 'state gardener' should always attend. The consumer is the actor towards whom all economic political decision-making should be directed (Eucken 1952).

Consequently, Eucken demanded a 'strong state' if and when OL should function as a political programme (Bonefeld 2012). Rather than a big-scope state, this is a state that is strong enough to protect 'the competitive order' (Eucken 1952). The robust and non-discretionary rules of an OL state also meant that technocrats were shielded from special interests (Beck and Kotz 2017c). Hence, the role of the state in Figure 7.1.

Generally, according to OL, the functioning of the competitive order and process cannot be entrusted to market mechanisms on their own, nor can the economy be entrusted to state intervention on a more or less permanent basis. Eucken stressed that the strong state should be responsible for creating a stable monetary policy and avoiding large public deficits. This is in contrast to the lean state promoted by modern neoliberalism (Beck and Kotz 2017b). The OL principles also differ from Keynesian demand management, which is where OL has been criticized for being old-fashioned in its rejection of any macroeconomic stabilizing intervention (Beck and Kotz 2017b). In post-World War II Germany, the government has also used the macroeconomic Keynesian stabilization instrument to some degree in times of economic crisis and unemployment, albeit less so than in other Western European countries (Schmidt 2017).

At the same time, the ideal OL state is also strong enough to be able to prevent the government from becoming the target of (in more modern public-choice parlance) special interests' rent-seeking activities (Vanberg 2004). This is in contrast to an interventionist strong state seeking permanently to intervene in the competitive order and process on behalf of sectorial interests, national pride, industrial policy concerns, and so forth (Clift 2008).

The notion that a strong state should act as guardian of the competitive order and process stands in contrast to liberalism as represented by Hayek (1960), in as

		Control over the 'economic order' via constitutive principles	
Control over the 'competitive order and process' via regulative principles		Private	State
	Private	Laissez-faire capitalism	Ordoliberal economy
	State	Crony capitalism with an interventionist state	State planning (Soviet economy, National Socialist economy)

Figure 7.1 An OL taxonomy of economic systems

Source: Zettelmeyer (2017), based on Eucken (1952)

much as he stressed that 'the method of specific orders and prohibitions' (which might be necessary for the 'cultivation' of the market forces, according to OL) is ruled out, as a matter of principle, by the laissez-faire liberal or neoliberal concept of 'spontaneous market order'. In other words, the freedom of contract (which was hailed by Hayek) cannot be accepted by ordoliberals to undermine the market through, for example, cartel agreements and beggar-thy-neighbour devaluations (Eucken 1952; Vanberg 2004). In contrast to this view on cartel agreements, one of the founding fathers of neoliberalism,[6] Murray Rothbard, sees no reason to object to cartel contracts. From his perspective, they are nothing but voluntary contracts among producers (Vanberg 2004, p. 12): 'To regard a cartel as immoral or hampering some sort of consumer sovereignty is therefore completely unwarranted' (Rothbard 1970, p. 570).

Figure 7.1 shows a matrix with the various economic models discussed in the section above. The two dimensions of the matrix are control over the 'economic order' via constitutive principles and control over the 'competitive order and process' via regulative principles.

OL and European economic integration processes

Since OL has been such a strong economic philosophy in Germany, one might expect it to have an impact on the EU economic integration processes, as well. Christian Joerges has pointed out that the Treaty of the European Community (EC) of 1958 has some OL elements based on a key idea that the treaty should establish 'the interdependence of a system of undistorted competition, individual freedoms and the rule of law – and protect this precious balance against discretionary political influence' (cited in Oksala 2017, p. 191). In other words, if we accept this claim, the EU is to a certain extent a political system of rules-based and non-discretionary Ordnungspolitik (Young 2017a). While this does not mean that the EU has suddenly come to 'conform to the ordoliberal play work in its entirety' (cited in Oksala 2017, p. 190), one should be open to the possibility that OL forms a pervasive rules-based way of German thinking that has also influenced European economic integration.

Michel Foucault (2008) also mentioned the influence of OL on European economic integration processes, claiming that OL broke with the preceding tradition of liberalism in denying that the political consequence of free markets should be laissez-faire. He saw OL as the earliest form of neoliberalism (and different from Chicago School neoliberalism) (see endnote 6). Generally, according to Foucault, OL rethought the relations between economy and politics, which in the EU can be seen in how the Common Agricultural Policy is designed regarding both its constitutive and regulative principles (Foucault 2008).

Hence, one *could* postulate that the European Economic Community forms a European economic constitution and a new transnational order that is attractive for OL. Nevertheless, this postulate is first and foremost an ex post rationalization. A much more influential line of thought in the 1950s was planification, which was a commonplace governance idea among the EU member states in all sectors of the economy. Jean Monnet, the founding father of the EC and greatest source of ideational inspiration in the early years of the EU, was director of the French Planning Commission (Young 2017a). The long-term perspective and non-discretionary character of the EU stems more from this tradition than from OL. At the same time, other sources claim that OL did influence the institutions of the original EC (Joerges 2017).

In addition, there *were* similarities between OL and the regulative principles of the economic integration process right from the beginning of European integration processes after World War II. From early on, the EC's integration initiatives placed a premium on principles, frameworks, and rules. This is not least found in the undistorted competition of European economic integration processes seen after the Internal Market since the mid-1980s has become the most richly developed aspect of the EU (Nedergaard 2013). The Internal Market has also increased depoliticization in the EU. More specifically, this means that many basic EU economic policy decisions are effectively removed from democratic decision-making, executed instead through legal instruments and by unelected economic experts and bureaucrats (á la Eucken's recommendations in 1952, cf. previous). In that sense, it is no accident that both OL and the EU are often met with the same criticism; namely, that of being authoritarian liberal constitutionalism in disguise (Young 2017a, 2017b).

There are numerous indications that both the Single European Act (with the Internal Market) and the Maastricht Treaty (with the European Monetary Union [EMU]) were conceptualized with OL in mind among many (not least German) decision-makers, and they were inspired by the rules-versus-discretion debate herein (Young 2017a). Nonetheless, the EU's Maastricht Treaty with the EMU was severely criticized by OL advocates for being too imprecise as an OL economic constitution and with inadequate sanctions (Feld et al. 2017). As far as the EMU (which is most relevant for the Eurozone crisis) is concerned, on 1 January 2002, the euro was physically introduced as the currency of 12 of the then 15 EU member states: Germany, France, Italy, Belgium, Luxembourg, the Netherlands, Ireland, Greece (one year later), Spain,

Portugal, Austria, and Finland. This was promptly followed by the introduction of low German interest rates in many Southern European member states, which resulted in booming consumer spending and construction (the balance between the two varying from country to country).

In accordance with OL, the EMU was established with the aim of low inflation. This is an important accession criterion and part of the statutes of the European Central Bank (ECB), which was the institution with the sole responsibility for the EMU monetary policy. The statute about low inflation was a strong demand from German decision-makers. The ECB pursues a monetary policy inflation objective of below, but very close to, 2 per cent. It also reflected the statute of the German Bundesbank, where low inflation has always been the order of the day. In that sense, the ECB is akin to a Bundesbank writ large (Beck and Kotz 2017b). Generally, an independent central bank for which the mandate of price stability is dominant, and with a no-bailout requirement that supposedly ensures an alignment of liability and control, are examples of how two of Eucken's constitutive principles – the primacy of currency policy (i.e. low inflation) and the liability principle – are implemented in EMU (Feld et al. 2017).

The ECB objective of price stability is an expression of an ordoliberal recommendation on monetary policy that coincides with monetarism. OL, however, came first in temporal terms. Monetarism only became an international trendsetting economic theory 25–30 years after OL had inspired the Western German economic model. No matter what, monetarism further strengthened the ordoliberal agenda in the making of the EMU and its guidelines, even though the sanctions were forgotten or put aside for political reasons (cf. ahead).

According to its statutes, the ECB is not assumed to play the role of 'lender of last resort', as central banks in nation-states otherwise often do. In principle, this can be seen as an ordoliberal guarantee against non-ordoliberal and discretionary disorder in an EMU with many intergovernmentalist traits. As shown ahead, however, the Eurozone crisis has cast doubt on this guarantee. Even though the ECB is an independent central bank, as recommended by Eucken, there have also been many attempts to put political pressure on the ECB board. This seems to be an essential part of the life of an institution like the ECB – especially in a political system like the EU – which is neither a unitary nation-state-based political system nor a real federal political system (Gabor 2012). This has not been the worst threat to the OL character of the ECB.

Some of the internal EMU causes contributing to the financial crisis since 2008 related to the design of the EMU (see also the next section). In the Maastricht Treaty, in accordance with OL, the EMU accession criteria consisted primarily of the required maximum 60 per cent of accumulated government debt-to-GDP-ratio and a maximum annual public budget deficit of 3 per cent of GDP. In principle, these were rules-based, non-discretionary, and anti-Keynesian criteria for public expenditures.

In order to ensure that the criteria were met after EMU accession, the Stability and Growth Pact was adopted after pressure from German decision-makers based on German experiences with federalism (Wyplotz 2017). The Maastricht

Treaty accession requirements thus became permanent, which was not least due to more countries joining the EMU than Germany, in particular, had envisioned. The Stability and Growth Pact was intended to ensure that these countries practised responsible economic policy in the OL sense of the concept. There are many indications that Germany had imagined that the EMU would initially consist solely of Germany, France, the Netherlands, Belgium, Luxembourg, and Denmark; that is, countries with economic policy not too dissimilar from that of Germany (Nello 2012, p. 224).

According to Wyplosz (2006, p. 217), the EMU basically reflected a German economic-philosophical view (i.e. OL). In practice, however, when the initial decision was taken in 1998 on which EU member states could join the euro, the first part of the German defence of the OL principles was lost, and many more EU states gained access to the EMU than envisioned (cf. previous). Hence, the problems of the future Eurozone crisis were created, with (not least) the Southern European member states causing problems. The second part of the German defence of the OL principles was abandoned when the regulative principles of the Stability and Growth Pact proved unenforceable due to a lack of robust German support; the rules-based system likely grew worse than had there been no rules at all (Beck and Kotz 2017c) (see ahead for a more detailed account of this second part of the lost defence of the OL principles of the pact).

The rather casual final interpretation of which countries were able to fulfil the EMU accession criteria probably owed much to the weakness of the German economy at the very moment when EU decision-makers were making membership decisions, Germany having huge public deficits at the time. In other words, Germany itself could not live up to the OL prescripts, which seriously undermined the German authority, and more member states were allowed to join the EMU.

The Stability and Growth Pact implied that the EcoFin[7] was continuously assessing the performance of the EMU countries to ensure compliance with the prescribed rules. In the event of drastic increases in unemployment, for example, the EcoFin could choose to accept the violation of rules.[8] In other cases, it could sanction non-complying countries with an interest-free deposit or fine.

The Stability and Growth Pact was originally introduced in response to German convictions regarding the need for a rules-based system that would ensure the coordination of budgetary policies (Heipertz and Verdun 2010; Nello 2012). Hence, the Stability and Growth Pact offered opportunity to continuously discipline the fiscal and economic policy of member states (Feld et al. 2017). Nevertheless, despite there having been numerous violations of the Stability and Growth Pact since its introduction, sanctions have yet to be enforced. In a rules-based OL perspective, this is a fundamental weakness of the EMU and has led to the delegitimization of its economic constitution (namely, the Maastricht Treaty and the Pact) since the Eurozone crisis.

There are numerous examples of short-term decisions taken by EMU decision-makers regarding the Eurozone economic and monetary policy, the worst probably being the annulment of sanctions against Germany and France and other member states for violating the Stability and Growth Pact (see ahead). Generally and in practice, short-term interventions have often prevailed over long-term ordoliberal recommendations. Breaking the Stability and Growth Pact rules soon became the order of the day. As a side effect, the de facto suspension of the Stability and Growth Pact in 2003 (intended to avoid a clash with EMU's two largest countries) also led to pro-cyclical fiscal policies in many Southern European member states, which exacerbated the Eurozone crisis (Wyplotz 2017).

OL and the Eurozone crisis

The Eurozone crisis hit in 2008 and continued thereafter. While it was triggered by the international financial crisis originating in the United States, internal EMU factors also worsened the crisis. The foundation for how the crisis was tackled was laid from 2002, when the EU economy began slowing and the Stability and Growth Pact was criticized for being far too rigid.[9] As mentioned previously, by late 2002, the excessive deficit procedure had been initiated for Germany by the European Commission, aiming at potential sanctions in case there was no extraordinary economic crisis resulting in mass employment.

However, Germany (supported by France, which a bit later also became the target of the deficit procedure) favoured revising the (easily interpretable as ordoliberal) European Commission's recommendations to sanction violations of the Pact (Heipertz and Verdun 2010). This dispute caused a deadlock in EcoFin, as a qualified majority could not be found for a decision on sanctions. Instead, a qualified majority annulled the sanctions of the Stability and Growth Pact against France and Germany in 2003. The ECB warned against this de facto suspension of the pact and claimed that the suspension was against the ordoliberal line of regulative principles (even though I did not use these words) (Nello 2012, p. 240). The main problem in an OL perspective was that upholding the rules of the Stability and Growth Pact was fatally abandoned by Germany, which had traditionally been the great defender of these rules. Consequently, why should other member states adhere to the rules when Germany itself would not?

Greece had also already violated the pact at the time, and has continued to do so ever since. Italy, Austria, and Belgium also violated it in most of the years since the introduction of the euro. Member states were able to avoid sanctions because, as in the German case, there was no qualified majority in EcoFin to impose them. The economic constitution of the Maastricht Treaty and the Stability and Growth Pact were therefore increasingly considered to be too weak as an institutionalized structure to ensure the necessary harmonization of economic policies embedded in the EMU. This confirms the hypothesis that rules-based policies that are not enforced can do more harm than no rules at all.

The Eurozone crisis triggered a sharp increase in public debt in several Eurozone countries. Growth slowed, even shifting to negative growth, resulting in lower private demand (consumption, investment, and exports), which in turn led to lower public revenue, higher public expenditures, and increased public debt (Dullien and Guérot 2012). There was a clear negative spiral at work.

This signalled that the decision-makers in the Eurozone countries had not really internalized the OL belief system concerning economic policy, as expressed in German Chancellor Angela Merkel's speech in the Bundestag on 2 December 2011 during a debate on the Eurozone crisis: 'The lessons are very simple: Rules must be adhered to, adherence must be monitored, non-adherence must have consequences' (Beach 2013, p. 35) – words taken from Eucken's mouth. This was also a lesson for German decision-makers themselves, however, who had been at the forefront of non-adherence in 2003.

As a result of the constitutive and regulative principles of the EMU not being considered strong enough, the decision-making procedure on sanctions was tightened by a number of initiatives. The mode of legitimizing the 'Politics of Necessity' early in the Eurozone crisis was often due to moralism: The emphasis on personal responsibility, the moral of condemnation of debts (often in the 'name of our children'), or the rigorism with which it defended the absolute necessity of 'playing by the rules'. It became a categorical imperative that rules are to be adhered to (Biebricher and Vogelmann 2017b). However, this only produced unsatisfactory results. The institutional incentives of the economic constitution of the EMU also had to be considered carefully (Zettelmeyer 2017).

The cooperation on economic policy in the EU and EMU was therefore strengthened institutionally, beginning approximately in 2011, both with respect to constitutive and regulative principles. This increased cooperation took the shape of some comprehensive EU legal acts under the names 'Six-Pack' and 'Two-Pack' (proposed in 2010–2011 and implemented in 2011 and 2013, respectively), which involved automatic sanctions for violations of EMU rules, which became far more difficult to avoid than previously,[10] and through the decision that national budgets were to be discussed in the EcoFin before adoption (the so-called European semester). These initiatives increased the EU's influence on national fiscal policy. While the initiatives included all EU member states, only full EMU members could be fined. Finally, an intergovernmental agreement (the Fiscal Compact) was adopted. In this process during the Eurozone crisis, even former French President Nicholas Sarkozy began voicing his support for the ordoliberal line regarding public deficits (Sarkozy 2011).

At the same time, the creation of Eurobonds and other forms of collective liability for member states' debt continued to be rejected by Germany in particular, they believing that an introduction in the midst of the Eurozone crisis would only increase uncertainty and further damage credibility.[11] The Ordnungspolitik-basis of the European competitive order and process would thereby also be undermined due to the inherent moral hazard problems associated with Eurobonds, meaning that a country could increase its public debt at the expense of other EMU member states, as Eurobonds do not distinguish between the debt of individual member countries. Such a situation would contravene both the intergovernmentalist national interest of Germany by making the EU a 'transfer union' and the recommendations of OL, but it was also contrary to Eucken's (1952) principle of liability in an OL economic constitution. Again, as mentioned above, German national interests and OL are basically indistinguishable in practice. From an OL perspective, the Eurozone crisis was fundamentally a result of a domestic policy mistake that called for reforms; however, the southern EU member states were unwilling reformers except under heavy pressure (Zettelmeyer 2017).

Hence, the German rejection of joint liability and Germany's unwillingness to support the European Commission's proposal in 2011 to issue government Eurobonds jointly can easily be viewed as being rooted in OL. The link between the interest in an OL rule-based EMU and the German rejection of joint liability is undeniable.

The increased attention to debt avoidance during the Eurozone crisis in EU member states included focus on the rules-based policy of maintaining balanced budgets in the EU member states as part of the EU treaty (an idea of James Buchanan in line with OL); however, this failed due to – mainly British – resistance. Instead, as mentioned earlier, the Fiscal Compact was adopted as an international treaty in December 2011 to be ratified by 25 member states (i.e. the whole of the EU, except for the UK and Czech Republic).

The official title of the Fiscal Compact was 'Treaty on Stability, Coordination, and Governance in the Economic and Monetary Union'. The goal was to introduce stricter fiscal discipline in order to reduce public debt, thereby restoring confidence in the euro and the public finances of the EU member states, which was achieved by implementing stricter constitutive principles. In concrete terms, this was pursued through five stabilization initiatives, e.g. member states can have an annual structural deficit (i.e. deficit adjusted for the effect of cyclical fluctuations) of no more than 0.5 per cent of nominal GDP. Member states should also pursue the stabilization of the balance between government revenue and expenditure, which the European Court of Justice was granted authority to ensure was done (Fiscal Compact 2012). It is difficult not to see the Fiscal Compact as an OL dream come true. While it is an OL economic constitution, the Fiscal Compact is also a weaker constitution than if it had been integrated into the core of the EU Treaty. Still, as before, the soft spot has related to questions of whether sanctions would be imposed in the case of non-adherence to these rules.

The Fiscal Compact was accompanied by an international agreement (i.e. not a treaty) on a number of structural policy initiatives in the form of the Euro Plus Pact (initially the Competitiveness Pact, a Franco-German initiative) in which all of the Eurozone member states participated together with Denmark, Poland, Latvia, Lithuania, Bulgaria, and Romania. It was also suggested that the European finance minister should be strengthened and provided with the competence to overrule national budgets if in conflict with the Eurozone rules (Gabor 2012). The latter proposal was not adopted, but French President

Emanuel Macron has again put it on the table. A Eurozone finance minister would be a strong 'coach' regarding the Eurozone fiscal policies. All of the elements mentioned previously are constitutive elements of the EMU and signs of ordoliberal influence, as Keynesians would never recommend such institutions due to how they would unnecessarily bind financial policies in EU member states; the emergent economic constitutionalism of the EU is generally contrary to everything that Keynesianism stands for.

Furthermore, the EU has established two emergency funds that are exclusively available to and funded by Eurozone countries. The European Financial Standing Facility (EFSF) was established in the context of the Greek debt crisis and was supplemented by the permanent European Stability Mechanism (ESM) in 2012. These funds are to be activated if a member state is hit by an economic crisis and extraordinary public expenditure and deficits. However, it has been discussed in OL circles whether the ESM might also be a violation of the joint liability principle.

The backdrop for establishing the EFSF/ESM initiatives was the debt crisis in the so-called PIIGS countries (Portugal, Ireland, Italy, Greece, Spain) since 2008, the Greek crisis being the most severe. The debt crisis was monitored by the 'Troika': ECB, IMF, and European Commission. OL was behind the insistence with the terms of the rescue package for Greece and the refusal to consider further 'haircuts' for Greek debt than the one implemented so far, cf. ahead (Schmidt 2017). The OL liability principle also meant that there was no debt cutting (except, however, a haircut in Greece in one instance) or Eurobonds (not accepted by Germany but proposed by the Commission) to avoid moral hazard.

The rescue packages implied that important non-political actors and the technocratic aspects and expertise from the ECB, the IMF, and the European Commission were drawn into the reform processes, which also corresponds to strong faith in science in OL (Biebricher and Vogelmann 2017b). At the same time, approximately since 2011, Germany took a clear lead for the first time since the start of the European integration process (Wyplotz 2017).

The proposed banking union from 2012 constitutes yet another initiative for rebuilding the credibility of the EMU policy and institutions as a well-functioning economic constitution. The banking union consists of a European supervisory authority under the ECB. It is possible for non-euro countries to become members of the banking union, but given that the ECB is the parent authority, only euro countries will enjoy voting rights. The banking union includes a single bank resolution mechanism, a single rulebook, and possibly a common deposit protection mechanism. Concerning the banking union, Germany pushed for rules-based governance and quasi-automaticity, and Germany did not want to be made liable for past losses incurred by others member states' banks, which was in accordance with Eucken's *Haftungsprinzip* or liability principle (Beck and Kotz 2017c). Moreover, regarding the banking union, the liability principle guided German positions.

Nevertheless, pragmatism also characterized German policy through the Eurozone crisis. For example, the Greek rescue package included a regular haircut and the acceptance of the ECB's expansive monetary policy, including Outright Monetary Transactions (OMT). The acceptance of the haircut could also be explained by how several German banks were exposed to Greek public debt (Wyplotz 2017); however, most experts also viewed it as a necessary initiative to help Greece. At the same time, as mentioned, Germany rejected any proposed mutualization of government debt (Feld et al. 2017).

The ECB's balance sheet has generally taken a central role as a stabilizing instrument in several ways during the Eurozone crisis. First, in the aftermath of the bank-funding freeze precipitated by the Lehman Brothers crash in September 2008, the ECB provided essential funding liquidity to banks. Second, in response to the sovereign debt crisis that followed, the ECB initially launched the Securities Markets Programme and in 2012 announced OMT. Third, in 2014, further ECB credit easing was required. As of 2015, the ECB expanded its asset purchases into the sovereign space to reverse a continued shortfall of inflation relative to price stability (Praet 2017). Germany was critical and feared hyperinflation due to the ECB monetary policy, allegedly breaking its mandate through its asset purchase programme; however, the inflation never came. Nevertheless, Germany wanted the ECB to stick to OL principles, and German decision-makers had no focus on possible asymmetric information or market imperfections in the financial sector (Praet 2017).

The ECB's role changed during the Eurozone crisis in a way that was sometimes interpreted as being contrary to OL. For example, ECB bailouts in the form of national bond purchases (i.e. OMT) were hardly informed by OL. While ordoliberals criticized the OMT initiative aimed at purchasing bonds from member states, Germany accepted this deviation from OL.

The EMU has also had serious problems with its macroeconomic management since it was established. Domestic spending initially soared in much of Southern Europe, whereas the German economy hardly grew at all. The ECB was more or less powerless. Its monetary policy was simultaneously much too tight for Germany and much too loose for the periphery. According to the German OL belief system, any demand stimulus is viewed as killing off incentives to start structural reforms. The Southern European belief system viewed structural reforms as ineffective in a demand-constrained economy (Landmann 2017).

The ECB generally considered OL as a kind of 'in-house economic philosophy' of the bank;[12] however, the ECB also occasionally deliberately broken with the regulative principles of an imagined OL economic constitution. It seems thus far as though the ECB has had success in the short- and medium-term perspectives with this new balance between rules and discretion within an overall OL frame.

Conclusion

Are there any linkages between OL and how the Eurozone crisis evolved and was tackled by decision-makers? As mentioned in the beginning, this is the overarching question that has been addressed in this chapter.

The answer is that OL has informed the development of the Economic and Monetary Union, and later the Eurozone crisis and how it was tackled. In fact, many such problems were created long before the crisis by the fact that OL prescriptions on sanctions were generally not adhered to – not even by Germany itself. Here, more OL would have helped. From an orthodox OL perspective, the foundation of the Eurozone crisis was fundamentally a result of a domestic policy mistake that called for reforms; however, not least the Southern European member states were unwilling reformers.

When the Eurozone crisis began, however, the strict OL prescriptions demanded by Germany and others vis-á-vis Southern European member states exacerbated the crisis due to a lack of discretionary willingness. Germany bears major responsibility for this, due to its taking a clear lead in the EU from approximately 2011 and onwards for the first time since the start of the European integration process.

Numerous emergency funds were established to tackle the debt crisis in the PIIGS countries. OL was behind the insistence on the terms of the Greek rescue package and credit facilities for the other countries. The OL liability principle also meant that there was no debt cutting (except, however, a one-time haircut for Greece) or Eurobonds (not accepted by Germany but proposed by the Commission) to avoid moral hazard.

The OL economic constitution came later (i.e. the Fiscal Compact), which was accompanied by an international agreement on a number of structural policies. All of the elements implemented were constitutive elements of the EMU and were also signs of ordoliberal influence, as Keynesians would never recommend such institutions due to the fact that they will unnecessarily bind the financial policies in the EU member states. Generally speaking, the EU's emergent economic constitutionalism is contrary to everything that Keynesianism stands for.

The ECB's role changed during the Eurozone crisis in a way that was sometimes interpreted as running contrary to OL. This was possible due to its role as a relatively free agent vis-à-vis its principals. For example, the ECB bailouts via the purchasing of national bonds (i.e. OMT) were not an idea informed by OL; nevertheless, Germany accepted this deviation from OL.

The ECB generally considered OL as a kind of 'in-house economic philosophy' of the bank; occasionally, however, the ECB also deliberately broke with the regulative principles of an imagined OL economic constitution. So far it seems as if the ECB has had success – at least in the short- and medium-term perspectives – with this new balance between rules and discretion within an overall OL frame.

Notes

1 Ordoliberalism (OL) is a theoretical school of German origin. After the Second World War OL was highly influential in (West) German policy-making. OL stresses the necessity of adhering to strict economy policy rules. Young (2017b) points out how there are various branches of OL and that the Freiburg School is merely one of them. Another branch of OL is the social market variant, with Wilhelm Röpke, Alexander Rüstow,

and Alfred Müller-Armack as representatives. In connection with the Eurozone crisis, however, I judge that it is not necessary to treat OL as a multi-branchial object.

2 'Ordo' is 'Ordnung' in Latin.

3 This signifies that the meaning hereof goes beyond a written constitution.

4 Eucken called this 'the primacy of monetary policy' (Praet 2017, p. 81).

5 Keynesian ideas about macroeconomic demand management were somehow delegitimized due the Nazi regime implementing Keynesian policies prior to World War II (see also Keynes' ignominious preface to the first German edition of the *General Theory*) (Burda 2017).

6 Here, there might be some confusion. The concept of neoliberalism was originally used instead of OL in contrast to Anglo-Saxon laissez-faire liberalism. The term was coined in 1938 at a seminar for exactly this purpose. OL was first called OL in the 1950s (Young 2017b). Today, neoliberalism refers to that which the founding fathers of OL called laissez-faire liberalism.

7 EcoFin is the acronym for the Economic and Financial Affairs Council of the EU.

8 Ecofin is also responsible for negotiating currency agreements with third-party countries and determining the EU's position vis-à-vis EMU (e.g. ensuring compliance with agreements on maximum public deficits).

9 In a speech on 18 October 2002 the then president of the Commission, Romano Prodi, even called it 'stupid'. Source: The Guardian, 17 October, 2002. Link: https://www.theguardian.com/business/2002/oct/18/theeuro.europeanunion.

10 Previously, the adoption of proposed sanctions required a qualified majority in the Council of Ministers. In the future, a qualified majority will be necessary to remove such sanctions. The burden of proof regarding sanctions has thus been reversed.

11 This can be seen as reflecting the idea of 'credible commitment' in modern political science.

12 For example, in a speech in 2013, Mario Draghi (2013) said: 'In this context, it is worth recalling that the monetary constitution of the ECB is firmly grounded in the principles of "ordoliberalism", particularly two of its central tenets:

- First, a clear separation of power and objectives between authorities;
- And second, adherence to the principles of an open market economy with free competition, favouring an efficient allocation of resources'.

References

Beach, D. (2013). Finanspagten og issue-linkage inden for eurosystemet. *Tidsskriftet Politik* 16: 31–41.

Beck, T., and H.-H. Kotz (eds.) (2017a). *Ordoliberalism: A German Oddity?* London: A VoxEU.org Book CEPR Press.

Beck, T., and H.-H. Kotz (2017b). Introduction. In: T. Beck, and H.-H. Kotz (eds.), *Ordoliberalism: A German Oddity?* London: A VoxEU.org Book CEPR Press.

Beck, T., and H.-H. Kotz (2017c). Banking union: Rules versus discretion? In: T. Beck, and H.-H. Kotz (eds.), *Ordoliberalism: A German Oddity?* London: A VoxEU.org Book CEPR Press.

Berghahn, V., and B. Young (2013). Reflections on Werner Bonefeld's 'freedom and the strong state: One German ordoliberalism' and the continuing importance of the ideas of ordoliberalism to Germany's (contested) role in resolving the Eurozone crisis. *New Political Economy* 18(5): 768–778.

Biebricher, T., and F. Vogelmann (eds.) (2017a). *The Birth of Austerity*. London: Rowman & Littlefield.

Biebricher, T., and Vogelmann, F. (2017b). Introduction. In: T. Biebricher, and F. Vogelmann (eds.), *The Birth of Austerity*. London: Rowman & Littlefield, 1–22.

Blyth, M. (2013). *Austerity: The History of a Dangerous Idea*. Oxford: Oxford University Press.

Böhm, F. (1937). Die Ordnung der Wirtschaft als geschichtliche Aufgabe und rechtsschöpferiche Leistung, Stuttgart/Berlin: Kohlhammer. Translated in T. Biebricher, and F. Vogelmann (eds.) (2017), *The Birth of Austerity*. London: Rowman & Littlefield, 115–120.

Bonefeld, W. (2012). Freedom and the strong state: On German ordoliberalism. *New Political Economy* 17(5): 633–656.

Burda, M. C. (2017). Ordnungsökonomik or Teutonomik? In: T. Beck, and H.-H. Kotz (eds.), *Ordoliberalism: A German Oddity?* London: A VoxEU.org Book CEPR Press.

Clift, B. (2008). Economic interventionism in the Fifth Republic. In: *The French Fifth Republic at Fifty: Beyond Stereotypes: French Politics, Society and Culture*. Basingstoke: Palgrave Macmillan.

Draghi, M. (2013). Speech by Mario Draghi, President of the ECB, Jerusalem, 18 June. Accessed 12 December 2017: www.ecb.europa.eu/press/key/date/2013/html/sp130618.en.html

Dullien, S., and U. Guérot (2012). The long shadow of ordoliberalism: Germany's approach to the Euro crisis. Paper ECFR/49. European Council of Foreign Relations.

Dyson, K. (2009). German Bundesbank: Europeanization and the paradoxes of power. In: K. Dyson, and M. Marcussen (eds.), *Central Banks in the Age of the Euro*. Oxford: Oxford University Press.

Eucken, W. (1940). *Die Grundlagen der Nationalökonomie*. Jena: Fischer.

Eucken, W. (1952). *Grundsätze der Wirtschaftspolitik*. Tübingen: J.C.B. Mohr.

Eucken, W., F. Böhm, and H. Grossmann-Doerth (1936). Unsere Aufgabe (English: The Ordo Manifesto of 1936) in *Frankfurter Zeitung*, 29 November. Translated in T. Biebricher, and F. Vogelmann (eds.) (2017), *The Birth of Austerity*. London: Rowman & Littlefield.

Feld, L. P., E. A. Köhler, and D. Nientiedt (2015). Ordoliberalism, pragmatism and the Eurozone crisis. *ERIS* 2(3): 48–61.

Feld, L. P., E. A. Köhler, and D. Nientiedt (2017). The 'dark ages of German macroeconomics' and other alleged shortfalls in German economic thoughts. In: T. Beck, and H.-H. Kotz (eds.), *Ordoliberalism: A German Oddity?* London: A VoxEU.org Book CEPR Press.

Fiscal Compact (2012). Treaty on stability, coordination and governance in the economic and monetary union. Accessed 27 December 2017: www.ecb.europa.eu/pub/pdf/other/art1_mb201205en_pp79-94en.pdf?ea087c02b73d02418533c67ea0d36c1c

Foucault, M. (2008). *The Birth of Biopolitics: Lectures at the College de France, 1978–1979*. Houndsmills: Palgrave Macmillan.

Gabor, D. (2012).The power of collateral: The ECB and geographies of bank funding. Social Science Research Network. Paper available from: http://eprints.uwe.ac.uk/1898.1 Accessed 25 March 2013.

Goldschmidt, N., and H. Rauchenschwandtner (2007). The philosophy of social market economy: Michel Foucault's analysis of OL. Paper 07/4. Freiburg: Walter Eucken Institut.

Hayek, F. A. (1960). *The Constitution of Liberty*. Chicago: The University of Chicago Press.

Heipertz, M., and A. Verdun (2010). *Ruling Europe: The Politics of the Stability and Growth Pact*. Cambridge: Cambridge University Press.

Hutchinson, T. W. (1981). *The Politics and Philosophy of Economics: Marxians, Keynesians and Austrians*. New York: New York University Press.

Joerges, C. (2017). Europe after ordoliberalism. In: T. Biebricher, and F. Vogelmann (eds.), *The Birth of Austerity*. London: Rowman & Littlefield, 197–220.

Landmann, O. (2017). What's wrong with EZ: Conflicting narratives. In: T. Beck, and H.-H. Kotz (eds.), *Ordoliberalism: A German Oddity?* London: A VoxEU.org Book CEPR Press.

Nedergaard, P. (2013). The influence of ordoliberalism in European integration processes: A framework for ideational influence with competition policy and the Economic and Monetary Policy as examples. Paper. University of Munich.

Nedergaard, P., and H. Snaith (2015). 'As I drifted on a river I could not control': The unintended ordoliberal consequences of the Eurozone crisis. *JCMS: Journal of Common Market Studies* 53(5): 1094–1109.

Nello, S. S. (2012). *The European Union: Economics, Policies and History*. New York: McGraw-Hill.

Oksala, J. (2017). Ordoliberalism as governmentality. In: T. Biebricher, and F. Vogelmann (eds.), *The Birth of Austerity*. London: Rowman & Littlefield, 181–196.

Praet, P. (2017). Unconventional measures: A case of realpolitik? In: T. Beck, and H.-H. Kotz (eds.), *Ordoliberalism: A German Oddity?* London: A VoxEU.org Book CEPR Press.

Rothbard, M. N. (1970). *Man, Economy and State: A Treatise on Economic Principles*. Vols. 1 and 2. Los Angeles: Nash Publishing.

Sarkozy, N. (2011). Speech in Toulon, 1 December. Accessed 1 December 2017: www.theguardian.com/business/2011/dec/01/sarkozy-new-european-treaty-euro

Schmidt, C.M. (2017). Don't shoot the messenger: About the diversity of economic policy conclusions in the face of severe identification issues. In: T. Beck, and H.-H. Kotz (eds.), *Ordoliberalism: A German Oddity?* London: A VoxEU.org Book CEPR Press.

The Guardian, 17 October, 2002. https://www.theguardian.com/business/2002/oct/18/theeuro.europeanunion. Accessed 20 December 2017.

Vanberg, V. J. (2004). The Freiburg school: Walter Eucken and OL. Paper 04/11. Freiburg: Walter Eucken Institut.

Walters, W., and J. H. Haahr (2005). *Governing Europe: Discourse, Governmentality and European Integration*. London: Routledge.

Winkler, A. (2017). Ordoliberalism, post-crisis monetary policy and the German 'Angst'. In: T. Beck, and H.-H. Kotz (eds.), *Ordoliberalism: A German Oddity?* London: A VoxEU.org Book CEPR Press.

Wyplosz, C. (2006). European Monetary Union: The dark sides of a major success. *Economic Policy*, 21: 207–261.

Wyplotz, C. (2017). The euro and ordoliberalism. In: T. Beck, and H.-H. Kotz (eds.), *Ordoliberalism: A German Oddity?* London: A VoxEU.org Book CEPR Press.

Young, B. (2017a). Is Germany's and Europe's crisis politics ordoliberal and/or neoliberal? In: T. Biebricher, and F. Vogelmann (eds.), *The Birth of Austerity*. London: Rowman & Littlefield, 221–238.

Young, B. (2017b). Ordoliberalism as an 'irritating German idea'. In: T. Beck, and H.-H. Kotz (eds.), *Ordoliberalism: A German Oddity?* London: A VoxEU.org Book CEPR Press.

Zettelmeyer, J. (2017). German ordo and Eurozone reform: A view from the trenches. In: T. Beck, and H.-H. Kotz (eds.), *Ordoliberalism: A German Oddity?* London: A VoxEU.org Book CEPR Press.

8 The evolution of the international monetary and financial system

Were French views determinant?

Alain Alcouffe and Fanny Coulomb

> The ideas of economists and political philosophers, both when they are right and when they are wrong, are more powerful than is commonly understood. Indeed the world is ruled by little else. Practical men, who believe themselves to be quite exempt from any intellectual influences, are usually the slaves of some defunct economist. Madmen in authority, who hear voices in the air are distilling their frenzy from some academic scribbler of a few years back.
>
> J. M. Keynes, 1936 (chapter 24, §V, p. 383[1])

Anthony M. Endres, in his 2005 book, has stressed the part player by some economists in the design of the international monetary system during the Bretton Woods era. He proposed a classification of their doctrines and proposals in a table where sixteen economists (Hansen, Williams, Graham, Triffin, Simons, Viner, Friedman, Johnson, Mises, Rueff, Rist, Hayek, Heilperin, Röpke, Harrod and Mundell) are mentioned for eight proposals[2]). Among them only one French economist, Jacques Rueff, is to be found, but he did not stand alone but merged with those of other "paleo-liberals". At the opposite, in his 2007 book, Rawi Abdelal pointed the predominant part played by French citizens in the evolution of the international monetary system during recent decades, especially during the building up of the euro area and the liberalization of the capital movements.

The article outlines the key stages in the evolution of the international monetary system and the part played by French actors in the forefront of the scene (Jacques Delors, European commission; Pascal Lamy, WTO) or in the wings (Chavranski, OECD). Among the six persons who are singled out by Rawi Abedal or made it in the book of Dyson & Maes, it is striking that four have been trained in the National School of Administration: Pascal Lamy (b. 1947), ENA 1975, Director-General of the World Trade Organization (WTO), 2005–2013; Michel Camdessus (b. 1933), ENA 1960, Chairman of the Monetary Committee of the EEC from Dec. 1982 to Dec. 1984, chairman IMF 1987–2000; Jacques de Larosière (b.1929), ENA 1958, Chairman IMF (1978–1987), Banque de France; and Henri Chavranski (b.1930), ENA 1957, chair OECD's Committee on Capital Movements and Invisible Transactions (CMIT). For his part, Jacques Delors graduated in law at Faculté de Droit of

Paris, where Charles Rist was an authority on monetary matters. Thereafter, he began his carreer at Banque de France. Paradoxically, most of these people had a background leaning towards a significant role of the state in the national economy, whereas Maurice Allais (1911–2010), the major figure of the French liberalism during the second half of the 20th century, was a tireless opponent of "laissez-fairism" and liberal globalization.

Our article aims to explain the French position in the negotiations on the international monetary system, from the post-war period to the 1980s. The influence of Charles Rist and Jacques Rueff is perceptible in France's positions. However, the opposition to the Anglo-Saxon position did not lead to the reforms sought by France (first section). The post-World War II European construction was supported by many French politicians, in a Keynesian line, challenging the dominant role of the dollar (second section). Finally, we will study the specific but convergent positions of four major French political figures, coming from the socialist current but in favour of economic liberalization: Delors, Chavranski, Lamy and Macron. (third section).

French economists and the IMFS from 1943 to 1982

The French vision of international monetary issues has sharply differentiated since the 1930s from the Anglo-Saxon conception, but it never succeeded in imposing itself on the international monetary scene.

The isolated position of France in the IMF after World War II

Even if France had not adopted the system of the Gold Exchange Standard settled at the Conference of Genoa in 1922, the country had signed a Tripartite Agreement with Great Britain and the United States in 1936, on the eve of the franc's devaluation and non-convertibility. The purpose was to avoid a monetary war (through competitive currency devaluations) and to promote cooperation and monetary compensation. The French economist Jacques Rueff was one of the initiators of this agreement. The stated aim was cooperation to favour equilibrium on the foreign exchange market. Two years after the agreement of September 25, a French economist reviewed a rather bad record of this agreement of monetary cooperation (cf. A. Piatier, 1938), which had not prevented capital movements and the currency fluctuations. However, a feeling of cooperation nevertheless remained, not least because France had no interest in letting its capital flow, nor the United States to face an influx, nor Great Britain to allow the franc to devalue, what would have been unfavorable to its trade.

The French plan for the post-World War II international monetary system is presented in *The New York Times*, May 9, 1943, p. 5. It was prepared by Hervé Alphand and André Istel (the latter being present at Bretton Woods, alongside Pierre Mendès France) and results of deliberations within the "France libre". It proposes the extension of the Tripartite Agreement, putting gold at the centre of international monetary relations in the future. It was midway between the gold standard system and the gold exchange standard, the foreign currency assets being liable to be exchanged only above a certain level, below which the debtor countries should only provide guarantees (M. Lelart, 1994, p. 522). This took the form of bilateral monetary agreements (with a long-term ambition of multilateral agreements) based on fixed exchange rates, allowing with certain limitations to use the partners' reserves without gold or foreign currency exchanges.

But this plan was not officially proposed at Bretton Woods by the French delegation. In 1944, France was no more able to directly influence international monetary relations, and also failed in imposing a discount on interest rates for countries that had been invaded (E. Monnet, 2017, p. 77)

So, France has little negotiating power at the conference of Bretton Woods and General Charles de Gaulle is there without any minister, to not give the impression that he is negotiating. The "commissaire aux finances" Pierre Mendès France is the chief of the French delegation. Despite his protestations concerning the insufficient consideration given to France, his role remains minor. The negotiations on the quota shares in the International Monetary Fund are tense, each country willing to be given a major place in the institution (the United States will have 25%, as well as a right of veto). Pierre Mendès France only obtains a small concession regarding his country's quota share, as well as the use of French as one of the official languages within the International Monetary Fund (IMF) (Muracciole, Piketty, 2015).

The negotiations open in Bretton Woods in 1944 are at once based on the American plan settled by H. D. White, the British government having in April agreed to waive the plan presented by J.M. Keynes in September 1941. Keynes based his plan on the departure from the gold standard, blamed as likely to cause economic adjustments unfavourable to growth, and the creation of an international currency, the bancor, based on a basket of currencies with associated weights based on the national incomes and on the share in the global trade. A kind of world central bank (the International Clearing Union) would organize transfers in bancor between countries in surplus and countries in deficit, to achieve an equilibrium of national trade balances which would not be automatic but required by the refund and loan mechanisms (the surplus countries, to be reimbursed for their loans in bancor, needing to import products from deficit countries).

This plan of international financial cooperation, which would have notably required large transfers from the United States to Great Britain, was not the liking of the US government. Its large gold reserves after World War II allowed the United States to place the dollar at the centre of the international monetary system, as its gold convertibility could easily be secured. The plan developed by Harry White as soon as 1942 was de facto the only one being presented at Bretton Woods (BW).

Though his plan was excluded, Keynes' influence was great in the setting up of BW's institutions, as they aimed to promote a stable international monetary order and international cooperation rather than trade and monetary wars. But during the following decade, the system of BW evolved from a system of equal currencies (the dollar and the pound sterling being key currencies) into a gold-dollar system, the American currency progressively gaining supremacy as an international reserve currency.

In 1949, Jean de Largentaye, member of the French delegation at BW and French translator of Keynes's *General Theory* in 1942, considered that the good intentions of monetary cooperation at the origin of the negotiations for the creation of the IMF were limited by the Anglo-American supremacy (cf E. Monnet, 2017).

Four years after BW, France is excluded from the IMF mechanism, as a sanction against its 1948 devaluation (the franc was devalued four times between 1948 and 1949) and its cross exchange rates policy being judged in violation of the official dollar/sterling parity and as liable to encourage the sterling devaluation, which will be effective in 1949. The country is excluded until 1952. This sanction has generated a huge resentment in Europe, and explains the choice of the International Settlement Bank for intra-europeans settlements as part of the Marshall plan (J. F. Crombois 2004).

The role of the IMF was therefore less important than expected when it was created in 1944, dethroned by the Marshall Plan and the reconstruction of Europe.

The French criticism of the Bretton Woods system

After the proclamation of the Fifth Republic, the influence of Jacques Rueff, of which Couve de Murville (minister of foreign affairs from 1958 to 1968) had been the treasury assistant in the interwar period, was considerable on the French monetary policy. He has been very close to Charles Rist, who was a major figure of economic liberalism in France. Rist had published in 1952 a book titled *Défense de l'or*, in total opposition to the Keynesian ideas, pleading for the return to gold convertibility. Following him, Jacques Rueff advocates for the revaluation of gold and denounces the gold exchange standard as the "monetary sin of the West" (see Rueff, 1971). He is convinced of the need for a return to the balances of payments equilibrium to avoid the resurgence of trade protectionism. In fact, fixed exchange rates prevented automatic balance of payment adjustments in the event of persistent structural imbalances and forced deficit countries like France to adopt austerity policies to contain inflation, and the devaluation had a significant political cost, considered as a national failure on the international scene.

Supporting a policy of budgetary austerity and a gradual return to the gold standard, Rueff is concerned about the considerable deficits in the US balance of payments allowed by the new international role of the dollar as a reserve currency. Through the metaphor of the tailor, he explains that the country with the key currency never suffers from the deficit of its balance of payments. He advocates the US buy-back, with the gold it held, of all dollar assets held by central banks. To that end, an increase in the price of gold is advocated.

These arguments will serve France to push the United States to reform the international monetary system (Bordo, Simard, White, 1994. However, the French Ministry of Finance is less favourable to a return of the gold standard than Rueff. In September 1964, minister Giscard d'Estaing made a proposal at the IMF annual conference in Tokyo for the creation of additional liquidity, the CRU (Currency Reserve Unit), ancestor of the IMF's Special Drawing Rights. This mechanism was recommended by Robert Triffin to avoid a shortage of liquidity resulting from possible deflationary temptations in the United States as a response to their deficit, which could have disrupted the international trade. Triffin had even proposed a system close to BW's Keynes plan, with the creation of a world central bank, but this project had no follow-up. His analysis was in contradiction with that of Rueff, who denounced the excess of money supply resulting from the GES.

The French policy begun in the 1960s and accelerated in 1965 to convert gold reserves into dollars was accused by the Americans of having precipitated the collapse of the Bretton Woods system. In fact, these conversion operations accelerated the demonetization of gold with the increase in dollar liquidity. General de Gaulle proposed in February 1965 the restoration of the gold standard, in line with the positions of Rueff (who recommended doubling the price of gold in dollars) and against Robert Triffin's recommendations. Throughout 1966, France and the United States were at war on this issue.

The French demands for a greater role for gold in the international monetary system were aimed at increasing the influence of Europe, which now had a large share of the world's stock. But France's demands did not lead to any significant decision to reform the system, nor did they permit the Common Market to obtain a right of veto in the IMF (1967 negotiations). In 1978, Rueff recalls that the diversity of exchange rates in Europe, generating deficits and inflation, prevents the proper functioning of prices. He writes: "L'Europe se fera par la monnaie ou ne se fera pas"[3] (Rueff, 1978, p. 388).

In 1967, the former president of the Council of Ministers, Pierre Mendès France, criticizes very severely the Rio de Janeiro agreement (validated by France) for the creation of new international liquidity by the IMF, advocating for the end of the pound as a reserve currency and for the creation of a new regulatory mechanism based not only on gold holdings but also on stocks of commodities and manufactured products listed on world markets. This mechanism would have the double advantage of stabilizing the terms of trade and constituting a sustainable form of development assistance (P. Mendès France, 1967).

From 1968 onwards, the decline in capital exports by the United States to limit the flight of their gold reserves prompted the Common Market countries to temper their support for French demands for the international monetary system reform against the United States (Bordo, Simard, White, 1994, op. cit.).

After the abandonment of the Bretton Woods system in 1971, the role of the IMF decreased considerably, as it was no longer necessary to support payment balances using credit from the institution.

In 1998, the French economist Maurice Allais renewed with the old debate by advocating a "new Bretton Woods" for a reform of the international monetary system, arguing in particular for the complete abandonment of the dollar as currency of account, exchange and reserve at the international level, for the fusion of the IMF and the WTO and for the progressive establishment of an international unit of account through a system of indexation in real values of the securities (Allais, 1999).

French views along the road to EMU (European Monetary Union)[4]

From 1943 to 1958 – Marjolin versus Mendès France

In the aftermath of World War II, Europe was not a central topic for French economists – least of all was it the case of monetary union. Nevertheless, the international economic relations were a matter of concern for them as the weaknesses of the pre-war Franch economy were seen as the causes of French defeat in 1940. We can devote some time to introduce Robert Marjolin (1911–1986). He was born in Paris, the son of an upholsterer. He left school at the age of 14 to begin work but took evening and correspondence courses at the Sorbonne. A 1931 scholarship from the Rockefeller Foundation enabled him to study sociology and economics at Yale University, which he completed in 1934. He also received a postgraduate doctorate in jurisprudence in 1936. During these years he had been in touch with Léon Blum as well as with a "tendance" (trend) of the SFIO, called *Révolution Constructive*, which was interested in planning ideas. In 1936, he was briefly special advisor to Léon Blum, whose policies towards Spain and labour duration he criticized. A turning point in his evolution came in 1938 as he took part in the Colloque Lippman, "a prestigious conclave" which reunited Hayek, Rueff and Röpke, paving the road to the Mont Pelerin society.[5] From 1938, he worked as a chief assistant to Charles Rist at the Institute of Economics in Paris. His research at this time as well as his later political work was strongly affected by the New Deal programmes of US President Franklin D. Roosevelt. He wrote then defended a thesis in 1941 whereby he displayed remarkable knowledge of leading economists of this period (Keynes, Hicks, Kuznets, Hayek, Myrdal), quoting them directly from German as well from English. It is difficult to find evidence sustaining Arena and Schmidt's assertion that Marjolin was "one of France's first prominent Keynesians" (Arena, Schmidt, 1999, p. 93). His thesis seeks to combine "the results of theoretical elaboration with statistical research" (ibid., p. 13). Actually, Marjolin surveyed the field of long swing economics devoting a special attention to the part played by marginal productivity of capital and anticipation while gathering a lot of French economic data at a time when national accounting was non-existent in France, but there is no more elaborated treatment than simple graphical representations. As the thesis focused on the period before the Word War I, it is not necessary to insist that it does not provide any insights on the metamorphosis of money in the interwar period.

Therefore, his evaluation of the Blum experiment is the more indicative of his supply-side approach (Marjolin, 1938). In his paper, he gave his explanation of the economic shortcomings of Blum's policies blaming the forty-hours work week as the culprit of the final failure. Besides, he confronted Kalecki's defence of Blum. Along with Marjolin, Kalecki had defended Keynesian policies and blamed "French economists, bankers and rentiers for continuing to adhere to the 'vulgar theory', according to which the budget deficit, above all if it is financed by the Central bank, constitutes an imminent threat to the currency". (ibid., p. 190). On the contrary, Marjolin argued that "the reduction in the length of the working week was the dominant factor of the whole experiment. It was that which, in the spring of I937, stifled the revival which had been going on for some months", and further:

> the legal length of the working week was reduced at one blow by 17 per cent at the close of 1936 and the beginning of 1937. The possibilities of further expansion were thereby destroyed owing to the consequent shortage of skilled labour. The result was a stagnation of economic activity during the greater part of the year 1937.
>
> (ibid., p. 191)

Consistenly with this supply-side approach, Marjolin while he was working for Jean Monnet's Commissariat du Plan in 1946 took side for free trade.

> France has a fundamental interest in a world of extremely active trade, rapidly developing imports and exports, in a world, therefore, where commercial transactions will be as free, with as little embarrassment as possible, where obstacles of every kind, Customs duties, quotas, will be as low as they can be.
>
> (Marjolin, 1946, p. 274)

He attacked consistently the protectionism asserting that "We must not fight against autarky by saying: it is harmful; But we must say: it is impossible" (ibid., p. 275). Meanwhile, he was confident that:

> In the space of ten years, economic technology has made considerable progress. Henceforth, the intervention of the State in economic life is no longer a matter of empiricism and trial and error. The war showed what a state could get when it was decided to intervene and that it had a public opinion behind it that supported it. There is no economic objective that can not be achieved, and the maintenance of full employment appears perfectly feasible.
>
> (ibid., p. 275)

But it is doubtful if this paean for economic interventionism is anything more than a last resort defence of market economy.

In 1948, Marjolin was appointed the first Secretary-General of the Organization for European Economic Cooperation (OEEC), which was established to implement the Marshall Plan and later became the OECD. In 1956 he joined Christian Pineau, the minister of foreign affairs, and took part in the negotiations of the Treaty of Rome, signed in 1957. The treaty makes no mention of economic and monetary union, and the single currency. The French national assembly ratified the treaty by a vote of 323 in favour and 287 against. Communists, gaullists, poujadists, but also some members of the radical party followers of Pierre Mendès France, were among the opponents.

As Mendès-France (1907–1982) was to become an iconic reference for Jacques Delors, we must devote some attention to his economic positions. Mendès-France devoted his thesis to the monetary policies of the Poincaré government (1926–1928). The book was published in 1928 and established his reputation as an expert in favour of rigour as he approved Poincaré's "courgeous financial policy, tense fiscal effort leading to large fiscal surpluses" (Mendès France, 1928, p. 90). Two years later, Mendès France took the opportunity of the creation of the Bank for International Settlements, intended to facilitate reparations imposed on Germany by the Treaty of Versailles after World War I, to discuss the European trade and finance problems. He advocated a European tariff union as a counterpart of the BIS, foreshadowing the EEC with features of a large market and a single currency (Baverez, 2001, p. 37). The decisive episode for Mendès France happened as the war approached its end. Pierre Mendès France was minister of the economy and René Pleven was minister of finance. The latter was the more important ministry of the two, and Pleven had been at de Gaulle's side since the early days of the Resistance in London. "Mendès France wanted to take advantage of the period of economic stagnation to take consolidation measures, particularly in the monetary field, and thus give economic development a solid starting position. His great concern was to ward off inflation and to stop the price and wage race"[6]. Pleven's approach was focused on the short term and was aimed at alleviating the suffering of the French people after four years of occupation. "His recipe was a raise in public sector salaries (of 40 per cent) and the floating of a national *Liberation Loan*"[7]. The result was a sharp increase in inflation. On 18 January 1945, Mendès France resigned though de Gaulle kept Mendès France briefly in the government, he decided in favour of Pleven. Mendès France left on 7 April 1945. It is difficult to assess clearly what was at stake because the dispute was not only about inflation, but also about alternative policy-mix. Mendès-France's proposals implied more public interventionism leading to a command economy while Pleven's ones gave more weight to market mechanisms. Mendès France's stance could be found in his position vis-à-vis the Treaty of Rome. For Mendès France, who was always in favour of an "organic construction of Europe" because old European countries are too small for the great activities of the 20th century, "the proposed common market as presented is based on classical liberalism of the nineteenth century, according to which pure competition rules out all problems" whereas "Ten grave crises, so much suffering endured, bankruptcy and periodic unemployment have shown the character of this classic theory of resignation". He denouced "our partners [that] want to retain the commercial advantage they have over us because of their social backwardness". He was especially critical of the foreseen free movement of capital. "It is evident that the natural movement of capital, especially of private capital, will be oriented towards low-burden countries, that is to say, countries where social policy is the least costly. Capital tends to leave the socialist countries and their departure to exert pressure in the direction of abandoning an advanced social policy". He sustained that a prerequisite should be "equalising the levels of obligatory social contributions and benefits: harmonization should be realized along the most advanced social progress" (Mendès France, 1957, p. 166).

Marjolin and Mendès France had both some acquaintance with Keynes and took economics seriously. We have argued previously that Marjolin did not stick to Keynesian policies to improve the French economy. His only departure from classical economics was his confidence in the state intervention to overcome economic difficulties. Mendès-France explicitly invoked Keynes, and his discourse of 1957 echoed the rejection of the Classics by Keynes. But it is doubtful that his repeated invocation of rigour is far from any version of Keynesianism.

French monetary policies in the 1960s

After the ratification of the Treaty of Rome, Marjolin became vice-president of the EEC commission and held the post from 1958 to 1967. His mandate covered the crucial months of 1958 when the Fourth Republic ended and was replaced by Charles de Gaulle's Fifth Republic. At this moment, De Gaulle – who has been an opponent to the treaty – changed his mind vis-à-vis the European construction. For the second time, de Gaulle turned his back to Mendès France and adopted economic policies directly inspired by the French opponent to Keynes, Jacques Rueff. They included a new devaluation in December 1958 of 17% of the franc.

During the 1960s, De Gaulle adopted Rueff's stance vis-à-vis the IMS invocating the return to Gold standard instead of the BW system. On 4 February 1965, President of France Charles De Gaulle noted in a famous press conference that there can be only one international reserve currency: gold.

The fact that many countries accept as a principle that dollars are as good as gold for the payment of the difference existing to their advantage in the US balance of trade leads Americans to get into debt, and to get into debt for free, at the expense of other countries, because what the United States owes them is paid, at least in part, with dollars only they are allowed to emit. Considering the serious consequences a crisis would have in such a domain, we think that measures must be taken on time to avoid it. We consider necessary that international trade be established as it was the case before the great tragedies of the world, on an indisputable monetary base and one that does not bear the mark of any particular country. Which base? Truly, it's hard to imagine how it can be any standard criterion other than gold.

Yes, gold – whose nature does not alter, which may be formed equally into ingots, bars or coins, which has no nationality and which has, eternally and universally, been regarded as the unalterable currency par excellence.

The supreme law, the golden rule – and indeed it's pertinent to say it – that must be enforced and honoured again in international economic relations, is the duty to balance, from one monetary area to another, by effective inflows and outflows of gold, the balance of payments resulting from their exchanges (De Gaulle, 1965).

President de Gaulle's political posturing was a weapon to further a French gold policy that was an extension of earlier policies dating back to the interwar period. The French government wanted a revision of the international monetary system along the lines of the gold exchange standard of the 1920s and of the Tripartite Agreement of 1936, which the de Gaulle government perceived as more in line with the non-aligned stance of France. Following Bordo, Simard, White (1994), periodic references to an orthodox gold standard by the French government were tactical threats to induce the United States to begin negotiations with the Common Market countries to make the existing system a more symmetrical one with an improved automatic balance of payments adjustment mechanism.

Eventually with all possible qualifications, a French approach emerged with several characteristics: mistrust vis-à-vis the US discretionary policy, preference for multilateral agreement, preferences for rules-based policies and indifference towards inflation, which is exemplified by the evolution of the rate of exchange between the franc and the Deutsche mark (Figure 8.1).

First steps on the road to EMU

Nevertheless, some concerns about the stability of exchange rates lead to the creation on 18 March 1958 of the Monetary Committee of the Council of the European Economic Community (EEC). Established by Article 105 of the EEC Treaty, the Monetary Committee is responsible for keeping under review the monetary and financial situation of member states and of the Community, as well as the general payments system of the member states, and must report regularly thereon to the Council and to the Commission.

Twelve years later, monetary turbulence was triggering the end of the Bretton Woods agreements. Therefore at the European Summit in The Hague in 1969, the heads of states and governments of the European Community agreed to prepare a plan for economic and monetary union. The Werner Report was drawn up by a working group chaired by Pierre Werner, Luxembourg's prime minister and minister for finances, and presented in October 1970. The three-stage plan proposed gradual institutional reform leading to the irrevocable

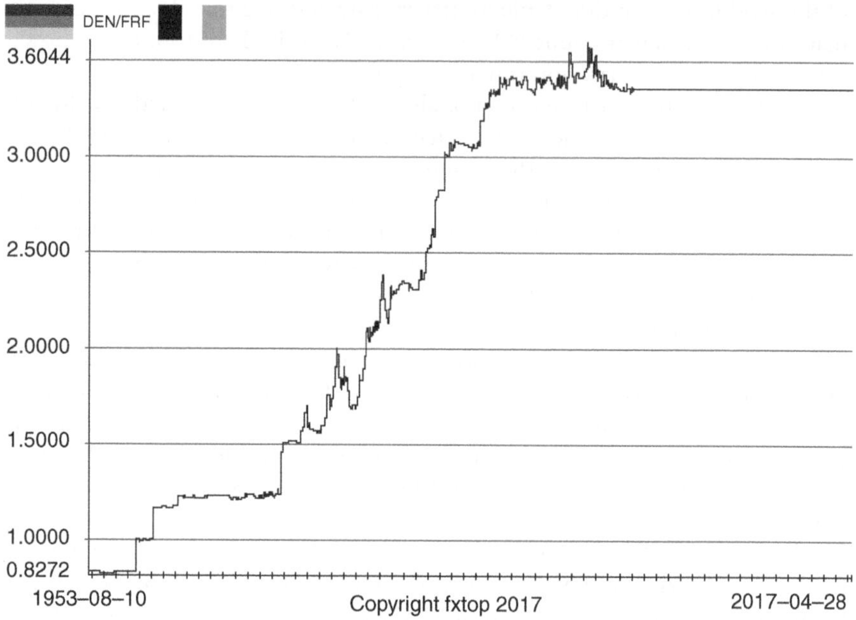

Figure 8.1 Parity between Deutsche mark and franc

fixing of exchange rates and the adoption of a single currency within a decade, but it did not recommend the establishment of a central bank. The plan was never implemented because of pressure of the United States: France retired its support after a France-US meeting in the Azores at the end of 1971.[8]

It was fourteen years before the European Community adopts in 1985 the project of a single European market. It soon becomes apparent that this will be supplemented by a single currency. Towards the end of the decade, in 1989 the Delors Report on Economic and Monetary Union proposes a three-stage plan culminating in the creation of a single currency and a European central bank. It triggers renewed discussion on the Treaty of Rome preparing the Maastricht Treaty which transformed the European Community into a full Economic and Monetary Union. The participants adopt a range of macroeconomic criteria which must be respected in order to qualify for membership of the Monetary Union. Eventually in 1997, the Stability and Growth Pact is adopted by all the member countries at the Amsterdam European Council. For the countries joining the euro, it lays down certain common constraints relating to public finance, mainly a 3% ceiling on the budget deficit, and provides for financial sanctions. These constraints are necessary in an asymmetrical system in which the countries of the euro area have a single monetary policy while retaining their national fiscal policy.

The liberalization of capital movements

The Treaty of Rome provided for the free movement of capital, but the abolition of capital restrictions between member states was to be "to the extent necessary to ensure the proper functioning of the common market"[9]. Many financial operations with other member states were subject to prior authorization requirements known as "exchange controls". This situation persisted until the early 1990s. The Council adopted a capital liberalization directive in 1988, providing for the removal of all remaining exchange controls by mid-1990 for most of those countries maintaining this mechanism. As part of the drive towards Economic and Monetary Union, the freedom of capital movements gained the same status as the other Internal Market freedoms with the entry into force of the Maastricht Treaty. From 1 January 1994, not only were all restrictions on capital movements and payments between EU member states prohibited, but so were restrictions between EU member states and third countries.

The free movement of capital has followed a unique and "non-linear" evolutionary trajectory. In contrast to the treaty provisions on goods, persons and services, whereby liberalization was driven by the court, a step ahead of the Union's political branches and often against the natural instincts of national governments, the development of the treaty rules on capital movements was for many years essentially left to the member states as a matter of policy. The court's decision to secede control over the pace and depth of capital market liberalization to the member states was made in Casati. In that decision, the Court of Justice (CJ) of the European Union, famously concluded that Article 67(1) EEC – the central provision on intra-EU capital movements in the founding EEC Treaty – was not directly effective. According to the court, the wording of that provision was non-absolute, requiring member states to liberalize intra-EU capital movements only "to the extent necessary to ensure the proper functioning of the common market"[10].

The court's ruling in Casati (November, 1981) effectively left the member states to manage the opening up of the EU capital market using their legislative competence in EEC Article 69. Now we can follow the presentation by Julien Brault of the French case:

> the election of François Mitterrand and the coming into power of the French left in 1981 leads to the short quantitative re-enactment of controls in 1982 and 1983, notably to prevent financial outflows to Switzerland. Competition appears then notably distorted by derogatory regimes given to certain big companies in their access to exchange authorizations. However, the role of professional associations, chambers of commerce and other ministries totally disappears. The final dismantlement of French foreign exchange control happens for the most part between 1983 and 1989. The third and definitive step of exchange control abolition comes between 1986 and 1989. The European

> directive of 1986 completes the liberalization of long-term capital flows, and the directive of 1988 organizes the definitive liberalization of capital flows. Foreign exchange control is abolished on 29 December, 1989, concluding a long-term movement affecting most of the countries of the world [. . .].
>
> (Brault, 2017, p. 25).

A French socialist U-turn in 1982–1983?

After giving the background of the IMFS (International Monetary and Financial System) and the EMU, we can turn our attention to the part played by the French socialists in the 1980s. In May 1981, the first socialist-communist government after the victory of the United Left in the 1981 presidential and legislative elections implemented:

> its program of "redistributive Keynesianism" in macroeconomics (to be achieved via public sector hires, reduction of the workweek, longer vacation time, increases in social transfers) and restoring the state's role in microeconomics (via a nationalization program and a return to active industrial policy), initially turned toward demand stimulation as a solution for pulling the economy out of the crisis.
>
> (Fourcade-Gourinchas, Babb, 2002, p. 565)

Lester Thurow, a longtime advocate of a political and economic system of the Japanese and European type, in which governmental involvement in the direction of the economy is far more extensive than is the case in the United States, coined the term "Keynesianism in one country" to describe the experiment which came to an end in March 1983 with the austerity turn (Thurow, 1983). Singled out by Abedal, there is a handful of politicans and civil servants who played an important part in this evolution: Laurent Fabius (b. 1946), ENA 1973, minister of budget; Jacques Delors (b. 1925) minister of the economy; Pascal Lamy (b. 1947), ENA 1975, head of cabinet of J. Delors; Michel Camdessus (b. 1933), ENA 1960, chairman of the Monetary Committee of the EEC from December 1982 to December 1984, chairman IMF 1987–2000; Jacques de Larosière (b.1929), ENA 1958, chairman IMF (1978–1987), Banque de France; Henri Chavranski (b. 1930), ENA 1957, chair OECD's Committee on Capital Movements and Invisible Transactions (CMIT).

Putting aside Laurent Fabius, whose involvement was not very strong, let us examine the part played by Delors, Chavranski and Lamy in the evolution of the international monetary and financial system and discover if it can be highlighted by some features of French political economy.

Jacques Delors and the EMU

Jacques Delors was born on 20 July 1925 in Paris. Already an economics graduate, he obtained the diploma of the Centre d'Etudes Supérieures de Banque

(CESB) in 1950. From 1945 to 1962, he worked for the Banque de France. Then he became a member of the Economic and Social Council (France). First chief officer for social affairs to the Commissariat Général du Plan from 1962 to 1969, he was next appointed general secretary of the prime minister for the "Formation Permanente et la Promotion Sociale", a post he held until 1973. He taught at the Université de Paris-Dauphine as external instructor from 1974 to 1979 and at the Ecole Nationale d'Administration (ENA). During this period, he was also a member of the General Council of the Banque de France, from 1973 to 1979, and joined the Parti Socialiste in 1974 and its Management Committee in 1979.

His European career began in 1979 with his election as a member of the European Parliament. There he was the chairman of its Economic and Monetary Committee until May 1981. From 1981 to 1984, he came back to French political affairs as Ministre de l'Economie et des Finances and as mayor of the town of Clichy, from 1983 to 1984.

From 1985 to 1995, he served as president of the European Commission within the European Economic Community (EEC), and then within the European Union (EU). At his instigation, on 14 June 1985, the Commission published the "White Paper", the aim of which was to urge on the economic recovery, free movement and the establishment of a common market. From 1988 to 1989, he was the chairman of the committee responsible for studying the project of an Economic and Monetary Union (EMU), resulting in the "Delors Report" which would contribute to the establishment of the Maastricht Treaty and of the euro. In 1995, he refused to stand in the French presidential election, which some people thought he might win.

He is also known for his commitment to Christian syndicalism. He has been a member of the French Confederation of the Christian Workers (CFTC) and of the think tank *Vie Nouvelle*.

Clearly, Delors was trained in economics while working at Banque de France, and he was probably permeated by the scepticism in regard to managed currencies and international agreements of the Bretton Wood type which characterized the French position in monetary matters as opposed to the typical Anglo-American and can be found in the two most important thinkers in the field, Charles Rist and Jacques Rueff (Cf. Dehem ([1987] 2017)

Henri Chavranski and the OECD code of liberalization

Born in 1930, Henri Chavranski graduated in Sciences Politiques, then by ENA (1955–1957). During an unspectacular career, he held several posts in French civil service in France and abroad (Morocco, Argentina, French representation by the EC), and eventually the Committee on Capital Movements and Invisible Transactions (CMIT) after 1980 which he chaired from 1982 to 1994. The CMIT was responsible for the Code of Liberalization of Capital Movement. The code was part of the OECD from its beginning in 1961. But while the 1960s and 1970s were decades marked by just few changes in the code, the 1980s and 1990s witnessed a speeding-up of capital account liberalization, as a result of a more market-based approach being adopted. The year 1989 can be regarded as a turning point since from then on, virtually all types of capital movements were covered by the code. It happens that Chavranski was the chairperson of the committee from 1982 to 1994 and in some sense presided over the extinction of capital controls in virtually all OECD member countries.

In his 1997 book based on first-hand experience, he starts from the observation that the OECD is not well known and if he does not intend "to completely remedy this deficiency and to be exhaustive", he sketches out an overall presentation of the organization, discussing the main problems it faces today and setting out some lines of thought on its prospects (Chavranski, 1997, p. 6).

Despite this limited scope, the book includes a discussions of the theses defended, often systematically, by the secretariat of the organization. Far from the emphasis which surrounders the definition of the OECD by Hilary Clinton, as "a community of shared values, open and effective markets, human rights, freedoms and the rule of law, accountable governments and leaders, free, fair and transparent competition" (Bonucci, 2011, pp. 249–50). Chavranski barely states that "no one in the OECD questions the principles and constraints of the market economy" but he sees a dividing line "about whether the market should be seen as a means of achieving stable, sustainable and non-inflationary growth or as an objective in itself, unconditionally in all cases, regardless of the consequences" (Chavranski, 1997, p. 80). He asserts that:

> there is a permanent tension within the Organization between the supporters of the two schools. Curiously, here we are witnessing a real reversal of preconceived notions about the behavior of each other: it is the Anglo-Saxons who continually rely on reference texts to elaborate their positions while others, Scandinavians, Germans and French in particular, are increasingly trying to build their own from the examination of concrete situations
>
> (ibidem, p. 80)

Despite his positions are presented with the reservation that befits a senior official, it is not difficult to guess where his preferences go. Eliane Mossé, a French left-leaning economist, summarizes Chavranski's developments as follows:

> the OECD moved from a militant keynesianism, which lasted until the late 1970s, to a Liberalism more and more assertive, the key words of which are flexibility, deregulation, supposed remedies for all the difficulties facing the Western economies, especially in the field of employment. The structural reforms advocated by the Secretariat have always been to the same effect: reduction of the weight of the public sector, privatization, liberalization of trade and capital movements, abolition of public support for industry and agriculture, wage rigidities, etc.
>
> (Mossé, 1997)

Chavranski himself criticizes himself the "one size fits all" recommendations advocated by the OECD regardless of the specificities of each economy and wonders: "Why, a priori, should we exclude considerations relating to history, demography, sociology and the evolution of political institutions, for example, since they obviously influence the structures and the evolution of economies?"(Chavranski, 1997, p.79). He rejects market orientation in fields as education or health. He does not hide his reservation vis-à-vis the GDP and regrets that no research had been done for an index of Gross Domestic Happiness. He complained that "the center of gravity of economic studies devoted annually to the Organization's member countries has shifted significantly in recent years. It was previously focused on the problems of what economists call the "magic square", namely full employment, growth, price stability and external balance. The organization's judgements on the policies pursued by the member states were closely related to the results achieved in relation to these fundamental objectives. They have progressively shifted to new and unavoidable priorities, the defence of balanced budgets, the rigour of monetary policy and the effectiveness of structural reforms" (ibidem, p. 81).

Obviously Chavranski did not appreciate some young economists he had to deal with during his presidency, and he deplores that fashion plays such a part in economics and that "schools of thought in vogue tend to advocate categorical solutions and to forget the recipes previously recognized" (ibid. p. 83). He goes so far as to question the benefits of free trade, which is a constitutive principle of the OECD. He does not partake in the "conviction . . . deeply rooted in the majority of minds in the OECD that openness and competition play to the benefit of the most effective and the best, and are beneficial to all actors, whatever their situation and, consequently, for all countries". Moreover, he is not fooled that opponents to public monopolies or state interventionism are less strident whenever giant firms exert a market power, often with the assistance of state. Instead of a fastidious argument again free trade, he stresses the incoherence of the report on Korea which recommended the dismantling of the policies that had been the basis of the country's economic take off and its continuing performances.

After this criticism of liberal principles, it is surprising that Chavranski celebrates the liberalization codes that have been implemented according to these principles but either it would have been too demanding to criticize his own part as chairman of the CMIT – a case of the "Bridge over the River Kwai" syndrome, or what matters for him is that each government keeps some room to mitigate the possible negative effects.

The French presence is very weak, or almost nil at the level of the decision, particularly in the two directorates which are generally considered as the OECD nerve centre (Department of Economic Affairs and Directorate of Financial Affairs), the French occupy only relatively secondary or marginal positions and the Anglo-Saxon preponderance there is very strong. Concerning the Committees, he judges that "the positions of Committee Chairperson can be used to influence the work and to exert a significant influence, assuming that it is recognized as being exercised wisely". (ibid., p. 143).

Pascal Lamy and the managed globalization

Pascal Lamy studied at Sciences Po Paris, HEC and later at ENA, graduating second in his year of those specializing in economics. He served as an adviser to Jacques Delors as economics and finance minister, and Pierre Mauroy as prime minister. When Delors became president of the European Commission in 1984, he took Lamy with him to serve as chef de cabinet, which he did until the end of Delors' term in 1994. During his time there, Lamy was seen as ruling Delors' office with a "rod of iron", with no-one able to bypass or manipulate him and those who tried being "banished to one of the less pleasant European postings".[11] Between 1999 and 2004, Pascal Lamy was Commissioner for Trade at the European Commission under Romano Prodi. As director-general of the World Trade Organization from September 2005 to April 2009, Pascal Lamy chaired the Doha Round of negotiations and witnessed a rapidly changing international trade environment.

Fortunately, Lamy has repeatedly defended his committment to socialist thinking or at least to some particular brand of socialist thinking so that it is easy to define his position which is very similar to those of Delors and Chavranski. He articulated very clearly his position during his hearing as commissioner-designate in 1999. For him:

> globalisation, a key element of which is international commerce, facilitated by liberalisation of trade and investment, is not a zero-sum game where some lose what the others gain. It is to my mind a win-win process, as post-war economic history shows. Europe has profited from it, and will continue to do so, provided that it preserves its long-term competitiveness, its capacity for innovation, and its social-market economy. . . . But if globalisation is to be both effective and fair, it must be controlled, steered and managed, according to the collective interests of European citizens.
>
> (Lamy, 1999)

In 2002, as he was already commissioner, with the economist Jean Pisani-Ferry he asserted that: "For the left-wing men and women, the challenge is to build, in Europe and by Europe, public regulations commensurate with the globalized economy and modernize a social system whose political family has powerfully built contributed" (Lamy, Pisani-Ferry, 2002, p. 9). Again two years later, he accepted to confront his positions with those of José Bové, a European representative and a world leader of anti-globalization. José Bové incriminated Lamy for considering "free trade as the main tool of development". Lamy argued as follows:

> No! I did not say that. I'm not a free trader. But I think, for historical, economic and political reasons that the opening up of exchanges is in the direction of the progress of humanity. That we have provoked fewer misfortunes and conflicts when we opened the exchanges than when we

closed them. . . . Where trade passes, the armies stop. Montesquieu said it better than I did.

(Bové, Lamy, 4 September 2003)

In his first book since leaving the WTO, Lamy (2014) reflects on his time there and outlines his views on the significance of open trade in generating global economic growth, reducing poverty and creating jobs around the world. He argues that trade can only act as a motor for growth if the correct mix of domestic and international economic and social policies is in place. This approach – the "Geneva Consensus" – requires deeper cooperation and policy coherence between the international organizations active in setting international economic, social and political policies. *The Geneva Consensus* describes the ongoing efforts to put this into effect, calling for more effective global governance to tackle the challenges of globalization.

Emmanuel Macron and the call for common initiatives against the excesses of finance and for economic growth

Emmanuel Macron is an enarque released inspector of finance, became managing partner of the bank Rothschild & Cie in 2010. Elected president of the French Republic in May 2017, at 39 years, making him the youngest French president of the history, he has had a meteoric political rise. Appointed in 2012 as deputy general secretary to the cabinet of Socialist President François Hollande, he two years later became minister of economy, industry and digital. To display a vision of gathering beyond the traditional political divisions, he created in 2016 a new party, "En Marche", and won the presidential election a year later in the second round against the candidate of the far right Front National.

The ideas championed by Emmanuel Macron are a mixture of support for economic openness and criticism of the excesses of deregulated finance and growing inequalities. His calls for investment aid and international cooperation have some Keynesian accents.

Defender of the European ideal, Emmanuel Macron considers, in his programme book of 2017 titled *Revolution*, that the measures taken after the financial crisis of 2008 did not make it possible to regulate all the excesses of the speculative finance and slowed down the activity of the banks and the insurance companies, even though these institutions play a central role in the financing of productive investment. He calls for abandoning "easy solutions", adopting international solutions and a "spirit of unity", rather than blaming only a few economic agents for the growing injustice felt by citizens. "In this regard, we have to be discriminating, by opposing finance for its own ends while encouraging finance that promotes investment" (p 40).

Considering that the Bretton Woods system had succeeded in introducing regulations to the financial sphere that created "a sorely needed new financial and monetary balance", he implicitly calls for a G20 initiative along the same lines. Placing this issue at the centre of the evolution of human civilization

("We have to rethink humanism for our times"), he criticizes the excesses of financial capitalism which limit the positive effects of globalization. (p 136)

In his Foreword of Bertrand Badré's book *Will Finance Save the World?* (2018a), Macron reaffirms the importance of finance but this one "is only a means to serve human ends". However, the deregulated finance resulting from the collapse of the Bretton Woods system is no longer at the service of "governments' greater goals". "The crucial lesson of the 2007 financial crisis is the urgent need to regain control of the global financial system" (p. viii). Money must be reallocated towards environmental innovation, new technologies and development. For this purpose, private institutions must be encouraged to take risks for the general interest.

In *Revolution* (2017), denouncing the growing inequalities arising from the excesses of finance, Macron calls for a central role for France to change capitalism: "I am convinced that France must take its rightful place in this essential undertaking – ensuring that human values prevail in globalisation" (p. 137).

According to Macron, the EU and the G20 must make it possible to find international agreements on several essential topics:

- applying rules to grey financing,
- regulating financial executives' remuneration worldwide,
- combating tax evasion and tax fraud (all existing tax agreements between European Union countries and tax havens must be renegotiated), and
- flying the flag of social and environmental responsibility.

> We need to ensure that by 2020 we can lay down the foundations of new rules for globalisation. This is not a battle to "prevent", or simply to "preserve", but a battle against devastating excesses, and for our common future. . . . Our sustained response must be to make globalisation more civilised, and to base our action in the heart of a Europe that has become even more indispensable.
>
> (p. 138)

Two years later, now president of the French Republic, he defended two other ideas in his speech at the World Economic Forum in Davos (24 January 2018) (Macron 2018b):

- To fight increased inequalities in the spreading of value added, investment mechanisms and investment criteria must include the value distribution within the company. In this perspective, he calls on China and the United States to join the OECD initiative on the base erosion and profit sharing (BEPS). Moreover, the taxation of the "Big tech" must be complete and not limited by "tax-attractive" hubs, which require tax cooperation within OECD countries.
- Concerning the financial regulation, he is "in favour of the IMF having the mandate to monitor the entire international financial system, entire sections

of which are currently unregulated", like cryptocurrencies and shadow banking. Increased regulation would permit to limit financial instability.

In *Revolution* (2017), regarding the euro crisis, he launches the idea of the creation of a "joint Eurozone fund" to deal with major problems: the widening gaps between its economies, the slow recovery and a lack of public and private investment. He proposes the creation of a post of European minister of finance "responsible to a Eurozone Parliament that would bring together all European parliamentarians from the Eurozone at least once a month, to ensure true democratic oversight" (p. 148). Implicitly, he calls on the least indebted countries of the Eurozone to finance this fund (p. 148).

In addition, he advocates the establishment of a five-year public investment plan in France, without waiting for European initiatives that would take too long to set up. "All future investments that can contribute to the plan will need to be dispensed from the debt and deficit objectives included in the EU Stability and Growth Pact" (p. 148).

In Davos (2018b), the French president renews his call for a collective action, including international institutions, to overcome the crisis of globalization. In France, it is a question of reorienting the financial system towards capital (finance risks and key innovations) and investment, through tax reforms and measures aiming at reducing labour costs, to bolster territorial attractiveness. The "refoundation of Europe" would concretize "in 10-year strategy . . . to make Europe an actual economic, green, social, scientific and political power" (Macron, 2018, p. 1). To combat inequalities and the concentration of wealth resulting from the process of economic globalization, the European cooperation on labour and tax law is necessary, as well as a common strategy to deal with the consequences of technical changes – artificial intelligence, for example, or Big Data, particularly in terms of job losses. A new global contract must be "included in the investors' model, banks' model, in the entrepreneurs' model" to prevent most of powers from becoming "free-riders of common goods".

Conclusion

The French position on the international monetary system has always been marked by a certain defence of orthodoxy, with a central role claimed for gold. In a weak position during the BW negotiations, France was not able to impose its views on the Anglo-Saxon countries, and the role of the IMF as the pivot of the international system will decrease rapidly, at the same time as the dollar becomes a key currency. Jacques Rueff's idea of a need to combat balance of payments imbalances did not succeed in bringing about reforms; the considerable deficits of the United States will be maintained over a long period. The influence of Europe is then very weak, and the hopes of international monetary cooperation are reduced.

After World War II, the ideas of the French politicians (especially Marjolin and Mendès France) played an important role in the drafting of a European ideal, with a Keynesian sensibility. The French contesting of the dominant role of the dollar exerted a reformist pressure that can be considered as having played a role in the implementation of the European project.

The French politicians who played an important role in the establishment of the EMU were engaged in a socialist government, which adopted a policy of austerity away from the previous Keynesian principles. The French position remains in the long term in line with the positions of Rist and Rueff. And several politicians who have had a major influence on the evolution of the European Union since the 1980s have defended the process of liberalization underlying economic globalization: this is the case of Chavranski, Delors, Lamy and of the current French president, Emmanuel Macron.

After the global financial crisis began in 2007 in the United States, questions about the viability of the current international monetary system have multiplied. The objective of combating external imbalances, which has been a central argument in the French contestations of the international monetary system since the end of World War II, is now widely supported. For example, Mervyn King, the governor of the Bank of England, points out in a 2011 speech the danger of the floating exchange rate system when "global imbalances" exist: "Today's IMFS has become distorted (King, 2011, p. 79). The major surplus and deficit countries are pursuing economic strategies that are in direct conflict". This puts the global economy at risk of a return to protectionism and of a deterioration in international relations like that of the 1930s. Nearly sixty-five years after the Bretton Woods conference, a new exchange rate and capital control interventionism is being invoked at the highest level of the international monetary and financial system.

Notes

1 The Bretton Woods Conference (July 1–22, 1944) was the gathering of delegates from all allied nations at the Mount Washington Hotel, situated in Bretton Woods, to regulate the international monetary and financial order after the conclusion of World War II.
2 See Table 10.1, What financial architects in the BW era believed: some generalizations, Endres, 2005, p. 209.
3 "Europe will happen through the currency or will not happen".
4 Source: www.nbb.be/en/notes-and-coins/brief-history-euro
5 In his *Memoirs* (Marjolin 1986, p. 370), he denied any evolution, asserting the following "From 1945 to 1967, I remained socialist leaning. I was social-democrat, or rather a liberal ready to adopt a moderate socialist program".
6 *Le Monde*, 7 April 1945, Statement of Mendès-France after his resignation.
7 See Cogan 2007, p. 228.
8 www.bullionstar.com/blogs/koos-jansen/gold-meeting-nixon-pompidou-1971-azores/
9 Treaty Establishing The European Community, Official Journal C 224, 31/08/1992 P. 0024.
10 Judgment of 11. 11. 1981 – Case 203/80 , European Court Reports 1981 –pp. 2595–2620.
11 www.bluebird-electric.net/oceanography/Global_Ocean_Commisioners/Pascal_Lamy.htm

Bibliography

Abdelal, R. (2005). Capital Rules: Institutions and the International Monetary System, www.princeton.edu/Meunier/Abdelal,%20The%20Rules%20of%20Globalization.pdf.

Abdelal, R. (2007). *Capital Rules: The Construction of Global Finance*. Cambridge, MA: Harvard University Press.

Abdelal, R., & Meunier, S. (2010). Managed Globalization: Doctrine, Practice and Promise, *Journal of European Public Policy*, Vol. 17, No. 3, pp. 350–367.

Abdelal, R., & Ruggie, J. G. (2009). The Principles of Embedded Liberalism: Social Legitimacy and Global Capitalism, in *New Perspectives on Regulation*. Ed. D. Moss and J. Cisternino. Cambridge, MA: The Tobin Project.

Aglietta, M. (1995). *Cinquante ans après Bretton Woods*. Paris: Economica.

Aglietta, M. (2011). Risque systémique et politique macroprudentielle: une nouvelle responsabilité des banques centrales, *Revue d'économie financière*, Vol. 1, No. 101, pp. 193–204.

Allais, M. (1999). *La crise mondiale d'aujourd'hui: pour de profondes réformes des institutions financières et monétaires*. Paris: C. Juglar.

Allais, M. (2002). *Nouveaux combats pour l'Europe: 1995–2002: un aveuglement suicidaire: pour une autre Europe*. Paris: C. Juglar.

Allais, M. (2005). *L'Europe en crise que faire? réponses à quelques questions, pour une autre Europe*. Paris: C. Juglar.

Annamaria, de C., Marta, G., & Anne-Christelle, O. Currency-Based Measures Targeting Banks: Balancing National Regulation of Risk and Financial Openness.

Arena R. and C. Schmidt, 1999, Keynes Before and After the General Theory: the Theoretical Contents of French Economists' Reactions, 1929–69, in L. Pasinetti & B. Schefold (eds.) *The Impact of Keynes on Economics in the 20th Century*. Cheltenham: Edward Elgar, pp. 73–98.

Armijo, L. E. (2002). *Debating the Global Financial Architecture*. Albany: State University of New York Press.

Bakker, A. (1996). *The Liberalization of Capital Movements in Europe: The Monetary Committee and Financial Integration, 1958–1994*. Dordrecht: Kluwer Academic Publishers.

Bastidon-Gilles, C., Brasseul, J., & Gilles, P. (2010). *Le système de Bretton Woods de 1946 à 1973*, in Histoire de la globalisation financière, Armand Colin.

Baverez, N. (2001). Gouverner la monnaie. In: Matériaux pour l'histoire de notre temps, n°63–64, 2001. Pierre Mendès France et la Modernité – Actes du colloque – Assemblée nationale – 15 juin. pp. 35–42.

Bonucci, N. (2011). The OECD at Fifty: Some Observations on the Evolving Nature of an International Organization, *The George Washington International Law Review*, Vol. 43, No. 2.

Bonucci, N., & Thouvenin, J. M. (2014). L'OCDE, site de gouvernance globale? http://pedone.info/sfdi/701/03-BONUCCI.pdf.

Bordo, M. D. The Bretton Woods International Monetary System: A Historical Overview, NBER Working Paper No. 4033.

Bordo, M. D., Simard, D., & White, E. (1994). France and the Bretton Woods International Monetary System: 1960 to 1968, NBER, Working Paper No. 4642, French trad.: Revue d'économie financière, Vol. 26 No. 3, pp. 249–286.

Bové, J. Lamy, P. (2003), "Bové-Lamy: Le choc des deux gauches", Le Nouvel Observateur, n°2026 – 4 September, http://trade.ec.europa.eu/

Brault, J. (2013). The International Transactions of France from the 1920s to the 1970s, PhD thesis in International Studies, Graduate Institute of International and Development Studies, Geneva.

Brault, J. (May 1, 2014). The Political Economy of French Foreign Exchange Control, Working Paper, www.academia.edu/4048741/The_Political_Economy_of_French_Foreign_Exchange_Control.

Brault, J. La Banque de France et les transactions internationales de la France des années 1930 aux années 1970, séminaire de la Banque de France, www.banque-france.fr/. ./banque_de_france/. ./. .

Brender, A., Pisani, F., Gagna, E., & Centre for European Policy Studies. (2012). *The Sovereign Debt Crisis: Placing a Curb on Growth*. Brussels, Belgium: Centre for European Policy Studies (CEPS).

Bush, O., Farrant, K., & Wright, M. (2011). Financial Stability Paper No 13: Reform of the International Monetary and Financial System, No 13, Bank of England Financial Stability Papers, Bank of England, http://EconPapers.repec.org/RePEc:boe:finsta:0013.

Büthe, T. (2008). Politics and Institutions in the Regulation of Global Capital: A Review Article, *The Review of International Organizations*, Vol. 3, No. 2, pp. 207–220.

Cassou, P.-H. (2001). Seize ans de réorganisation bancaire en France. *Revue d'économie financière*, No 61. 15 ans de restructuration bancaire. Dynamique financière et création de valeur. pp. 13–30.

Chavranski, H. (1997). *L'OCDE: au coeur des grands débats économiques*. Paris, la Documentation française.

Chwieroth, J. M. (2007). Testing and Measuring the Role of Ideas: The Case of Neoliberalism in the International Monetary Fund, *International Studies Quarterly*, Vol. 51, No. 1 (Mar.), pp. 5–30.

Chwieroth, J. M. (2010). *Capital Ideas: The IMF and the Rise of Financial Liberalization*. Princeton, NJ: Princeton University Press.

Cogan C. G., From the Fall of France to the Force de Frappe: The Remaking of French Military Power, 1940–62. Edited by Talbot C. Imlay, Monica Duffy Toft, pp. 224–248.

Cohen, B. J. (2001). Contrôle des capitaux. Pourquoi les gouvernements hésitent-ils? *Revue économique*, Vol. 52, No. 2, pp. 207–232.

Crombois, J. F. (2004). Le Fonds Monétaire International, le plan Marshall et la reconstruction des économies européennes 1946–1951, *Revue belge de philologie et d'histoire*, Vol. 82, No. 4, pp. 995–1019.

Davidson, P. (October, 1998). Efficiency and Fragile Speculative Financial Markets: Against the Tobin Tax and for a Creditable Market Maker, *The American Journal of Economics and Sociology*, Vol. 57, No. 4, pp. 639–662.

Davidson, P. (2002). *Financial Markets, Money, and the Real World*. Cheltenham, UK: Edward Elgar.

de Gaulle, C. February 4, 1965. Press Conference.

de Grauwe, P. (1999). *La monnaie internationale: théories et perspectives*. Paris; Bruxelles: De Boeck Université.

Dehem, P. ([1987] 2017). Rist, Charles (1874–1955), in *The New Palgrave Dictionary of Economics*. Second Edition. Ed. S. N. Durlauf and L. E. Blume. Palgrave Macmillan.

Deutsche Bundesbank. (2001). *The Monetary Transmission Process: Recent Developments and Lessons for Europe*. Houndmills; Basingstoke; Hampshire: Palgrave.

Deutsche Bundesbank, & Monatsbericht, J. (2001). *Grenzüberschreitender Kapitalverkehr und die Rolle des Internationalen Währungsfonds. (Cross-Border Capital Movements and the Role of the IMF)*.

Deutsche Bundesbank Monthly Report. (July 1985). *Freedom of Germany's Capital Transactions with Foreign Countries.*

Dewatripont, M., Rochet, J.-C., Tirole, J., & Tribe, K. (2010). *Balancing the Banks: Global Lessons from the Financial Crisis.* Princeton, NJ: Princeton University Press.

Dillingham, A. J. (1995). The Evolution of France's European Monetary Diplomacy.

Dirk Ehnts, Bard College Berlin from Wicksell to Le Bourva to Modern Monetary Theory: A Wicksell Connection.

Donges, J. B., & Stiftung Marktwirtschaft. (2010). *Öffentliche Finanzen dauerhaft sanieren – in Deutschland und Europa.* Berlin: Stiftung Marktwirtschaft.

Drouin, M. (2001). *Le système financier international.* Paris: Armand Colin.

Durand, D. Guerre monétaire internationale: l'hégémonie du dollar contestée? *Géoéconomie*, Vol. 2008/4, No. 47, pp. 69–84.

Dyson, K. H. F., & Maes, I. (2016). *Architects of the Euro: Intellectuals in the Making of European Monetary Union.* Oxford: Oxford University Press.

Eichengreen, B. J. (1995). *Europe's Post-War Recovery.* Cambridge: Cambridge University Press.

Eichengreen, B. J. (2004). *Capital Flows and Crises.* Cambridge, MA: MIT Press.

Eichengreen, B. J. (2008). *Globalizing Capital: A History of the International Monetary System.* Second Edition. Princeton, NJ; Oxford: Princeton University Press.

Eichengreen, B. J., & Mathieson, D. J. (July 2000). The Currency Composition of Foreign Exchange Reserves: Retrospect and Prospect IMF Working Paper Research Department.

Endres, A. M. (2005). *Great Architects of International Finance: The Bretton Woods Era.* London: Routledge.

Escrivá, José Luis Alicia Garcia-Herrero, Galo Nuño, Joaquin Vial (June, 2008). After Bretton Woods II * †BBVA Research Department.

European Commission. (2009). *Economic Crisis in Europe: Causes, Consequences and Responses.* Luxembourg: Office for Official Publications of the European Communities.

Financial institutions in Europe under new competitive conditions edited by Donald E. Fair and Christian de Boissieu; with contrIbutions frOI Ole Aerthej, let al.l. p. cm.-(Financial monetary policy studies; 20).

Fernandez-Bollo, E. (2013). *Structural Reform and Supervision of the Banking Sector in France.* (OECD Journal: Financial Market Trends, 2013, Vol. 1, pp. 31–38). Paris: OECD Publishing.

Fiorentini, R., & Montani, G. (2010). Global Imbalances and the Transition to a Symmetric World Monetary System (July 13, 2009), *Perspectives on Federalism*, Vol. 2, No. 1, 2010. Available at SSRN: http://ssrn.com/abstract=1433248.

Fischer, S. (2004). *IMF Essays from a Time of Crisis: The International Financial System, Stabilization, and Development.* Cambridge, MA: MIT Press.

Fourastié. (1963). *Jean La planification économique en France.* Paris: Presses universitaires de France.

Fuchs, T. K. (1998). *The Tardieu Moment: Andre Tardieu's Failure as Prime Minister of France, 1929–1930, B.A.* Georgia Southern University.

Fourcade-Gourinchas, M., & Babb, S. L. (2002). The Rebirth of the Liberal Creed: Paths to Neoliberalism in Four Countries, *American Journal of Sociology*, Vol. 108, No. 3 (Novem ber), pp. 533–579.

Giraud, G. Pour un second Bretton Woods, *Revue Projet*, Vol. 2009/2, No. 309, pp. 67–75.

Goodman, J. B., & Pauly, L. W. (January 1, 1993). The Obsolescence of Capital Controls? Economic Management in an Age of Global Markets, *World Politics*, pp. 50–82.

Henry, P. B. (January 1, 2007). Capital Account Liberalization: Theory, Evidence, and Speculation, *Journal of Economic Literature*, Vol. 45, No. 4, pp. 887–935.

Howarth, D., Sadeh, T. (December 2011). In the Vanguard of Globalization: The OECD and International Capital Liberalization, *Review of International Political Economy*, Vol. 18, No. 5, pp. 622–645.

Imlay, Talbot C., & Monica Duffy Toft. (2007). *The Fog of Peace and War Planning: Military and Strategic Planning under Uncertainty*. London: Routledge.

International Monetary Fund. (March 13, 2012). Liberalizing Capital Flows and Managing Outflows, Policy Papers.

Keynes, J. M. (1936). *The General Theory of Employment, Interest and Money*. London: MacMillan.

Keynes, J. M. (1941). Post-War Currency Policy. British Treasury Memorandum, September. In *The Collected Writings of John Maynard Keynes*. Ed. D. Moggridge. Vol. 25. Cambridge: Cambridge University Press, 1980, 31.

Keynes, J. M. (1942). Plan for an International Currency (or Clearing) Union. In *The Collected Writings of John Maynard Keynes*. Ed. D. Moggridge. Vol. 25. Cambridge: Cambridge University Press, 1980, 129–130.

Keynes, J. M. (1980). *The Collected Writings of John Maynard Keynes*. Ed. D. Moggridge. Vol. 25. Cambridge: Cambridge University Press.

King, M. A. (2011). Global Imbalances: The Perspective of the Bank of England, *Banque de France Financial Stability Review*, No. 15, February, pp. 73–80.

King, M. A. (2016). *The End of Alchemy: Money, Banking and the Future of the Global Economy*. New York: W. W. Norton & Company.

Kydland, F. E., & Prescott, E. C. (1977). Rules Rather Than Discretion: The Inconsistency of Optimal Plans, *Journal of Political Economy*, Vol. 85, pp. 473–491.

Laïdi, Z. (2008). *Norms over Force: The Enigma of European Power*. New York: Palgrave Macmillan.

Lamy, P. (1999). *Hearings of Commissioners-Designate*. Brussels: European Parliament.

Lamy, P. Pisani-Ferry, J. (2002), L'Europe de nos volontés, Notes de la Fondation Jean Jaurès, N°27 – janvier.

Lamy, P. (2014). *The Geneva Consensus: Making Trade Work for All*. Cambridge: Cambridge University Press.

Lelart, M. (1994). De Gênes à Bretton Woods, *Revue d'économie financière*. Hors-série. Bretton Woods: mélanges pour un cinquantenaire, pp. 521–524.

Loriaux, M. M. (1991). *France after Hegemony: International Change and Financial Reform*. Ithaca, NY: Cornell University Press.

Macron, E. (2017). *Revolution*, London: Scribe, 2017.

Macron, E. (2018a). *Foreword* of Badré Bertrand, *Will Finance Save the World?*, Berret-Koehler.

Macron, E. (January 24, 2018b). Speech at the World Economic Forum in Davos. Retrieved from https://in.ambafrance.org/Address-by-Prez-Emmanuel-Macron-at-Davos .

Maes, I. (2004). Belgium National Bank Macroeconomic and Monetary Policy-Making at the European Commission, from the Rome Treaties to the Hague Summit", Working Paper No. 58.

Makin, J. H. (1974). Capital Flows and Exchange-Rate Flexibility in the Post-Bretton Woods Era. Princeton, NJ: International Finance Section, Princeton University.

Mangenot, M. (1998). Une école européenne d'administration? L'improbable conversion de l'ENA à l'Europe, *Politix*, Vol. 11, No. 43, 3 trimestre, pp. 7–32.

Mangenot, M. (2001). La revendication d'une paternité: Les hauts fonctionnaires français et le "style" administratif de la Commission européenne (1958–1988), *Pôle Sud*, No. 15, pp. 33–46.

Marcy, G. (1958). Quelques aspects de l'évolution de la réglementation française du commerce extérieur depuis 1945. Contrôle des changes et règlements internationaux, *Revue économique*, Vol. 9, No. 3, pp. 348–384.

Marjolin, R. (1938). Reflections on the Blum Experiment, *Economica*, New Series, Vol. 5, No. 18, pp. 177–191.

Marjolin, R. (1941). *Prix, Monnaie et Production. Essai sur les mouvements économiques de longue durée with a preface by Charles Rist*. Paris: Alcan.

Marjolin, R. (1946). Les perspectives de l'économie française dans l'économie mondiale, *Politique étrangère*, Vol. 11, No. 3, pp. 263–277.

Marjolin, R. (1958). Coopération intergouvernementale et autorités supranationales, *Revue économique*, Vol. 9, No. 2, pp. 267–277.

Marjolin, R. (1986). *Le travail d'une vie, Mémoires, 1911–1986*. Paris: Laffont.

Marshall, J., & Great Britain. (2009). *The Financial Crisis in the US: Key Events, Causes, and Responses*. London: House of Commons Library.

Mendès France, P. (1928). *L'oeuvre financière du gouvernement Poincaré*. Paris: LGDJ.

Mendès France, P. (1930). *La banque internationale. Contribution à l'étude du problème des Etats-Unis d'Europe*. Paris: Valois.

Mendès Frace P. (1957), Discours lors de la séance du 18 janvier 1957, *Journal officiel du Samedi 19 Janvier 1957*, pp. 159–166.

Mendès France, P. (1967). M. Mendès France juge très sévèrement le plan adopté à Rio-de-Janeiro pour la création de nouvelles liquidités internationales, *Le Monde*, November 18.

Messerlin, P. A. (January 1, 1995). The Impact on Trade and Capital Movements on Labour: Evidence of the French Case, *OECD Economic Studies*, Vol. 24, pp. 89–124.

Michler, A. F., Seitz, F. Internationale Kapitelströme vor dem Hintergrund der Finanzmarktkrise, in *Die aktuelle Finanzkrise: Bestandsaufnahme und Lehren für die Zukunft*. Ed. A. F. Michler, and H. D. Smeets (2011). Stuttgart: Lucius & Lucius, 325–352.

Monnet, E. (2017). French Monetary Policy and the BW System: Criticisms, Proposals and Conflicts, in *Global Perspectives on the BW Conference and the Post-War Order*. Ed. G. Scott-Smith and J. Simon Rofe. Palgrave Macmillan.

Mossé, E. (1997). Henri Chavranski. OCDE: au coeur des grands débats économiques, *Politique étrangère*, No. 4–62[e]année, pp. 670–671.

Muracciole, J.-F., Piketty, D. (2015). *Encyclopédie de la seconde guerre mondiale*. Paris: Robert Laffont.

O'Brien, J. (2010). The Future of Financial Regulation: Enhancing Integrity through Design, *Sydney Law Review*, Vol. 32, No. 1, p. 63.

OECD (1963). Code of Liberalization of Capital Movements. Paris: OCDE.

OECD (2002). Forty Years' Experience with the OECD Code of Liberalisation of Capital Movements, Paris: OECD.

Palais Royal Initiative, Reform of the International Monetary System: A Cooperative Approach for the Twenty-First Century. (May 1, 2011). *Global Journal of Emerging Market Economies*, Vol. 3, No. 2, pp. 185–193.

Papers presented at the 15th colloquium arranged by the Societe unlversitaire europeene de recherChes financieres (SUERF), Nice, France. October 1989.

Patat, J-P. (1986). *Histoire monétaire de la France au XXe siècle*. Paris: Économica.

Patat, J.-P. (2005). *Histoire de l'Europe monétaire*. Paris: La Découverte.

Patat, J.-P., Lutfalla, M., & Raymond, R. (1986). *Histoire monétaire de la France au XXe siècle*. Paris: Economica.

Piatier, A. (1938). Les mouvements de capitaux et l'Accord Tripartite, *Politique étrangère*, No. 3–1938–3e année, pp. 280–300.

Quatrepoint, J.-M. (2013). Mars 83 ou comment la France a perdu la guerre monétaire, *Le Débat*, Vol. 2, No. 174, pp. 10–25.

Quinn, D. P., & Inclan, C. (July, 1997). The Origins of Financial Openness: A Study of Current and Capital Account Liberalization, *American Journal of Political Science*, Vol. 41, No. 3, pp. 771–813.

Ramos-Tallada, J. (2013). Le FMI et la gestion des flux de capitaux: la longue route vers une approche pragmatique, *Bulletin de la Banque de France*, No. 192, pp. 95–110.

Rueff, J. (June 1965). The Role and the Rule of Gold, *Essays in International Finance*, No. 47.

Rueff, J. (1971), Le Péché Monêtaire de l'Occident, Paris: Plon, English translation, *The Monetary Sin of the West*, New York: Macmillan, 1972.

Rueff, J. (1978). L'Europe se fera par la monnaie ou ne se fera pas, *Commentaire*, No. 3, pp. 386–388.

Singer, D. A. (2007). *Regulating Capital: Setting Standards for the International Financial System*. Ithaca, NY: Cornell University Press.

Singh, A. (2003) Capital Account Liberalization, Free Long-Term Capital Flows, Financial Crises and Economic Development, *Eastern Economic Journal*, Vol. 29, No. 2 (Spring), pp. 191–216.

Tirole, J. (2002). *Financial Crises, Liquidity, and the International Monetary System*. Princeton, NJ; Woodstock: Princeton University Press.

www.xerficanal-economie.com/mobile/ensavoirplus/Le-graphique-Xerfi-le-cours-euro-dollar-les-lecons-de-l-histoire_i2431.html.

Thurow L. (1983), Macroeconomics by Wynne Godley and Francis Cripps, *London Review of Books*, Vol. 5 No. 16 1 September.

9 Economic culture and the role of economists

The crisis on European newspapers (2008–2013)

Monika Poettinger

Introduction

Usually the history of economic thought – and specifically the history of economic analysis – concentrates on the evolution in time of a certain system or theory, in respect to which all divergences are termed as heterodox or simply false. Theories are followed back and forth in time, collecting precursors, systematizers and followers. Schools of thought are defined, economists cataloged and neatly subdivided manuals printed. The relation between economic thought and economic facts is only hinted at by describing how the economic policy of certain countries followed the dictates of some theoretician or school of thought. Little attention is given, instead, to the formation and development of economic culture and its influence on policymaking or to the influence that generic culture had on the development of economic thought or on individual theoreticians (Brunnermeier, James, Landau, 2016, 56).

At the origin of this lack of interest lies the presumed scientific status of economic theory and the specialization of disciplines, with economic history rarely interacting with economics and history of economic thought (Poettinger, Tusset, 2016). If economics is considered a science with the ambition of unveiling in time an absolute truth, then an history of economic analysis that studies the evolution in time towards this teleological end would be completely justified. Such an evolution could be researched with complete disregard for facts, politics or culture.

The present research, instead, presumes economic thought to be part of general culture and its development a worthy subject of sociological analysis. Despite older debates (Einaudi, 1932; Michels, Einaudi, 1932), more recent methodological help is to be found in the writings of Walt Whitman Rostow (1990). Beside individual decisions, Rostow allows the existence of *broad collective decisions*, based on long-term cultural traits unconsciously applied at societal level (Rostow, 1990, 15), and *social decisions*, consciously taken by the collectivity (Rostow, 1990, 15), through a political decision process determined by economic and uneconomic rationales (Ternisien, Rosen, 2010; Giacometti, Péron, 2010). In the following, economic culture is so defined as the sum of all economic concepts and theories that at a given time influences individual choices, but also broad collective decisions and social decisions. While individual choice is an object of study for economists, the determinants of the other two typologies of decision-making are not. John M. Keynes hinted at the fact that dead economists' ideas had much more an influence on individual and collective decisions than was commonly believed (Keynes, 1936, 383), but such idealistic belief was not shared by many colleagues, then or now. There are some exceptions, though. In the same years, Amintore Fanfani (1939) described economic ideas as being at one time the agent of change in society when answering to changes in technology, while becoming a hindrance to development when transformed in institutions and immutable theories. Federico Caffè (1966), also, in the aftermath of World War II stressed the role and responsibility of economists in shaping the future by influencing, as every other intellectual, the set of beliefs on which the decision-making of individuals and collective actors rely.

The recent economic crisis (2008–2013) represents an interesting case to delineate on one hand which economic theories, from times past, exerted an influence on contemporary economic culture, shaping broad collective responses to the economic turmoil, and on the other hand, if and how contemporary economists consciously intervened in the public and specifically political debate to influence public opinion and shape social decisions. The analysis concerned three European countries and four European newspapers: *Corriere della Sera* and *Repubblica* for Italy, the *Frankfurter Allgemeine Zeitung* for Germany and *Le Monde* for France.[1] Newspapers were chosen to represent an expression of broad economic culture when articles were written by journalists, and of academic influence on public opinion when articles were written by leading economists. In the first case, the analysis has been pursed quantitatively, with simple word counts measured annually on newspapers' archives, while in the second case, the research was mostly done qualitatively. Other indicators of economists' political influence (Pühringer, 2015) as direct political involvement, consultancy contracts and think tank activities are only cited in passing.

Economic culture in times of crisis

> So true is it that, in science as elsewhere, we fight for and against not men and things as they are, but for and against the caricatures we make of them.
>
> (Schumpeter, 2006, 86)

The problem of intra-European relations during the crisis 2008–2013 had many layers (Poettinger, 2014). The recrudescence of nationalist and populist attitudes in the years of the crisis depended on old rivalries and prejudices, grounded in the historical past, but also on the influence and diffusion of different economic schools (Fressoz, Wieder, 2013; Brunnermeier, James, Landau, 2016). An analysis of the frequency of citations of individual economists shows how economic culture was still imbibed with economic thought of the past. The foremost example is Karl Marx. Although the 1980s witnessed the crumbling of communism in Eastern Europe, wiping out the political realization of his utopia, and his economic theory has long vanished from universities' programs, Marx remains the most quoted economist in all newspapers considered in this research, with no regard for nationality or political orientation. In Italy the analysis, including the *Corriere della Sera* and *La Repubblica*, covered Adam Smith, Karl Marx, John M. Keynes, Luigi Einaudi and Piero Sraffa (Table 9.1). In Germany, the *Frankfurter Allgemeine Zeitung* was searched for quotations of Adam Smith, Karl Marx, John M. Keynes, Ludwig Erhard and Piero Sraffa (Table 9.2). The French *Le Monde* was analyzed in regard to Adam Smith, Karl Marx, John M. Keynes, Piero Sraffa, Jacques Attali, Jean-Paul Fitoussi and Olivier Blanchard[2] (Figure 9.1).

Marx's quota, on the total of articles naming the previously mentioned economists, persistently remained around 50%, peaking at almost 70% on *La Repubblica* in 2010. In Germany, Marx seemed also to enjoy the advantage of a national champion, because, although *Frankfurter Allgemeine Zeitung* is a right-wing newspaper, Marx is not only the most quoted economist among the chosen ones, but shows an advantage over the second placed only comparable with the one of the Italian left wing *La Repubblica*. *Corriere della Sera*, instead,

Table 9.1 Articles citing relevant economists on *La Repubblica* (white rows) and *Corriere della Sera* (gray rows) in the years 2008–2013

Articles containing the words	*2008*	*2009*	*2010*	*2011*	*2012*	*2013*
Marx	140	156	131	131	128	76
Marx	595	380	458	499	347	207
Keynes	54	64	42	45	43	31
Keynes	155	126	87	152	143	71
Sraffa	6	0	3	2	6	5
Sraffa	3	3	2	0	10	6
Liberism	127	60	43	74	90	48
Liberism	268	120	134	171	239	90
Adam Smith	19	24	25	17	25	14
Adam Smith	76	27	26	18	53	28
Luigi Einaudi	50	31	42	87	100	70
Luigi Einaudi	97	91	94	182	115	73

Table 9.2 Articles citing relevant economists on *Frankfurter Allgemeine Zeitung* in the years 2008–2013

Articles containing the words	*2008*	*2009*	*2010*	*2011*	*2012*	*2013*
Marx	485	449	423	405	455	463
Keynes	88	159	117	113	131	162
Sraffa	1	2	1	0	0	2
Adam Smith	57	107	57	44	67	77
Ludwig Erhard	199	218	142	109	102	177

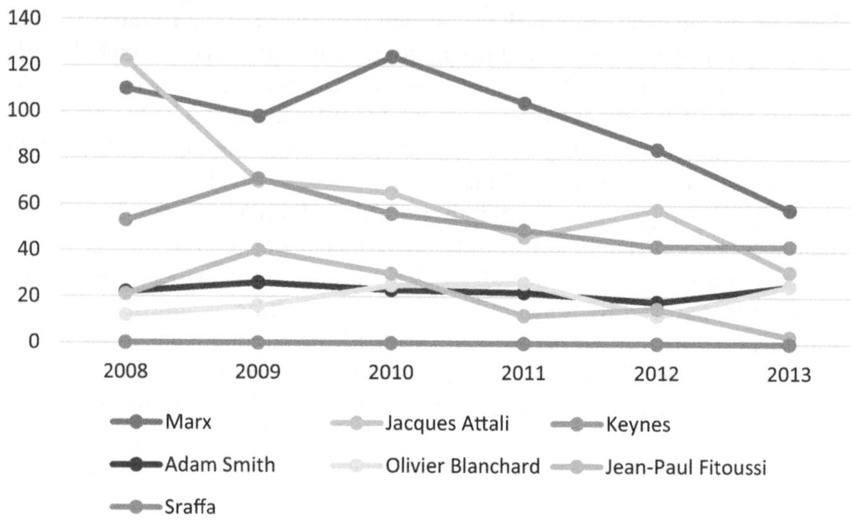

Figure 9.1 Number of articles quoting relevant economists in *Le Monde* during the years of crisis

appears more equilibrated: in 2013, Marx's quotations almost converge with those of Luigi Einaudi, Italy's renowned liberal economist and founding father of the Republic. *Le Monde* is no exception: Marx is by far the most quoted economist among past and present rivals. Only in 2008 was Jacques Attali able to overcome him due to the wide discussion on the results of the works of the *Commission pour la libération de la croissance française.*

Clearly, Karl Marx still dominates the realm of economic culture, and economic problems are discussed using his categories and vocabulary. As Keynes observed, the long-term effect of theoreticians is not to directly inspire individual, social or political decisions, but to determine how people at large categorize the world they live in, through concepts and relations that are not questioned but accepted as axioms. This way, long-dead economists define the conceptual language that people learn from the cradle, without questioning it. Although the direct influence of Marx' theories on politics and economics has almost vanished, his name has become something of a "brand" in which people can recognize themselves and as such worthy of continuous quotation. It could easily be said that, at least in Germany, Italy and France, we all live in a "Marxian" world. Such profound and pervasive impact has not escaped historians, and critical studies on Marx's writings have been flourishing in the years analyzed (Truong, 2011).

A more recent example is German *ordoliberalism*. As in the case of Marxism, the ordoliberal school, although academically dead already in the 1970s, kept a lasting impact on German economic culture (Braunberger, 2008) and still exerts a strong influence on present politics, as recognized in recent studies (Dullien, Guérot, 2012, 2). Ordoliberalism conditioned entire generations of journalists, bankers and politicians: Germany's elite (Wegner, 2014). Its principles are still diffused by the *Frankfurter Allgemeine Zeitung* (Brunnermeier, James, Landau, 2016, 64). Ordoliberalism, as a noun, hardly finds expression in the columns of the newspaper, although showing a significant peak during the first years of the US financial crisis. Ludwig Erhard, instead, one of the main offshoots of ordoliberal thinking, successfully contends with J.M. Keynes, in four out of six years, for second place in the frequency of quotations in articles. The same can be said for political programs of German parties regarding the European economic crisis. A recent study analyzed these programs in respect to ordoliberal normative indications, proving that, although never referring to the originating school of thought, their content constantly refers to it, in positive or negative (Dullien, Guérot, 2012, 9).

As economic theories gradually become the intellectual domain of elites, guiding politics and dominating academia, and then transform into widespread culture, their influence is delimited to the precise space where they have taken roots. In the case of ordoliberalism, such space overlapped with the national boundaries of Germany. Outside such space theories are ignored, if not in narrow circles,[3] except for their political and cultural consequences. When the originating theory suddenly crosses frontiers, having caught the attention of foreign politicians or media, it undergoes a process of interpretation and adaptation, and curious things happen. In the first years of the crisis, for example, ordoliberalism, considered in Germany a liberal economic philosophy and as such championed by a newspaper like *Frankfurter Allgemeine Zeitung*, would be particularly appreciated in Italy by left wing *La Repubblica*, because it is assumed to be synonymous with state intervention.

Past ideas rule the present in this form of broad culture, but, having lost in time the originating theoretical background, they can also become object and subject to prejudices and therefore be reduced to populist and nationalistic propaganda. This holds particularly true in times of crisis[4] when past economists and theories are evoked and invoked to foster traditional ways of thinking and conservative policies (Brunnermeier, James, Landau, 2016, 7) or to confirm old judgments and prejudices. Contemporary economists have, then, to decide how to react and interact to this use of economic thinking, assuming the role of impartial popularizers or taking the side of one of the political parties, underwriting its economic policy indications.

Economists in the public arena of social decisions

> But, strange to say, nobody seems to have known all these bricks or to have understood that they were bricks awaiting the hand that could combine them in a comprehensive structure.
>
> (Schumpeter, 2006, 746)

Not all interpretation of economic facts is based on socialized tradition. Political maneuvers and social interplay deliberately influence mass media and ignite public opinion, which in turn determines the political decision process and the resulting social decisions. In this case, dead economists have less an influence than living ones, in particular those writing in newspapers and journals, or lending their voice to political parties or other social actors. The role of economists as intellectuals is so called into question. Should economists represent the voice of reason, criticizing the instrumental use of economics made by political parties, or should they intervene directly in the political scene, advising politicians and even taking part in governments (Pühringer, 2015, 3–7)? Examples of both attitudes can easily be found analyzing European newspapers during the years of crisis.

From 2008 onward, obviously, the primary economic question occupying the attention of European public opinion has been the understanding of the economic crisis. Crises defy theories centered on equilibrium or growth, fostering alternative interpretations. Past theories, particularly those blaming the inherent unstable structure of capitalism, are brought back to life, often in the form of prejudicial knowledge to be used to interpret economic facts. In the subsequent turmoil of past and present, orthodox and unorthodox thinking, the intrinsic scientific dignity of economics is often menaced by the call for normative judgments, ethical and religious guidance, and institutional primacy.

In Europe, the external financial crisis of 2008 was immediately interpreted as the result of extreme speculative practices in the US (Stiglitz, 2008; Zucconi, 2008a; Rossi, 2008b; Calabresi, 2009; Villari, 2009; Bragantini, 2011): Gatsby's green light having bewitched America again (Rampini, 2009a). After all, the financial sector has historically been the first and preferred scapegoat on which the miseries of economic crises were blamed (Bocconi, 2008), and bankers always had, in the imagination of the public, a more evil reputation than entrepreneurs – an easy target of prejudice. The crisis of the new millennium was no exception. "The crisis has a name and surname: banks and rating agencies" titled *La Repubblica* (Bonafede, 2008), while Giulio Tremonti, the Italian minister for the economy, even called entrepreneurs and labor unions to judge and watch over banks and their practices (Lopapa, 2008). The devil of speculation had been evoked around the ultimate bonfire of vanities (Giannini, 2008a) and economists had to confront it (Bolopion, Nougayrède, 2008). Liberalists couldn't do otherwise than defend the freedom of markets. Francesco Giavazzi, remarking on the presumed speculation on oil prices in 2008, immediately recalled how Alessandro Manzoni described in his "I Promessi Sposi" the terrible famine of 1628–1629 and the consequent human chase on imaginary speculators (Giavazzi, 2008). History seemed to continuously repeat itself, and all the while people found it easier to mistake the scarcity of goods as the cause of a crisis and not as a consequence. Likely voices were those of Angelo Panebianco and Piero Ostellino (Ostellino, 2008), all writing in *Corriere della Sera*.

The majority of economists, though, called for some form of regulation in financial markets. As one of the earliest, Marcello de Cecco, in the columns of *La Repubblica*, blamed American monetary policies and the absence of controls for the collapse of the US economy (De Cecco, 2008), while Jean-Paul Fitoussi denounced on *Le Monde* the irresponsible increase in systemic risk following the financial deregulation of the last decade of the twentieth century (Fitoussi, 2008b). Christian de Boissieu, president of the *Conseil d'analyse économique*, called for a new Bretton Woods to construe an international order for financial markets ("Il faut refonder", 2008). The bailout of Freddie Mac and Fannie Mae and the spectacular maneuver of 700 billion dollars in September 2008 to save the American financial sector where then greeted as "the revenge of Keynes" (Zucconi, 2008b). Supply-side economic policy had been abruptly substituted by measures that to Italian observers easily recalled the experience of IRI (Zampaglione, 2008). Ugo Marani in *La Repubblica* even glorified the economic crisis as the cause for the anti-liberal change in American economic policy (Marani, 2008). A line of reasoning followed also by the economist Daniel Cohen in the Magazine of *Le Monde* (Joignot, 2008). On the contrary, Nicolas Baverez underlined on the same newspaper how the crisis could not be considered as the end of liberalism, but only the beginning of a new form of capitalism governed by new rules (Baverez, 2008b). The left-wing French association *Les Gracques*[5] advocated on *Le Monde* "more regulation, better regulation and more than everything else, more extensive regulation" ("La Bourse ou la vie", 2008).

German Chancellor Angela Merkel herself, at the World Economic Forum at Davos, January 2009, boasted of the virtues of extending the German ordoliberal model to Europe, with guidelines to dampen the excesses of speculation, comparing them to the catastrophic consequences of the absence of regulation in Anglo-Saxon capitalism. Merkel even invoked the creation of a UN Economic Council to lay down a charter for a global economic order and transpose the German model to the entire world economy (Dougherty, 2009). In Italy, in the columns of *La Repubblica*, the speech was praised as "the revenge of Europe" over liberalist America (Rampini, 2009b).

The recurring desire for revenge shown by the Italian left-wing newspaper in the name of Keynes or a European way to the regulation of the economy, is a telltale sign of the frustration of interventionists about the diffusion of liberalist theories and policies at national and international levels at the end of the twentieth century (Rossi, 2008a).

> Yes. This is the moment to defend the market from all who demonize it and want to get rid of it. – Tommaso Padoa Schioppa observed in an interview to *La Repubblica* – But a market that does not dominate political economy. Because the market is not a value, nor an idol to be sacrificed to; the market is a useful instrument if regulated and used well.
>
> (Giannini, 2008b)

Sergio Bocconi, on *Corriere della Sera*, relating the works of a congress titled: "Liberals taking capitalism on trial", likewise contended that capitalism could be absolved from all charges, but needed new rules (Bocconi, 2009). Gilles Dostaler in *Le Monde* would also underline that a natural return to an economic equilibrium was a myth, not a reality. To be liberal in this sense would be an absurdity, while an interventionist stance, even if professed as a liberal, would be more appropriate, as Keynes had demonstrated (De Tricornot, Dostaler, 2009).

Data collected on the analyzed newspapers confirm that, in this early phase, the crisis was generally perceived as a financial disaster due to a lack of control over speculation (Tables 9.3 and 9.4). The exact phrase "financial crisis" is most frequently quoted in 2008 in all newspapers and subsequently steadily declines. The same evolution is shown by the number of articles mentioning "capitalism" and "crisis" together (Tables 9.3 and 9.4, Figure 9.2). The historian and linguist Massimo Arcangeli even counted, for *La Repubblica*, the thirteen times that the Italian President Giorgio Napolitano quoted the word "crisis" – financial, global or profound – in his New Year's address of 2009, a frequency never reached before, in all the years the speech had been held (Arcangeli, 2009).

As in the wake of 1929,[6] the spectacular failing of US liberalism provoked in all newspapers a lively debate about the possible end of capitalism.[7] Francis Fukuyama, in one of his typical flamboyant announcements, denounced the bankruptcy of America Incorporated (Fukuyama, 2008). In Italy and Germany, "statism" and "liberalism" confronted with a virulence unseen in previous or later years (Tables 9.3 and 9.4). *Le Monde* shows, in the years 2008–2010, a peak for quotations of Keynes and liberalism, even if *etatisme* remains a stable and widespread concept for the whole period considered[8] (Figures 9.1 and 9.2). Marx, as seen, held the center of the stage. Articles referring to the German economist peaked in 2008 on *La Repubblica* and *Frankfurter Allgemeine Zeitung*, in 2009 on *Corriere della Sera* and in 2010 in *Le Monde*. Keynes showed a similar pattern on Italian newspapers, with a maximum of quotations in 2008 on *La Repubblica* and in 2009 on *Corriere della Sera*. Germany had its own ordoliberal bias, and instead of Keynes it was Erhard who reached the highest number of citations in 2008 and 2009. All possible alternatives to capitalism, or to free market economy (Giannini, 2008b), as Padoa Schioppa suggests because easier to define, were at some point proposed for discussion: statism, ordoliberalism, Keynesianism and even, if rarely, protectionism (Hautcoeur, 2011; Morelle, 2011; Zucconi, 2009; "Smith oder List", 2008).

In France, the debate on economics and economic policy was particularly lively in these first years of the crisis. From 2008 to 2010, quotations of all economists considered reach their highest frequency (Figure 9.1). The electoral campaign of 2007 and the financial breakdown of 2008 both ignited widespread discussions on the desirability and feasibility of different economic and social orders (Mermet, 2008; Lepage, 2008; Baudet, 2008a; Dorra, 2008). Jacques Attali (2005) ventured to ask, rhetorically, if Marx had reason in the end, predicting the end of capitalism and its transformation in socialism (Werling, 2009). The role of economists was called into question, given their incapacity to foresee and solve the crisis (Dufrénot, 2012; "Sortons l'enseignement", 2009; Daniel, 2009a; Cédelle, 2008; Moynot, 2008; Cypel, 2008). Had the economist become a *homo demens*, detached from reality, incapable of logical thinking, dedicated to media appearances instead than to serious studies? (Matouk, Gadrey, 2011; Matouk, 2012). *Le Monde* went so far as resurrect seven past economists who had been able to predict change, as a useful example for present-day colleagues: Jean-Charles Sismondi, Karl Marx, Nikolaï Kondratiev, Joseph Schumpeter, Fernand Braudel, Jean Fourastié and Paul Romer (Daniel, 2009b) – assuredly not a list of mainstream economists. Political economy, pleaded Nicolas Baverez (2011), should be completely reconstructed, having in mind the exigency to set new rules for the European and the Monetary Union, the necessity to manage globalization processes and the need to gain a better understanding of monetary issues in their relation to the economic cycle.

As if all this criticism would not be enough, also the Pope readily attacked the deteriorating market economy. "Money vanishes, only God's word is eternal" proclaimed *La Repubblica* in 2008, citing the head of the Catholic Church ("Mutui, Papa", 2008). At the same time, Nicolas Baverez (2008a), in *Le Monde*, declared: "Marx is dead, but God lives on well". A call for the return to more values that continued for all the duration of the crisis.[9] The same can be said for the laical demand for more ethics in the economy. *Frankfurter Allgemeine Zeitung* openly denounced the crisis of an economy without values in New Year's Eve 2008 ("Wertlose Ökonomie", 2008), while *La Repubblica* hosted in 2009 many articles pleading for a return to morals, among them those by Jean Paul Fitoussi (2009a) and Giorgio Ruffolo (2009). In the same year, on the columns of *Corriere della Sera* Antonio Marzano (2009) discussed at length the ethical crisis of the economy. *Le Monde* published the *plaidoyer (pleading)* of Pascal Bruckner (2008) for a profound change in European society and a return to morals. In the same newspaper, Jean Paul Fitoussi (2009b) denounced the ethical scandals of contemporary capitalism: the mundialization of poverty and the inacceptable divergence in income distribution.

With the subprime crisis, the adventure of capitalism seemed so at its end (Kaufmann, 2008), at least in its liberalist form (Dardot, Laval, 2009), as institutions reclaimed their role in the economy (Taino, 2013). Not everyone agreed. In Germany, Werner Plumpe (2009) maintained that "where a functioning market economy existed, capitalism transformed 'egoism' into society's interest". "Only someone ignoring Europe's historical past" – concluded Plumpe – "could affirm the contrary". The already quoted Italian liberalists repeatedly warned that speculation was the result of erroneous state policies, not absence of regulation, and *Corriere della Sera* remained detached toward the new economic order advocated by the German chancellor at Davos at the beginning of 2009 (Taino, 2009). German newspapers, too, were doubtful of the Chancellor's idea, as the forecasts for the world economy continuously worsened (Ward, 2009).

The subsequent profound crisis of the Mediterranean countries inside the European Union ("Banken zittern", 2010), the "Greek Tragedy" (Fitoussi, 2009c) could not so easily be attributed to extra-UE countries or some devilish speculative monster. The resurgence of the pejorative acronym PIIGS (Portugal,

Ireland, Italy, Greece, Spain) in 2010 (Gros, 2010; Gatinois, Lacombe, 2010), clearly indicated that the once external shock had become an internal issue of the European Union (Toussaint, 2012).

Europe's newspapers demonstrated that in 2010, the attention of the public in economic matters had shifted from the US speculation and finance toward Europe and its institutional construction (Tables 9.3–9.4 and Figure 9.2). In the *Frankfurter Allgemeine Zeitung*, during the course of 2009, the primacy of citations switched from "financial crisis" to "European Union" and the couple "Europe" and "crisis" and "Monetary Union" started a climb that would peak in 2012.

In Italy's newspapers, the evolution of quotations is similar, ignoring political coloring. The only difference with Germany is the primacy of the pair "Europe" and "crisis" over "European Union" and "Monetary Union". A confirmation that in Italy, in respect to Germany, Europe was perceived much more in relation to the hardships of a deepening crisis than in itself. Otherwise, the tendency of the citations is the same, growing from 2009 to 2012. In *Le Monde*, the couple "Europe" and "crisis" overcame the primacy of "financial crisis" in 2010, while discussion of the "European Union" and the "Monetary Union" peaked in 2011 and 2012.

At this point, European media started a blaming game recurring to whatever old prejudice could ignite public opinion.[10] Many economists, instead, charged the institutional construction of the Monetary Union and of the Economic Union for those continued imbalances that had transformed the American financial crisis into a European affair of gigantic proportions.[11] Bertram Schefold (2011), writing in *Frankfurter Allgemeine Zeitung* in 2011, observed that the greatest obstacle on the way of Europe toward integration was the discrepancy between the European Union, including Great Britain, and the Monetary Union, excluding it. This hiatus prevented EU's representative institutions to manage a coordinated fiscal policy that could constitute the missing fundament for the euro. Charles B. Blankart (2014) instead insisted on the profound differences existing in the fiscal systems of European states like Italy, France and Germany. While Germany's system was based on the economic and hence political responsibility of the institutions spending the taxpayers' money, the French system, as the Italian one, centralized public income and at the same time decentralized public expenses. The absence of economic responsibility, in these cases, constrained the central state to guarantee the debts of local institutions. Incentives implied by such fiscal systems created in the long run a deficit bomb, that could be defused only recurring to inflationary monetary policy or devaluation of the currency. Every partner state expected Europe to replicate its own fiscal system at the Union level, generating a decisional impasse that impeded the needed establishment of a common European fiscal policy. The excessive debt and loss of financial control of Southern European states was the cause of the euro crisis also for renowned German economists as Wolfgang Franz, Clemens Fuest, Martin Hellwig and Hans-Werner Sinn (2010).

Clearly the hypothesis underlying these interpretations of the European debt crisis was that, given no institutional differences, the crisis would have had a much lesser impact, because the inherent equilibrating forces of markets or the intervention of the individual states would have quickly resolved the question. In such a view, be it based on Keynesian or liberalist assumptions, a national state with its economic construction and its monetary and fiscal sovereignty represented the ideal framework for a well-functioning market economy and the ideal regulating agency if a market economy would not function so well. The only efficient way to exit the crisis, then, would have been to break up the Union, returning to fully sovereign national states, or replicate the institutional framework of the national state at the European level,[12] an idea that had commonly circulated among economists during the advent of the euro. Padoa Schioppa, for example, in the mentioned interview in 2008, reaffirmed: "I warned at the beginning of the Euro, against the perils of a 'money without a State'. It is clear that more European State was necessary, not less European money: without the euro, Europe today would experience a catastrophe" (Giannini, 2008b).[13]

Aside from breaking up the Monetary Union ("Die Griechen und der Euro", 2010), possible solutions of the crisis could be to transfer fiscal sovereignty at the European level to empower the democratically elected European Parliament with real legislative and governing power, or similar measures, a view shared by Jürgen Habermas (2014) and Anthony Giddens (2012). The imbalances and the restructuring of production along comparative advantages, caused by different factor endowments and factor prices in European regions, could then be overcome by direct transfers and development policies, as would easily be done inside a single national body. What could not be achieved through interaction and cooperation among national states, having different institutional settings and different economic and political philosophies of reference (Romano, 2011; Tajani, 2012; Galli Della Loggia, 2012a), could so be obtained by transferring power to a supra-national body and its bureaucracy, legitimized by democratic election. Such a proposal was supported by the French government under the presidency of Nicolas Sarkozy and also of François Hollande (Ricard, 2013).

A different way to look at the problem was to consider the Monetary Union and/or the European Union in the light of game theories, as Giacomo Vaciago (2012) suggested in 2012 in the journal *Il Mulino*. Europe was so seen as a constraining environment with good guys watching over bad guys, and rules inciting the spendthrift countries to cheat, while making parsimonious countries incapable of accepting the partner's bankruptcy – a continuously worsening scenario, leading the Union to an inevitable bad end. Similar to this, with a more optimistic outcome, was the idea that the Monetary Union created a competitive arena for differing institutional settings, so that virtuous states would emerge and vicious ones would be constrained by disastrous economic results to adopt better institutions (Wegner, 2014). A theory that presumes a positivistic attitude according to which the evolutionary selection of national institutions would automatically lead to the rise of the best one: a matter of faith.

Both these last interpretations, moreover, equate European states to individuals, playing a game or competing in a market environment. But there is more to a state than a community of private interests, as the *Frankfurter Allgemeine Zeitung* underlined in 2010, remembering Wilhelm Röpke, one of the founding fathers of the social market economy (Spieker, 2010), and Europe needed more than just additional bureaucracy, as Alberto Quadrio Curzio (2010) wrote in *Corriere della Sera* during the same year. Opposed to such liberal and ordoliberal views were the renewed calls for Keynesian policies, this time not in contrast to ruinous American deregulation as in the beginning of the crisis, but with the aim of reducing the deflationary effects of Europe's recession (Baccaro, 2009). German and Italian newspapers testify how, between 2010 and 2012, the number of articles quoting Keynes form a peak, with no difference in regard to nationality or political stance of the newspaper considered (Tables 9.1–9.2). The same can be said for citations of Adam Smith (Gaggi, 2010) and in Italy also of Luigi Einaudi, having a relative maximum in 2011.

France went its own way, as already hinted at. The liveliest debates on economics occurred from 2008 to 2010. The subsequent political alliance between Nicolas Sarkozy and Angela Merkel, stigmatized as "Merkozy", assured that political economy more or less followed the German lead.[14] The resilience of Germany's economy to the crisis made it a model for French politics (Hadas, 2009). All the while, internal discussion concentrated on the future of the European Union, particularly on the political level.[15] Journals and newspapers also debated, still, the survival of capitalism (De La Bruslerie, 2011; Philippe Arnaud, 2011; Faujas, 2011), or devoted their attention to non-economic issues.

In Italy, instead, the European recession and its disastrous consequences on the debt/GDP ratio of Mediterranean countries (Ferraris, 2013) sparked a profound debate opposing Keynesianism to liberalism not only in reference to European policies, but also to national traditions of thought and national economic policies. Particularly in 2011 and the beginning of 2012, during the brief government led by the liberal economist Mario Monti, *Corriere della Sera* came so to discuss at length Italian liberalism, while *La Repubblica* championed with polemical vigor the opposite Keynesian view.

Writing in *Corriere della Sera* in 2011, two weeks before Monti's assignment, renowned historian Giuseppe Galasso (2011) revived the historical debate between Benedetto Croce and Luigi Einaudi distinguishing *liberalismo* and *liberismo*, liberalism as a political philosophy the first, liberalism in the economy the second – a debate, not incidentally, raging when the effects of the crash of 1929 had reached Italy. While Croce affirmed that liberalism as an end could be achieved, under given circumstances, even by the means of an illiberal economic policy, Einaudi harshly dissented, sustaining the non-neutrality of means like economic policy toward the chosen end of liberty. Easy comparisons to the situation of Italy in 2011 were not incidental. Massimo L. Salvadori, likewise a famed historian, of left-wing sympathies, analyzed, in a book reviewed by Paolo Mieli (2011) only days after Monti's assignment, the biggest failure of

Italian liberalism: the incapacity to generate a real democratic alternation of governments. Reference could obviously be made to the extraordinary situation of Monti's "technical" prime ministry, delaying the possible democratic election of a political government led by the left.

The greatest contradiction of Italian liberalism, though, concluded Ernesto Galli Della Loggia (2012b) in 2012, again in *Corriere della Sera*, had been its obstinate refusal of economic liberalism in the wake of Croce's lesson. None of the Italian generations of liberals since unification in 1861 had ever really believed in free trade and its normative expressions, except for a bunch of isolated academics. According to the analysis of *Corriere della Sera*, then, the recession needed a liberal solution like it had never really been adopted in Italy and was hoped for by the newly assigned Prime Minister Monti. Giuseppe Bedeschi (2011) and Alberto Alesina (2012), conscious of the ecumenical support needed by Monti from right- and left-oriented parliamentarians, even went so far as to propose, through the columns of the newspaper, such extreme liberal agenda to Italian left-wing parties. Answers were trenchant (La Malfa, 2011; Mucchetti, 2012). Although accused of offering no solution to the contemporary economic crisis (Franchi, 2011), left-wing parties stuck to their Keynesian credo, while social democratic Giorgio La Malfa counter-proposed the German social market economy as the best solution to present hardships (Bedeschi, 2012).

In the last tormented months of the Monti government in 2013, *La Repubblica* started a campaign in favor of Keynesian policies, citing the positive results of expansionary measures adopted in the United States. In January, Federico Rampini (2013) wrote "Europe Tries the American Recipe: 'Enough Austerity, It's Time for Growth'", comforted by positive economic data arriving from the other side of the Ocean (Tessitore, 2013). Austerity, though, remained on the agenda of the Italian government, even if by then led by the leftist Enrico Letta. In December 2013, Giorgio Ruffolo and Stefano Sylos Labini (2013) indignantly wrote:

> It is time to close the season of rigor and launch a grand plan of investments in order to reverse the atrocious policy of 'delay' that is driving Europe to disaster. That Germany is again responsible for Europe's tragedy is a circumstance that defies the belief according to which history cannot repeat itself.

At the end of the period considered by this research, seemingly, a perfect circle had been drawn: *La Repubblica* proposed to its readers a prejudiced image of Germany, as a country devoted to economic imperialism, based on the historical past of the Third Reich. In reality, the analysis of national newspapers contradicts such conclusion. The effort of *La Repubblica* to demonize Chancellor Merkel in 2013 must be considered a rather rare offshoot of a permanent electoral campaign, devoid of any general significance. It might suffice to remember how enthusiastically *La Repubblica* celebrated in 2009 Merkel's call for a worldwide ordoliberalism to prove it, but looking at the data on the frequency of citations, a renewal of populist nationalism in Italy can definitively be ruled out. All indicators for *La Repubblica* and *Corriere della Sera*, be they relative to articles referring to Europe, crisis, or single economists, significantly diminish in the course of 2013 (Tables 9.1 and 9.2, Figure 9.1).

In effect, due to its better economic performance, Germany became, in the consideration of French and Italians, an example to be followed (Angeloni, 2010; Di Vico, 2010; Bedeschi, 2012). In Italy, the crisis was increasingly interpreted as a structural one, caused by internal problems and calling for a local solution (Magris, 2011; Alesina, 2011; Reichlin, 2012; Romano, 2013). Economists described Italy's bad performance, in comparison to other European partners and OCSE countries in general, as the result of institutional problems, regarding taxation, economic responsibility and diffused corruption, but also of economic issues like insufficient investments, private and public; infrastructural deficiencies; collapsing productivity and scarce competition (Bini, 2014). All these questions, unresolved since the 1980s, slowly eroded Italy's competitiveness, greatly accelerating the collapse of the economy after the external shock of the American financial crisis.[16] Surely, the easiest solution would have been to reclaim the possibility of discretionally using the monetary policy by exiting from the Monetary Union. In the long run, however, the best answer to Italy's structural crisis would be to politically tackle the cited questions, guaranteeing the institutional environment and the functioning markets needed for a stable economic growth.

In France, also, the attention was increasingly devoted to the national economy and to the enactment of structural changes. Nicolas Sarkozy had championed Germany as a model to be copied (Leparmentier, De Vergès, 2009; Lemaître, 2012b; "L'Allemagne est 'un exemple'", 2012; De Tricornot, 2012), particularly in regard to the reforms enacted under the chancellorship of Gerhard Schröder (Thureau-Dangi, 2012). This vision was increasingly questioned, though, after the rumor spread that the German government had asked for a study to solve the French problems through a proposed package of policy measures (Madelin, 2012; Schieritz, 2012): was France as the novel Greece, a problem to be solved with policies imposed by Germany?

The presidential campaign in 2012 in effect revolved around the relationship with Germany, the institutional structure of Europe and reviving economic growth (Chopin, 2012; Kauffmann, 2012; Lemaître, 2012c; Brunnermeier, James, Landau, 2016, 34–35). François Hollande inherited the need for reforms along with the presidency (Blas, 2012). Reforms were expected in the public administration and in the private sector, to particularly enhance the fabled competitiveness of France ("Si vous n'avez rien compris", 2012). In this sense, the Gallois Report ("Shock treatment", 2012) and the renewed call for regulations of the labor market along the lines of the Schröder reform ("Les enseignements des réformes Schröder", 2012). In Europe, also, a lunge forward was asked for, toward a common economic policy and a federative form of state. Economists like Stefan Collignon, Nelly Morisot and Gabriel Richard-Molard (2012), explicitly invoked a revision of the "Merkozy" model, based on the German policy of competitive disinflation. Other voices, though, asked for a serious discussion on the German model of a social market economy as a basis for the future common European policies (Bouaffre, 2012). The ensuing debate on the *Europe Allemande* shows, in any case, that from the presidential elections onward German policies were increasingly perceived as an imposition. France had lost its status as an equal partner (Revault d'Allonnes, Ricard, Wieder, 2012), while Germany had gained an absolute political power over Europe.[17]

One last notation emerges from studying how European newspapers represented the economic crisis in the years 2008–2013, and it concerns Germany. In 2013, in contrast to France and Italy, indicators about single economists and economic schools increase significantly. In this case, nonetheless, the debate had less to do with the economic crisis – articles quoting crisis significantly diminish – as with Germany's role inside Europe. The renewed discussion, in fact, concerned the economic order that, in the eyes of Germans, Europe should adopt (Fabre, Syfuss-Arnaud, 2011), and in consequence Germany's involvement in a future Union with fiscal competences (Van Renterghem, 2010). The shift of power inside Europe toward Berlin (Brunnermeier, James, Landau, 2016, 27–33) is also confirmed by the growing number of articles quoting Merkel during the whole crisis (Lemaître, 2012a; Mastrobuoni, Cavallaro, 2012; Jacquin, 2013; Askenazy, 2013).

Table 9.3 Articles containing sample words in *La Repubblica* (white rows) and in *Corriere della Sera* (gray rows) during the years 2008–2013

Articles containing the words	*2008*	*2009*	*2010*	*2011*	*2012*	*2013*
Capitalism and Crisis	251	265	145	145	173	132
Capitalism and Crisis	699	490	363	427	447	249
Europe and Crisis	1469	1737	1603	2119	2348	1104
Europe and Crisis	4778	3865	4274	6382	5862	3614
Financial Crisis	785	612	423	464	360	288
Financial Crisis	3780	1093	1011	3085	691	386
European Union	1026	1020	1003	1121	867	115
European Union	4036	2321	3331	3926	3185	2342
Monetary Union	15	13	79	103	150	10
Monetary Union	99	32	232	268	297	105
Merkel	462	604	598	1033	1394	734
Merkel	793	866	998	2424	2497	1059
Statalism	60	32	18	40	48	33
Statalism	84	55	33	48	47	17
Liberism	127	60	43	74	90	48
Economic Liberalism	268	120	134	171	239	90

Table 9.4 Articles containing sample words in *Frankfurter Allgemeine Zeitung* (gray rows) and in *Le Monde* (white rows) during the years 2008–2013

Articles containing the words	*2008*	*2009*	*2010*	*2011*	*2012*	*2013*
Capitalism and Crisis	181	290	98	139	162	130
Capitalism and Crisis	314	461	231	233	243	152
Europe and Crisis	1279	1566	1444	2173	2704	1766
Europe and Crisis	1672	2093	2063	2612	2604	1991
Financial Crisis	5552	5221	3466	3167	2784	2683
Financial Crisis	2456	2110	1852	2159	1585	1168
European Union	4887	4374	4706	7679	9478	8211
European Union	3068	2608	2946	3417	3384	3123
Monetary Union	175	198	868	1214	1719	899
Monetary Union	223	232	698	917	774	571
Merkel	2702	3614	3430	3915	4201	4499
Merkel	535	669	733	1109	1079	937
Social market economy	349	390	179	237	229	262
Ordoliberalism	7	18	9	8	7	13
Statalism	10616	11055	11756	11996	12348	11080
Liberalism	118	103	110	192	142	211
Liberalism[18]	381	295	271	300	342	250

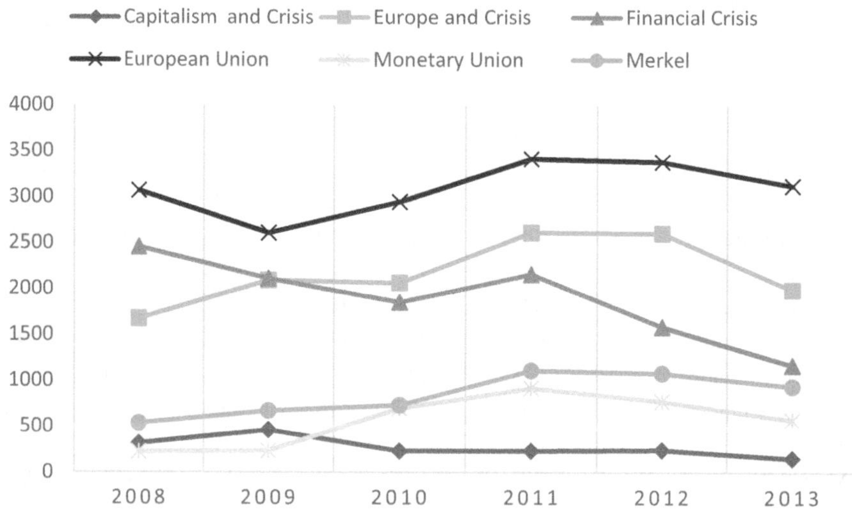

Figure 9.2 Number of articles quoting relevant concepts in *Le Monde* during the years of crisis

Conclusion

The recrudescence of populism and nationalistic sentiments in Europe during the economic crisis started in 2008 called for a more in-depth understanding of how economic theories are popularized into general culture, prompting social decisions and broad collective decisions. To this end, one German, one French and two Italian newspapers were analyzed over the period 2008–2013, exemplifying how prejudiced categorizations, past economic thought, political interference and theories of contemporary economists have been mixed and filtered by media to inform public opinion about the economic crisis.

The research unveiled a common economic culture, the "Marxian" world we live in, and the widespread diffusion of the same economic thought, based on the alternative between Keynesianism and liberalism. The crisis stirred many debates among differing views but also acted as a potent agent of diffusion for those theories, like ordoliberalism, that had until then mainly remained rooted inside a single country. The first spectacular phase of financial breakdown in 2008 and 2009 was accompanied by the usual victorious cry over the death of capitalism. All possible alternatives were so invoked by the press: statism, Keynesianism, ordoliberalism, morals and even religion. Apart from national champions, the pattern was similar in the countries observed, with no distinction due to the political coloring of the newspapers analyzed. As the crisis became real, conquering Europe, media hosted a vivid debate over the institutional construction of the European and the Monetary Union. This phase, lasting from 2010 to 2012, witnessed the maximum diffusion of prejudiced interpretations and the frequent insurgence of nationalistic tendencies. In 2013, the lessening of the debt crisis and the contemporary good economic results in the US and Germany sobered the economic debate on European newspapers. Only at this point did indicators really differ between countries. Economists in France and Italy proposed alternative Keynesian and liberalist solutions to solve the structural crises of their countries. In Germany, instead, the debate centered on the future institutional structure of Europe and the related economic order.

The study confirmed the relevance of economists long dead and of the historical past in the structuring of present categories of thought and symbolic imagining. It also showed how economic theories are used in relation to the political cycle and to ignite nationalistic sentiments. Last, it testified how economists interacted with media and politics as a critical voice against a judgmental evaluation of theories or as part of the political decision process, even in governments.

Notes

1 Some preliminary results of this research have been published in Poettinger (2014).

2 Contrary to the cases of Germany and Italy, the analysis of *Le Monde* did not single out a champion from the past among French economists. Neither Walras nor French 19th

century liberals gave significant results in terms of quotations. The most quoted economists, with the exception of Marx and Keynes, were contemporary ones.

3 In Italy, a recent publication on Ordoliberalism, not accidentally dates to the first year of the economic crisis (Felice 2008).

4 A precocious analysis of the diffusion of "Euroscetticism" and "populism" in European countries during the crisis is to be found in Galli Della Loggia (2009). A more recent analysis of the complex phenomena of literary narratives of the crisis and the figure of the "populist economist" is in Gotor (2012).

5 www.lesgracques.fr

6 For an early and critical comparison between the crisis of 1929 and that of 2008 see Fitoussi (2008a).

7 For example, Eugenio Scalfari, director of *La Repubblica*, quoted the economists Joseph Stiglitz and Luigi Einaudi, forecasting the end of a capitalism based on consumption (Scalfari, 2008). Other examples are: Ruffolo (2011); Giannini (2012). A critical appraisal of such early interpretations of the economic crisis can be read in Weimer (2013). On *Le Monde*, Immanuel Wallerstein forecasted the end of capitalism (Reverchon, Wallerstein, 2008).

8 As underlined by Brice Teinturier (director of the département stratégies d'opinion, TNS Sofres), the faith in the intervention of the state is a peculiar characteristic of French citizens, in Rostow's terms a *broad collective decision* (Baudet, 2008b).

9 See for example: "Il Papa" (2008); Vecchi (2009, 2011); Ventura (2011); Livini (2013); Hank (2014).

10 To quote just a few examples on both sides: Hank, von Petersdorff (2010); Taino (2010); "Die Italiener" (2010); Battista (2011); "Angriff auf die deutschen Steuerzahler" (2012); Hasan (2012); Montefiori (2013); Debenedetti (2013). A linguistic analysis of German articles blaming the euro crisis on the indebtedness of Southern European countries is to be found in: Polonyi (2012).

11 Some economists, like Paul Krugman and Lorenzo Bini Smaghi, had begun early to question the positive effects of the Monetary Union. See: Fubini (2008); Krugman (2008).

12 See: Habermas, Bofinger, Nida-Ruemelin (2012); Ruffolo, Sylos Labini (2012); Montefiori (2012); Ravaschio (2013); Carioti (2013).

13 See also: Padoa Schioppa (2004).

14 There were discrepancies of view between France and Germany in relation to the "Greek tragedy", but nothing compared to other European partners (Fournier, 2011).

15 See for example: Bofinger, Habermas, Nida Rümelin (2012); "L'euro, victime" (2011); Kateb (2011); Birnbaum (2011); "Trop de rigueur" (2010).

16 To cite just one influential example of this interpretation of the Italian crisis, see: Ciocca (2007, 2012).

17 The expression *Europe Allemande* has entered in common use and still describes Angela Merkel as the "patronne incontestée de l'Europe" (Leparmentier, 2015).

18 The voice "liberalism" includes a word count of "liberalisme" and "laissez-faire".

References

Alesina, A. (2011). "I Virtuosi Tedeschi Non hanno Colpe", *Corriere della Sera*, 6 July.

Alesina, A. (2012). "Gli Antichi Pregiudizi Economici della Sinistra Welfare, tasse e flessibilità La sinistra abbatta i tabù", *Corriere della Sera*, 13 December.

Angeloni, I. (2010). "A lezione di tedesco", *Corriere Economia*, 29 March.

"Angriff auf die deutschen Steuerzahler" (2012). *Handelsblatt*, 22 June.

Arcangeli, M. (2009). "Un 'linguaggio della verità' dominato dalla parola 'crisi'", *La Repubblica*, 1 January.

Arnaud, P. (2011). "Le Capitalisme peut-il survivre, de Joseph Schumpeter", *Le Monde Economie*, 17 October.
Askenazy, P. (2013). "Inquiétante Allemagne", *Le Monde*, 20 May.
Attali, J. (2005), *Karl Marx: ou l'esprit du monde*, Paris: Fayard.
Baccaro, A. (2009). "Draghi: lavoro e debito, i nuovi problemi all'orizzonte", *Corriere della Sera*, 23 October.
"Banken zittern mit den schwachen Euro-Staaten" (2010). *Frankfurter Allgemeine Zeitung*, 5 February.
Battista, P. (2011). "I fantasmi dell'egemonia tedesca", *Corriere della Sera*, 3 December.
Baudet, M. (2008a). "Six crises qui bousculent l'ordre économique mondial", *Le Monde Economie*, 28 April.
Baudet, M. (2008b). "Crise: les Français réclament le retour de l'Etat", *Le Monde Economie*, 24 November.
Baverez, N. (2008a). "Le XXIe siècle, entre passions et raison", *Le Monde*, 23 September.
Baverez, N. (2008b). "Les leçons de la crise: 'Cette crise est celle du capitalisme, pas du libéralisme'", *Le Monde.fr*, 30 October.
Baverez, N. (2011). "Refonder la politique économique", *Le Monde Economie*, 24 October.
Bedeschi, G. (2011). "Una sinistra davvero moderna deve farsi carico delle battaglie liberali", *Corriere della Sera*, 6 October.
Bedeschi, G. (2012). "La Terza via liberale di Einaudi e Roepke", *Corriere della Sera*, 31 May.
Bini, P. (2014). "How to escape from the crisis: The divergent opinions of Italian economists", in: Varsori, A., Poettinger, M. (eds.), *Economic Crisis and New Nationalisms: German Political Economy as Perceived by European Partners*, Bruxelles: Peter Lang, pp. 115–152.
Birnbaum, J. (2011). "Europe fantôme", *Le Monde des Livres*, 22 September.
Blankart, C. B. (2014). "From friends to foes? The Euro as a cause of new nationalism", in: Varsori, A., Poettinger, M. (eds.), *Economic Crisis and New Nationalisms: German Political Economy as Perceived by European Partners*, Bruxelles: Peter Lang, pp. 99–114.
Blas, N. (2012). "Le temps du réformisme radical est venu", *Le Monde.fr*, 10 December.
Bocconi, S. (2008). "Speculazione peste del secolo: Duello Tremonti-Guido Rossi", *Corriere della Sera*", 15 July.
Bocconi, S. (2009). "Processo al capitalismo: assolto, ma ora nuove regole", *Corriere della Sera*, 1 December.
Bofinger, P., Habermas, J., Nida Rümelin, J. (2012). "Plus que jamais, l'Europe", *Le Monde*, 4 September.
Bolopion, P., Nougayrède, N. (2008). "A l'ONU, les pays du Sud dénoncent un système financier 'cupide'", *Le Monde*, 24 September.
Bonafede, A. (2008). "La crisi ha nome e cognome: banche e società di rating", *La Repubblica*, 15 December.
Bouaffre, A. (2012). "Et si l'UE pensait à un modèle social européen pour régler la crise économique?", *Le Monde.fr*, 12 January.
"La Bourse ou la vie, le chantage des marchés, par les Gracques" (2008). *Le Monde*, 12 November.
Bragantini, S. (2011). "Se la finanza (incontrollata) scommette contro gli Stati", *Corriere della Sera*, 8 July.
Braunberger, G. (2008). "Das verwaiste Erbe der Freiburger Schule", *Frankfurter Allgemeine Zeitung*, 19 June.
Bruckner, P. (2008). "L'inévitable métamorphose", *Le Monde*, 15 October.
Brunnermeier, M. K., James, H., Landau, J.-P. (2016). *The Euro and the Battle of Ideas*, Princeton, NJ: Princeton University Press.
Caffè, F. (1966). *Politica economica. Sistematica e tecniche di analisi*, Torino: Bollati Boringhieri.

Calabresi, M. (2009). "La finanza americana tra intrighi ed eccessi", *La Repubblica*, 20 February.
Carioti, A. (2013). "Europeismo rivoluzionario", *Corriere della Sera*, 8 February.
Cédelle, L. (2008). "Les professeurs d'économie s'estiment menacés . . . malgré la crise", *Le Monde.fr*, 17 October.
Chopin, D. (2012). "Sarkozy-Hollande: deux conceptions du modèle économique allemand", *Fondation Jean-Jaures*, 29 February.
Ciocca, P. (2007). *Ricchi per sempre? Una storia economica d'Italia (1796–2005)*, Torino: Bollati Boringhieri.
Ciocca, P. (2012). "Se la Bce aiuta i 'Paesi illiquidi'", *Sole 24 Ore*, 25 January.
Collignon, S., Morisot, N., Richard-Molard, G. (2012). "France-Allemagne: pourquoi François Hollande a une chance historique de changer l'Europe", *Le Monde.fr*, 31 May.
Cypel, S. (2008). "Les libéraux tentent de se rassurer sans vraiment se remettre en cause", *Le Monde*, 13 October.
Daniel, J. (2009a). "Tout n'est pas à jeter dans les Prix Nobel d'économie", *Le Monde*, 9 October.
Daniel, J. (2009b). "Comment les économistes annoncent les mutations", *Le Monde Economie*, 7 December.
Dardot, P., Laval, C. (2009). "Vers un krach du sujet néolibéral ?", *Le Monde*, 3 April.
Debenedetti, F. (2013). "Fare la morale non cancella i debiti L'Europa si cura con il realismo", *Corriere della Sera*, 29 July.
De Cecco, M. (2008). "Il mondo affondato dal dollaro", *La Repubblica*, 10 March.
De La Bruslerie, H. (2011). "Un nouveau capitalisme se dessine", *Le Monde.fr*, 8 November.
De Tricornot, A. (2012). "Pourquoi le modèle allemand est une mode", *Le Monde Economie*, 20 February.
De Tricornot, A., Dostaler, G. (2009). "Le retour naturel à l'équilibre économique est un mythe", *Le Monde Economie*, 9 June.
Di Vico, D. (2010). "Imbroglio liberista e modello renano", *Corriere della Sera*, 10 September.
Dorra, M. (2008). "Malaise dans la mondialisation", *Le Monde*, 25 April.
Dougherty, C. (2009). "Merkel, at Davos, calls for a 'global economic charter'", *The New York Times*, 30 January.
Dufrénot, G. (2012). "On peut être un économiste engagé, voire médiatique, sans être un imposteur", *Le Monde Economie*, 2 July.
Dullien, S., Guérot, U. (2012). "The long shadow of ordoliberalism: Germany's approach to the euro crisis", *ECFR*, 49.
Einaudi, L. (1932). "Roberto Michels, Introduzione alla storia delle dottrine economiche e politiche, Bologna, Zanichelli, 1932", *La Riforma Sociale*, 39, 2,. 207.
"Les enseignements des réformes Schröder pour François Hollande" (2012). *Le Monde*, 28 December.
"L'euro, victime des pièges de l'idéologie ?" (2011). *Le Monde*, 10 November.
Fabre, T., Syfuss-Arnaud, S. (2011). "L'Europe à l'heure allemande", *Challenges*, 25 November.
Fanfani, A. (1939). *Introduzione allo studio della storia economica*, Milano: Giuffré.
Faujas, A. (2011). "Le Capitalisme à l'agonie, de Paul Jorion: le spectre de Karl Marx", *Le Monde*, 7 April.
Felice, F. (2008). *L'economia sociale di mercato*, Soveria Mannelli: Rubbettino.
Ferraris, M. (2013). "L' illusione economica. Come lo spread è diventato il reale", *La Repubblica*, 12 January.
Fitoussi, J. (2008a). "La leçon de la crise de 1929 a été tirée", *Le Monde.fr*, 8 October.
Fitoussi, J. (2008b). "Le capitalisme sous tente à oxygène", *Le Monde*, 29 October.
Fitoussi, J. (2009a). "Se torna l'etica nel capitalismo", *La Repubblica*, 23 February.

Fitoussi, J. (2009b). "La crise économique et l'éthique du capitalisme", *Le Monde*, 2 March.
Fitoussi, J. (2009c). "La Grèce: une tragédie européenne", *Le Monde*, 4 May.
Fournier, A. (2011). "Crise grecque: ce qui oppose Sarkozy et Merkel", *Le Monde.fr*, 20 July.
Franchi, P. (2011). "Le (non) terapie della sinistra europea", *Corriere della Sera*, 4 November.
Franz, W., Fuest, C., Hellwig, M., Sinn, H. W. (2010)."Zehn Regeln zur Rettung des Euro. Appell an die Bundesregierung", *www.oekonomenstimme.org*, 29 June.
Fressoz, F., Wieder, T. (2013). Bruno Le Maire: "L'attitude de l'UE nourrit le populisme", *Le Monde*, 9 March.
Fubini, F. (2008). "Dieci anni di euro: il costo di un successo", *Corriere della Sera*, 14 September.
Fukuyama, F. (2008). "La chute d'America Inc.", *Le Monde*, 9 October.
Gaggi, M. (2010). "La 'mano invisibile' di Adam Smith, precettore del mercato. Il filosofo conteso tra Destra e progressisti", *Corriere della Sera*, 15 December.
Galasso, G. (2011). "Le ragioni del liberalismo alle radici dell'Occidente", *Corriere della Sera*, 2 November.
Galli Della Loggia, E. (2009). "Europa, la fine di un ciclo", *Corriere della Sera*, 11 June.
Galli Della Loggia, E. (2012a). "Un' Antica Diversità. Europa Tedesca e Mediterranea", *Corriere della Sera*, 25 July.
Galli Della Loggia, E. (2012b). "Il Vestito fuori Misura dei Liberali Italiani La cultura liberale in Italia rimane un fantasma senza eredi", *Corriere della Sera*, 10 December.
Gatinois, C., Lacombe, C. (2010). "L'année où l'euro a failli mourir", *Le Monde*, 31 December.
Giacometti, P., Péron, A. (2010). "La crise renforce les exigences et le pouvoir des opinions publiques", *Le Monde*, 9 February.
Giannini, M. (2008a). "Capitalismo al gran falò delle vanità", *La Repubblica*, 30 June.
Giannini, M. (2008b). "Padoa-Schioppa: Ora si muova l'Ue. Bisogna difendere il libero mercato", *La Repubblica*, 6 October.
Giannini, M. (2012). "La fine della civiltà capitalista", *La Repubblica*, 27 February.
Giavazzi, F. (2008). "La vera origine della crisi. Il Nuovo Shock Petrolifero", *Corriere della Sera*, 4 July.
Giddens, A. (2012). "L'Union est morte? Vive l'Union!", *Le Monde*, 25 January.
Gotor, M. (2012). "Il Romanzo dell'Economia", *La Repubblica*, 7 October.
"Die Griechen und der Euro. Ein Austritt wäre langfristig besser" (2010). *Frankfurter Allgemeine Zeitung*, 12 October.
Gros, D. (2010). "Greek burdens ensure some Pigs won't fly", *Financial Times*, 28 January.
Habermas, J. (2014). "Un'altra Europa è possibile quattro mosse per costruirla", *La Repubblica*, 7 February.
Habermas, J., Bofinger, P., Nida-Ruemelin, J. (2012). "Il passo decisivo per salvare l'Europa", *La Repubblica*, 4 August.
Hadas, E. (2009). "La crise montre que le modèle rhénan n'est pas dépassé", *Le Monde*, 10 November.
Hank, R. (2014). "Ethik in der Wirtschaft. Kirchen wettern gegen Gier und Maßlosigkeit auf den Finanzmärkten", *Frankfurter Allgemeine Zeitung*, 22 February.
Hank, R., Von Petersdorff, W. (2010). "Die Deutschen werden gepiesackt", *Frankfurter Allgemeine Zeitung*, 28 February.
Hasan, M. (2012). "Angela Merkel's mania for austerity is destroying Europe", *New Statesman*, 20 June.
Hautcoeur, P. (2011). "Vous avez dit protectionnisme ?", *Le Monde Economie*, 5 December.
"Il faut refonder le système financier international" (2008). *Le Monde.fr*, 16 September.
"Die Italiener rechnen anders" (2010). *Frankfurter Allgemeine Zeitung*, November.
Jacquin, J.-B. (2013). "Le mystère Merkel", *Le Monde*, 21 May.

Joignot, F. (2008). "Crise: le procès d'une perversion du capitalisme", *Le Monde Magazine*, 17 October.

Kateb, A. (2011). "L'Europe souffre d'un déficit de puissance", *Le Monde.fr*, 2 November.

Kauffmann, S. (2012). "Le front du refus européen", *Le Monde*, 24 April.

Kaufmann, F. K. (2008). "Der Kapitalismus ist ein großes Abenteuer Wehe, wenn es schiefgeht!", *Frankfurter Allgemeine Sonntagszeitung*, 21 December.

Keynes, J. M. (1936). *The General Theory of Employment, Interest and Money*, London: MacMillan.

Krugman, P. (2008). "La recessione e le colpe della Merkel", *La Repubblica*, 16 December.

"L'Allemagne est 'un exemple', selon Mario Draghi" (2012). *Le Monde*, 22 March.

La Malfa, G. (2011). "Le frontiere del liberalismo tra mercato e intervento pubblico", *Corriere della Sera*, 16 October.

Lemaître, F. (2012a). "L'après-'Merkozy' s'écrit désormais à Berlin", *Le Monde*, 23 January.

Lemaître, F. (2012b). "L'Allemagne, un modèle d'équilibre?", *Le Monde*, 23 March.

Lemaître, F. (2012c). "Modèle allemand: les candidats en ont tiré des arguments opposés", *Le Monde*, 3 May.

Lepage, C. (2008). "Le temps de l'économie durable est arrivé", *Le Monde*, 22 August.

Leparmentier, A. (2015). "La fin de l'Europe allemande", *Le Monde*, 16 September.

Leparmentier, A., De Vergès, M. (2009). "Au cours d'un meeting commun avec Angela Merkel à Berlin, Nicolas Sarkozy érige l'Allemagne en modèle", *Le Monde*, 11 May.

Livini, E. (2013). "Il Papa contro la finanza selvaggia: Il denaro serve, non governa", *La Repubblica*, 27 November.

Lopapa, C. (2008). "Sindacati e aziende vigileranno sulle banche", *La Repubblica*, 11 December.

Madelin, T. (2012). "Berlin étudierait un plan pour remettre la France sur le chemin de la croissance", *Les Echos*, 9 November.

Magris, C. (2011). "Il primato tedesco. Solidarietà, efficienza, comunità e modernità senza indulgenze pop", *Corriere della Sera*, 13 February.

Marani, U. (2008). "Le virtù della spesa pubblica", *La Repubblica*, 16 October.

Marzano, A. (2009). "La crisi etica dell'economia", *Corriere della Sera*, 8 July.

Mastrobuoni, T., Cavallaro, R. (2012). "Angela Merkel vue par 'La Stampa'", *Le Monde.fr*, 25 January.

Matouk, J. (2012). "Economistes incompétents, vendus ou dans l'impasse?", *Le Monde.fr*, 13 July.

Matouk, J., Gadrey, J. (2011). "L'économie comme science citoyenne", *Le Monde.fr*, 21 November.

Mermet, G. (2008). "Profitons de la crise pour refonder la société", *Le Monde*, 13 October.

Michels, R., Einaudi, L. (1932). "Ancora intorno al modo di scrivere la storia del dogma economico", *La Riforma Sociale*, 39, 3, 303–313.

Mieli, P. (2011). "Liberalismo all' italiana: l'alternanza impossibile", *Corriere della Sera*, 29 November.

Montefiori, S. (2012). "Lo sconforto di Delors: 'Avremmo fatto meglio a lasciare fuori gli inglesi'", *Corriere della Sera*, 25 November.

Montefiori, S. (2013). "'Merkel egoista' Vacilla l'asse tra Parigi e Berlino", *Corriere della Sera*, 28 April.

Morelle, A. (2011). "La démondisalisation inquiète les partisans d'un libéralisme aux abois", *Le Monde.fr*, 7 September.

Moynot, P. (2008). "Nobel d'économie: coup de maître", *Le Monde*, 15 October.

Mucchetti, M. (2012). "La strana pretesa dei liberisti Chiedere alla sinistra di fare la destra", *Corriere della Sera*, 4 December.

"Mutui, Papa: I soldi scompaiono solo la parola di Dio è solida" (2008). *La Repubblica*, 6 October.

Ostellino, P. (2008). "Il capitalismo e la politica", *Corriere della Sera*, 19 September.
Padoa Schioppa, T. (2004). *Regulating Finance: Balancing Freedom and Risk*, Oxford, New York: Oxford University Press.
"Il Papa: La crisi alimentare è causata dalla speculazione" (2008). *La Repubblica*, 12 December.
Plumpe, W. (2009). "Eigennutz macht alle reich", *Frankfurter Allgemeine Zeitung*, 7 December.
Poettinger, M. (2014). "Introduction", in: Varsori, A., Poettinger, M. (eds.), *Economic Crisis and New Nationalisms: German Political Economy as Perceived by European Partners*, Bruxelles: Peter Lang, pp. 13–38.
Poettinger, M. franco Tusset (eds.) (2016), *Economic Thought and History: An Unresolved Relationship*, London: Routledge.
Polonyi, A. (2012). "Protestantische Scheinheiligkeit", *The European*, 4 January.
Pühringer, S. (2015). "Wie wirken ÖkonomInnen und Ökonomik auf Politik und Gesellschaft?", *ICAE Working Paper Series*, 35.
Quadrio Curzio, A. (2010). "All' economia dell'Europa servono rigore e crescita, non burocrazia", *Corriere della Sera*, 7 October.
Rampini, F. (2009a). "L' America della crisi e lo specchio buio del ' 29", *La Repubblica*, 25 January.
Rampini, F. (2009b). "La rivincita Europea", *La Repubblica*, 31 January.
Rampini, F. (2013). "L'Europa prova la ricetta americana: Basta austerity, è l'ora dello sviluppo", *La Repubblica*, 11 January.
Ravaschio, S. (2013). "Dalla crisi la spinta verso un'Europa che non sia solo euro", *Corriere della Sera*, 20 January.
Reichlin, L. (2012). "La malattia italiana nasce prima dell'euro", *Corriere della Sera*, 17 May.
Revault d'Allonnes, D., Ricard, P., Wieder, T. (2012). "Hollande-Merkel, l'histoire d'un couple sans exclusive", *Le Monde*, 22 September.
Reverchon, A., Wallerstein, I. (2008). "Le capitalisme touche à sa fin", *Le Monde*, 16 December.
Ricard, P. (2013). "François Hollande et la vieille idée du gouvernement économique européen", *Le Monde*, 18 May.
Romano, S. (2011). "Le dimensioni dell'UE troppi cuochi in cucina", *Corriere della Sera*, 21 December.
Romano, S. (2013). "Per la terapia della crisi non sbagliare la diagnosi", *Corriere della Sera*, 7 May.
Rossi, G. (2008a). "Come combattere il liberismo globale", *La Repubblica*, 10 January.
Rossi, G. (2008b). "Così il supercapitalismo uccide la democrazia", *La Repubblica*, 30 May.
Rostow, W. W. (1990). *The Stages of Economic Growth: A Non-Communist Manifesto*, Cambridge: Cambridge University Press.
Ruffolo, G. (2009). "L' economia e il ritorno alla morale", *La Repubblica*, 9 March.
Ruffolo, G. (2011). "Le promesse tradite", *La Repubblica*, 24 November.
Ruffolo, G., Sylos Labini, S. (2012). "Una Federazione Contro La Crisi", *La Repubblica*, 5 October.
Ruffolo, G., Sylos Labini, S. (2013). "L'ideale che manca nell'Europa in crisi", *La Repubblica*, 15 December.
Scalfari, E. (2008). "Campane d'allarme e trombe stonate", *La Repubblica*, 7 December.
Schefold, B. (2011). "Die Engländer sind schuld", *Frankfurter Allgemeine Zeitung*, 25 November.
Schieritz, M. (2012). "Deutsche Wirtschaftsweise sollen Reformprogramm für Frankreich ausarbeiten", *Die Zeit.de*, 9 November.
Schumpeter, J. A. (2006). *History of Economic Analysis*, London: Routledge.
"Shock treatment" (2012). *The Economist*, 3 November.
"Si vous n'avez rien compris au débat sur la compétitivité" (2012). *Le Monde.fr*, 9 November.
"Smith oder List: Wer gewinnt? Lists 'Nationales System' in neuer Auflage" (2008). *Frankfurter Allgemeine Zeitung*, 15 December.

"Sortons l'enseignement de sa bulle" (2009). *Le Monde*, 9 October.
Spieker, M. (2010). "Der Staat ist mehr als eine Aktiengesellschaft", *Frankfurter Allgemeine Zeitung*, 23 December.
Stiglitz, J. (2008). "La Follia dei Mercati e il Sonno delle Autorità", *La Repubblica*, 6 May.
Taino, D. (2009). "Per fermare la crisi la Merkel vuole un'Onu dell'economia", *Corriere della Sera*, 31 January.
Taino, D. (2010). "La doppia vita del cancelliere Merkel. Prussiana ed europea, senza complessi", *Corriere della Sera*, 17 December.
Taino, D. (2013). "Le Istituzioni, non la Geografia creano la Fortuna delle Nazioni", *Corriere della Sera*, 4 June.
Tajani, A. (2012). "L'unità di intenti che serve all'Europa", *Corriere della Sera*, 21 November.
Ternisien, X., Rosen, J. (2010). "Les journaux doivent montrer qu'ils ont une vision du monde et la défendre", *Le Monde*, 7 September.
Tessitore, F. (2013). "La miope Italia del rigore finanziario", *La Repubblica*, 5 January.
Thureau-Dangi, P. (2012). "La vérité sur l'Allemagne", *Courrier International*, 1110, 9–15 February.
Toussaint, T. (2012). "Identité européenne: la face cachée de la crise", *Le Monde.fr*, 18 July.
"Trop de rigueur ou trop de relance ?" (2010). *Le Monde*, 4 October.
Truong, N. (2011). "La crise européenne réveille le spectre de Karl Marx", *Le Monde*, 17 December.
Vaciago, G. (2012). "A che gioco giochiamo?", *Il Mulino*, 23 October.
Van Renterghem, M. (2010). "Allemagne: le droit à l'ego", *Le Monde*, 30 June.
Vecchi, G. G. (2009). "Etica e crisi L' appello del Papa ai politici", *Corriere della Sera*, 13 January.
Vecchi, G. G. (2011). "Giustizia sociale e rendite tassate La ricetta anticrisi del Vaticano", *Corriere della Sera*, 25 October.
Ventura, M. (2011). "Primato della Politica sulla Finanza la Visione economica del Vaticano", *Corriere della Sera*, 4 November.
Villari, L. (2009). "Quando La Finanza Divora L' Economia", *La Repubblica*, 6 June.
Ward, J. (2009). "The world from Berlin: Davos health spas won't heal the global economy", *Spiegel Online International*, 2 February.
Wegner, G. (2014). "The genealogy of German ordo-liberalism and the European project", in: Varsori, A., Poettinger, M. (eds.), *Economic Crisis and New Nationalisms: German Political Economy as Perceived by European Partners*, Bruxelles: Peter Lang, pp. 15–172.
Weimer, W. (2013). "Schuld an der Krise ist der Supernanny-Staat", *Handelsblatt*, 22 February.
Werling, J. (2009). "Et si Marx avait raison?", *Le Monde*, 23 January.
"Wertlose Ökonomie Die Krise" (2008). *Frankfurter Allgemeine Zeitung*, 31 December.
Zampaglione, A. (2008). "Finanza americana, i giorni dell'Iri", *La Repubblica*, 22 September.
Zucconi, V. (2008a). "L'America e il falso mito dell'identità tra due libertà", *La Repubblica*, 25 May.
Zucconi, V. (2008b). "La rivincita di Keynes", *La Repubblica*, 20 September.
Zucconi, V. (2009). "Protezionismo/Quando la paura fa alzare le barriere", *La Repubblica*, 10 February.

Index

Note: Page numbers in *italic* indicate a figure and page numbers in **bold** indicate a table on the corresponding page.

For Product Safety Concerns and Information please contact our EU representative GPSR@taylorandfrancis.com Taylor & Francis Verlag GmbH, Kaufingerstraße 24, 80331 München, Germany